D0464617

THE EATING DISORDER SOURCEBOOK

THE
EATING DISORDER
SOURCEBOOK

CAROLYN COSTIN, M.A., M.ED., M.F.C.C.

LOWELL HOUSE
LOS ANGELES

CONTEMPORARY BOOKS
CHICAGO

LIBRARY OF CONGRESS CATALOGING-IN-PUBLICATION DATA

Costin, Carolyn.
    The eating disorder sourcebook/by Carolyn Costin.
        p.   cm.
    Includes bibliographical references and index.
    ISBN 1-56565-463-3
    1. Eating disorders, Title.
RC552.E18C67 1996
616.85'26—dc20   96-32363
                                                        CIP

Requests for such permissions should be addressed to:
Lowell House
2020 Avenue of the Stars, Suite 300
Los Angeles, CA 90067

Lowell House books can be purchased at special discounts when ordered in bulk
for premiums and special sales. Contact Department TC at the address above.

Publisher: Jack Artenstein
Associate Publisher, Lowell House Adult: Bud Sperry
Managing Editor: Maria Magallanes
Text design: James Schlesinger

Manufactured in the United States of America
10 9 8 7 6 5 4 3 2 1

ACKNOWLEDGMENTS

I gratefully acknowledge and express deep appreciation to the many incredible and wonderful human beings who have both made my life and this book the way it is:

—to my patients and their families, who shared deeply, struggled valiantly, and taught me well.

—to my colleagues in the field who suffered (and will continue to suffer) my endless quest for knowledge, clarification, and understanding.

—to my late-night readers and typists (they know who they are) who corrected my mistakes, turned illegible handwriting into printed words, and gave me encouragement and happy faces to keep me going.

—to my dearest friends, who allowed me to put the book before watching the sunset with them, even though it should always be the other way around.

CONTRIBUTORS

AUTHORS (CONTRIBUTED TO OR WROTE A CHAPTER FOR THE MANUSCRIPT)

THE PSYCHIATRIST'S ROLE AND MEDICATION
Timothy Brewerton, M.D.
Associate Professor and Director
Eating Disorder Program
Department of Psychiatry and
    Behavioral Sciences
Medical University of South Carolina
171 Ashley Avenue
Charleston, SC 29425

NUTRITION EDUCATION AND THERAPY
Karen Kratina, M.S., R.D.
Renfrew Center
7700 Renfrew Lane
Coconut Creek, FL 33073

MEDICAL MANAGEMENT OF ANOREXIA
    NERVOSA AND BULIMIA NERVOSA
Philip Mehler, M.D.
Chief, General Internal Medicine
Department of Health and Hospitals
777 Bannock Street
Denver, CO 80204-4507

Linda Schack, M.D.
3400 Lomita Boulevard, #305
Torrance, CA 90505

EXERCISE RESISTANCE
Francie White, M.S., R.D.
White Seminars & Productions
P.O. Box 835
Santa Ynez, CA 93460

EDITORIAL CONSULTANTS

MALES WITH EATING DISORDERS
Charles Portney, M.D.
2336 Santa Monica Boulevard, #100
Santa Monica, CA 90404

Michael Strober, Ph.D.
Program Director
Eating Disorder Program
UCLA Neuro Psychiatric Institute
760 Westwood Plaza
Los Angeles, CA 90024

TREATMENT PHILOSOPHY AND
    APPROACHES, INDIVIDUAL THERAPY
Jeff Redant, M.F.C.C.
Program Director
The Rader Institute
Washington Medical Center
12099 Washington Boulevard, #204
Los Angeles, CA 92066

Contents

PREFACE xi

INTRODUCTION xv

1 DISORDERED EATING PAST AND PRESENT 1

2 NOT FOR FEMALES ONLY 23

3 ACTIVITY DISORDER: TOO MUCH/LITTLE OF A GOOD THING 29

4 SOCIOCULTURAL INFLUENCES ON EATING, WEIGHT, AND SHAPE 45

5 EATING DISORDER BEHAVIORS ARE ADAPTIVE FUNCTIONS 53

6 HEREDITY AND BIOCHEMICAL INDIVIDUALITY 61

7 ASSESSING THE SITUATION 65

8 GUIDELINES FOR SIGNIFICANT OTHERS 85

9 TREATMENT PHILOSOPHY AND APPROACHES 95

10 INDIVIDUAL THERAPY: PUTTING THE EATING DISORDER OUT OF A JOB 109

11 SHARING THE PAIN AND THE PROMISE IN GROUP 143

12 ALL IN THE FAMILY 155

13 NUTRITION EDUCATION AND THERAPY 177

14 THE PSYCHIATRIST'S ROLE AND MEDICATION 193

15 MEDICAL MANAGEMENT OF ANOREXIA NERVOSA AND BULIMIA NERVOSA 211

16 WHEN OUTPATIENT TREATMENT IS NOT ENOUGH 223

17 INCREASING AWARENESS AND PREVENTION 247

APPENDIX A TREATMENT PROGRAMS 255

APPENDIX B RESOURCES 267

BIBLIOGRAPHY 271

INDEX 279

PREFACE

This eating disorder sourcebook was written with a large audience in mind and thus provides information for those suffering from eating disorders, their significant others, and the various professionals who encounter or treat them. This work was a formidable task since entire books have been written on topics to which I could only devote a chapter, such as males with eating disorders, compulsive exercise, family therapy, and medical management. Furthermore, my publisher wanted the book to include anorexia nervosa, bulimia nervosa, and binge eating disorder (compulsive overeating). Binge eating disorder is not yet an established DSM diagnosis, and information on it is scarce. Furthermor, binge (or compulsive) eating is seen by many as being fundamentally different than anorexia nervosa and bulimia nervosa, which seem to share more similarities than differences. Many professionals and authors in the field of eating disorders do not mix these individuals in research studies, in writing, or even in treatment programs. In fact, the American Psychiatric Association (APA) guidelines for eating disorders do not even include binge eating disorder. Philip Mehler, M.D., who wrote chapter 15 on medical management chose to write only on anorexia nervosa and bulimia nervosa noting that medical management of binge eating will involve the same considerations as when treating obese individuals. Readers who want more information on medical considerations for binge eating or any other aspect of binge eating disorder and feel that it is not sufficiently covered in this book are referred to Dr.Christopher Fairburn's book on this subject, Overcoming Binge Eating Disorder.

The overall theme of the book is to provide readers from all walks of life with the most current information available on what we know about the cause, identification, treatment, and prevention of eating disorders. Each chapter was written to answer a variety of questions commonly posed by both professional and lay people about eating disorders, including:

How do I know when a diet has turned into a disorder? (asked by a mother or father)

What are the successful techniques for therapy? (asked by a therapist)

What is the latest in medical management and the use of psychotropic medications in treating these disorders? (asked by a doctor or psychiatrist)

How do I help someone I know who has an eating disorder, and how can I prevent this from happening to others? (asked by a teacher, friend or coach)

The first chapter of the book, "Disordered Eating, Past and Present" is a discussion of disordered eating in all its various forms and provides both a historical look and the current status and statistics in regards to eating disorders in our society. The following two chapters, "Not for Females Only" and "Activity Disorder, Too Much/ Little of a Good Thing" discuss the special topics of males with eating disorders and exercise addiction, both important topics for which available literature is scarce.

Chapters 4, 5, and 6 will provide both the general reader and professionals with a thorough understanding of the complex nature of eating disorders and the three main reasons attributed to their development in an individual and as an epidemic in society. Each chapter is devoted to the current information available on the social, psychological and biochemical causes of disordered eating, exercise, and body image.

The core of the book describes in detail how to assess and deal with individuals who have eating disorders, whether coming from the professional or the significant other position. Those suffering from eating disorders can also benefit from the material. Chapter 7, "Assessing The Situation," provides checklists for various areas to cover during a comprehensive assessment. Standardized assessment tools are also reviewed and a thorough description of the recommended components of a physical exam and lab testsare delineated. The following chapter offers "Guidelines for Significant Others," for those who need help, not only in how to deal with the individual who has the eating disorder, but in how to care for other members of the family including themselves. Chapters 9 through 16 all deal, in one way or another, with the philosophy, technique, modality, and art of treatment. The three main theoretical perspectives on the nature and treatment of eating disorders are discussed and compared: the psychodynamic, cognitive behavioral, and addiction models. A combination of the psychodynamic model and cognitive behavioral model has been shown, in research and in my own clinical experience, to have greater efficacy, so the book emphasizes this approach.

The question of whether eating disorders are addictions and if eating disordered individuals can ever be fully "recovered," as opposed to in a state of "recovering," as in the case of alcoholism or drug addiction, is addressed. This issue has been a heated debate in some circles and warrants continued discussion because treatment of these disorders should always begin with the end result in mind. My own experience as a "recovered" anorexic and as a therapist treating patients for almost seventeen years, many of whom are today "recovered," heavily influenced the discussion of this topic and the material in the therapy chapters.

Individual, group, family, and nutrition therapy are all described in chapters 10, 11, 12, and 13, respectively. These chapters provide examples of real cases, excerpts from patient's journals and transcribed sections of actual therapy sessions, enriching the clinical material for both lay and professional reader. Professionals will learn such things as the importance of contacting and working with the eating disorder self; how to structure a successful group; and important tasks for the family therapist. Family members will learn about roles that the eating disordered individual may play in the family and the stages that family members or significant others go through when dealing with a loved one suffering from an eating disorder.

Necessary components of a thorough treatment plan involve "Nutrition Education and Therapy," so chapter 13 points out the goals of nutrition therapy and the various models that can be utilized.

Karen Kratina, R.D., a specialist in eating disorders and coauthor of this chapter, discusses how to choose a nutritionist and questions to ask when interviewing. Karen also provides her response to these questions to help guide the reader in what to look for.

Chapters 14 and 15, both dealing with medical issues, are two very technical ones: "The Psychiatrist's Role and Medication" and "Medical Management of Anorexia Nervosa and Bulimia Nervosa." These chapters were written with the physician in mind but lay people can greatly benefit from the knowledge and may even want to share it with their doctors or other treating professionals. These chapters discuss critical issues, covering signs and symptoms to look for, how and why certain medications are often useful, and how to deal medically with certain issues such as laxative abuse and refeeding syndrome.

"When Outpatient Treatment Is Not Enough" (chapter 16) discusses the alternatives that must be considered. Knowing when and where to turn to for more intense care is important. This chapter discusses criteria for hospitalization and other treatment options such as residential facilities or halfway houses. Ingredients of a good treatment program are described, along with questions to ask when exploring options. For a better understanding of what takes place at a treatment program, I have included a summary description and schedule of my own program, Monte Nido (Mountain Nest) which is a residential facility for anorexia nervosa, bulimia nervosa, and exercise addiction. Appendix A lists other programs around the country.

Finally, but what should come first, is the topic of prevention. Ideas on this subject are given for teachers, families, coaches, doctors, counselors, and generally to anyone interested in the cause. Suggestions include how to avoid criticizing your own body, educate people about healthy dieting, love regardless of looks, provide literature and guest speakers, and so on.

This sourcebook will answer many questions and clarify much about the cause, treatment, and prevention of eating disorders. Hopefully, it will also stimulate further questions and a quest for more knowledge. The appendix section at the end of the book is a guide to further resources including literature, organizations, and treatment programs that are available to help in this quest.

INTRODUCTION

As an eating disorder specialist for the last sixteen years, and a recovered anorexic myself for over twenty years, I have witnessed with great attentiveness the epidemic increase in the great number of eating disorder cases reported, as well as the great number of theories and modalities developed to treat these disorders. Many questions are still being asked: Are eating disorders addictions? Are they treatable? Do certain medications really help? Can eating disorder patients fully recover?

With all of our study, research, technology, and expertise, we are still uncertain as to the exact origins of these disorders. We have clues, we have ideas, we have indications of why someone develops an eating disorder, but we still cannot say "A" leads to "B." For example, we know that cultural pressure, especially on women, in our "thin-is-in society" has contributed to an increase in dieting and eating disorders. It is no surprise that 95 to 97 percent of all reported eating disorder cases are female. According to Naomi Wolfe, in her book *The Beauty Myth*, dieting is at the top of the list in risk factors for eating disorders. However, if dieting or cultural pressures were "the cause," then why wouldn't every dieter develop an eating disorder? Furthermore, what causes one person to diet to the extreme of anorexia nervosa, another to become a binge eater, and yet another to binge and purge twenty times a day?

Today, we have a better understanding of the biochemical factors that may predispose one to develop an eating disorder and/or help perpetuate it once it has started. We have discovered that bingeing, purging, starving, and compulsive exercise all affect brain chemistry neurotransmitters such as endorphins and serotonin. Serotonin is interesting in many ways. Studies indicate that increased serotonin activity could be a trait which contributes to the development of pathological feeding behavior, obsessive-compulsive behaviors, and weight loss. However, our increased understanding of brain chemistry involvement in eating disorders has not led to their eradication through medication. We do see improvement of symptoms through medication, such as the new league of antidepressants which are selective serotonin reuptake inhibitors (see chapter 14) (for example, Prozac, Zoloft, and Paxil), but these medications have either not helped or have had limited success in many cases. Furthermore, there still exists the question of whether the chemical disturbance is the cause of, or is caused by, the disorder.

There are nutritional deficiencies associated with eating disorder patients, but we don't know which came first, the deficiency or the disorder. For example, one result of dieting, zinc deficiency, can be particularly problematic. Zinc deficiency actually causes loss of taste acuity and appetite and thus will enhance or perpetuate a state of anorexia. Several investigators, including this author, have discovered zinc deficiency is common in individuals with anorexia nervosa and, to a lesser degree, those with bulimia nervosa. Furthermore, when treated with zinc supplementation, many of these individuals experience positive results and, in some cases, even remission of symptoms.

To imply that a nutrient like zinc or a medication could cure or that abstinence from certain foods could resolve eating disorders is making leaps in the application of a limited amount of knowledge due to an eagerness to find causes and solutions. Yet, this is what often happens without adequate clinical trials which include controls. The application of the term *addiction* to eating disorders and the consequent twelve-step approach is one of those leaps.

Some people with eating disorders may have a problem with, and do well abstaining from, certain food items like sugar and white flour. Although I cannot support the ingestion of these food items as good nutrition, I stop short of calling them addictive and blaming them as a causative factor in eating disorders. In rare cases this might be true, yet for the most part, it is the attitude regarding the food, the meaning the food has, and the relationship with food—not the food itself—that is the problem. Patients who binge eat will ultimately binge on anything including roast beef, whole-wheat pasta, chips, and

French fries. Proclaiming abstinence from sugar and white flour, while continuing to binge on other foods, is truly missing the point. Individuals with bulimia nervosa often choose to binge on food items with white flour and sugar, but close inspection reveals that this choice is driven by the imposed restriction of these very foods in the first place. Finding a bulimic who does not have a history of dieting is like finding a needle in a haystack. Many bulimics will eat and purge anything, including a single peach or a glass of water. Yet eating disorders are still being referred to and treated by some as addictions. If they are addictions, why is one person afflicted and not the next? Why haven't drugs helped more people, and why do bulimics binge and purge vegetables and roast beef? If an addict is someone who surrenders to something habitually or obsessively in spite of aversive consequences, is secretive about the behavior, and experiences withdrawal without it, then eating disorders perhaps are addictions, but not in the normally perceived way. Rather than blaming "addictive foods," there may be other components of a biochemical and psychological nature that tend to foster the addictive pattern of disordered eating styles in individuals with anorexia, bulimia, and binge eating disorder. Our knowledge in the area of biochemical individuality and its role in the development of eating disorder is growing by leaps and bounds. Evidence indicates that there may very well be biochemical predispositions for eating disorders that can be identified and treated. These discoveries will not only enhance the treatment of eating disorders, but will aid in prevention.

In the psychological realm, it is generally understood that eating disorders are symptoms of other underlying issues (for example, self-esteem, control, perfectionism, and so on). Disordered eating and other weight-related behaviors serve as adaptive functions for the individual pondering such things as a way of nurturing or protecting oneself, soothing tension, expressing anger, dissociating from a traumatic event, or creating an identity. But why would a person need to have such an adaptive function? What real function was not supplied, what need not met, that the person would have to turn to such measures?

Human beings all have certain developmental needs which require caregiving responses of a particular nature in order for them to experience a sense of well-being. These responses are necessary for the emergence, maintenance, and completion of the self. It seems that individuals with eating disorders have unconsciously, over time, turned to food or eating rituals, rather than people, for meeting certain needs, perhaps because previous attempts with caregivers have brought about disappointment, frustration, or even abuse. The problem is that neither food nor food rituals (starving, bingeing, purging) can work, because these behaviors do not provide the necessary responsiveness or self-growth. By turning to food, or food rituals, the person only negates the true need and circumvents the hurt—nothing internal changes and no greater capacity to deal with problems and meet needs is internalized. The result of this behavior is that the individual has to keep repeating the food ritual behaviors to get the needed result, whether it be a sense of calmness, control, accomplishment, or love. One often hears comments from eating disorder patients such as "eating calms me down," "food doesn't talk back or ask anything of me," "I can relax after I purge," "I feel successful if I have lost a pound." Whether conscious or unconscious, the repetition of the behavior becomes necessary for the person to continue to meet the need or feel whole. The continued repeated behavior becomes addictive. This kind of psychological addiction is no less powerful than a biochemical one. With this in mind, it is easy to see how the disease model and addiction approach to treating these disorders falls short.

Abstinence is an all-or-nothing, black or white issue in drug and alcohol addiction treatment. Food, however, is a particularly difficult "substance" to abstain from or try to control. Abstinence from certain foods can be achieved but this does not always lead to the cessation of binge eating or purging and has little to do with starving. Furthermore, restricting food as part of a treatment plan for anorexia nervosa seems particularly contraindicated. Treating eating disorders involves controlling thoughts and behaviors. Recovery from an eating disorder also involves not only symptom management but cognitive behavioral therapy (see chapter 9) to deal with black-and-white thinking as well as psychotherapy to discover the function that the bingeing, starving, or purging is fulfilling and to resolve the underlying issues.

If treatment focuses on symptom management, without due attention paid to underlying etiology (the origins and causes of the symptoms), it will not eradicate the need for symptomatic behaviors. Therefore, behaviors such as bingeing and purging, if they stop at all, may just become some other form of negative behavior immediately or later. I have seen patients treated with an overemphasis on their symptons cease their eating disorder behaviors only to switch to drugs, alcohol, or self-mutilating behaviors like cutting and burning.

Treatment is further complicated because there is a variety of biochemical disturbances that may have been present before the eating disorder, or are the result of the eating disorder behaviors. These disturbances create, or exacerbate, problems such as loss of appetite, depression, lack of concentration, mood swings, even "highs" created by certain behaviors. It is often difficult to sort out what is causing what. The American Psychiatric Association's rule of thumb in the treatment of eating disorders is nutritional rehabilitation first, before medication. This certainly makes sense, as we know that many mood disorders and other psychological symptoms experienced by eating disorder patients clear up with nutrition rehabilitation. Even brain wave and neurotransmitter disturbances have been shown to return to normal after weight restoration. However, nutritional rehabilitation is not always easy to come by, and treating professionals often prescribe medication such as antidepressants in the hope of helping the patient to eat in order to achieve nutritional rehabilitation. This presents a sort of "Catch 22."

With eating disorder patients, there is a critical need for continued monitoring, assessing, and reevaluating the nature and form of treatment and treatment response. When to give medication and what medication to give are a part of this difficult picture.

Last, eating disorders are difficult to prevent and to treat due to the intense, increased, continuous positive feedback that individuals (mostly women) get from their peers, strangers, and our society in general for "achieving control" over food and the sleek bodies attained as a result. If an adolescent girl never gets asked out on a date until she begins an extreme regimen of dieting and vomiting after meals, thus losing twenty pounds, the message is "to be accepted and desirable is to be thin at any cost." Sad as it is, an anorexic's body is her trophy, displayed for the admiration it receives. "Oh, how I wish I could be anorexic even if for just a short time" is a common female refrain.

I believe that, like myself, people with eating disorders can be cured. However, to help individuals afflicted with eating disorders to fully recover, we must help them understand how they have given up all of their strivings and longings for an obsession. We must help them see how their internal conflicts have shifted from the real and vital issue of their own development to the symbolic issue of the size of their bodies and the amount of food they eat. What was written about one of the first documented eating disorder cases, the patient known as Ellen West, can be said about any woman suffering now. "Her rage, which arose initially because of the restrictions imposed upon her self-development, is now directed, through her body, at the 'inner self' which hungers for its development. It is a costly and tragic reversal . . . her obsession with her body is, fundamentally, an expression of violence towards her soul."

We still have a lot to learn about eating disorders and the individuals who have them. In the meantime, every individual who has an eating disorder should be treated with a multidimensional approach, involving nutritional, biochemical, and psychological perspectives. An understanding of the importance of all of these areas is necessary for those suffering from eating disorders, their significant others, and the people who treat them. My purpose in this book is to provide a summary of the current knowledge in the field, to examine the continued mystery we still must deal with in terms of our full understanding of how someone could binge or starve themselves into a ruined life or even death, and to provide the available information on how, by whom, and in what manner these disorders can be prevented, dealt with, and overcome.

Carolyn Costin, M.A., M.Ed., M.F.C.C., Director,
Eating Disorder Center of California
(805) 495-9629 or (310) 457-9958

1

DISORDERED EATING
PAST AND PRESENT

Anorexia nervosa and bulimia nervosa have become familiar house-hold words. As recently as the 1980s, it was difficult to find anybody who knew the true meaning of these terms, much less to know someone truly suffering from one of these syndromes. Today disordered eating is common, and having an eating disorder is almost trendy. Anorexia and bulimia have become, for approximately 2 percent of the female population, the acceptable weight loss methods of the 1990s. Binge eating disorder, a newly named syndrome, seems in part to be a backlash response to the rampant overuse of strict dieting. Eating disorders are becoming so common that the question seems to be not, "Why do so many people develop eating disorders?" but rather, "How is it that anyone, particularly if female, does not?"

The first hint that eating disorders might become a serious problem was introduced in 1973 in a book by Hilde Bruch called *Eating Disorders: Obesity, Anorexia Nervosa, and the Person Within.* It was the first major work on eating disorders, but was geared to professionals and was not readily available to the public. Then in 1978, Hilde Bruch gave us her pioneer work, *The Golden Cage* which continues to provide a compelling, passionate, and empathetic understanding of the nature of eating disorders, particularly anorexia nervosa, and of those who develop them. Finally, the public, for better or worse, began to be educated. With the book and the television movie *The Best Little Girl in the World*, Steven Levenkron brought the knowledge of anorexia nervosa into the average home. And in 1985, when Karen Carpenter died from heart failure due to anorexia nervosa, eating disorders made the headlines as the emaciated picture of the famous and talented singer haunted the public from the cover of

People magazine and in the national news. Since then, women's magazines began and have not ceased to run feature articles on eating disorders, and we learned that people who we thought had everything—beauty, success, power, and control—were lacking something else, as many began admitting that they, too, had eating disorders. Jane Fonda told us she had bulimia and had been purging food for years. Olympic gold medalist gymnast Kathy Rigby revealed a struggle with anorexia and bulimia that almost took her life, and several others followed suit: Gilda Radner, Princess Di, Sally Field, Elton John, Tracy Gold, Paula Abdul, and the late gymnast Christy Heinrich, to name just a few.

Characters with eating disorders started appearing in books, plays, and television series. Hospital treatment programs sprang up across the country, marketing to those afflicted with phrases such as, "It's not what you're eating, it's what's eating you," "It's not your fault," and "Are you losing it?" Eating disorders finally made it to top billing when Henry Jaglom produced and directed a major motion picture titled simply but provocatively, *Eating*. The scenes in this film, many of which are unrehearsed excerpts of monologues or dialogues happening between women at a party, are revealing, compelling, sad, and disturbing. The film and this book are in part about the war in which females in our society are engaged, the war between the natural desire to eat and the biological reality that doing so deprives them of attaining the standard of appearance held up for them to achieve. Talk shows on eating disorders are at an all-time high, featuring every possible eating disorder angle one can imagine: "Anorexics and Their Moms," "Pregnant Women with Bulimia," "Males with Eating Disorders," "Eating Disordered Twins," "Eating Disorders and Sexual Abuse."

When people ask, "Are eating disorders really more common now or have they just been in hiding?" the answer is, "Both." First, the numbers of individuals with eating disorders do seem to be continually increasing, paralleling society's increasing obsession with losing weight. Feelings that may have been brought out in other ways in the past now find expression through the pursuit of thinness. Second, it is easier to admit that a problem exists when that problem is better understood by society and there is help available to treat it. Even though individuals suffering from eating disorders are reluctant to admit it, they do so more now than in the past because they and their significant others are more likely to know that they have an illness, the possible consequences of that illness, and that they can get help for it. The trouble is, they often wait too long. Knowing when problem eating has become an eating disorder is difficult to determine. When is the line between disordered eating and an eating disorder crossed? We can begin with the fact that to be officially diagnosed with an eating disorder, one has to meet the clinical diagnostic criteria.

DIAGNOSTIC CRITERIA FOR EATING DISORDERS

The following clinical descriptions are taken from *The Diagnostic and Statistical Manual of Mental Disorders, Fourth Edition.*

ANOREXIA NERVOSA

A. Refusal to maintain body weight at or above a minimally normal weight for age and height (for example, weight loss leading to maintenance of body weight less than 85 percent of that expected, or failure to make expected weight gain during period of growth leading to body weight less than 85 percent of that expected).

B. Intense fear of gaining weight or becoming fat, even though underweight.

C. Disturbance in the way in which one's body weight or shape is experienced, undue influence of body weight or shape on self-evaluation, or denial of the seriousness of the current low body weight.

D. In postmenarcheal females, amenorrhea (for example, absence of at least three consecutive menstrual cycles). A woman is considered to have amenorrhea if her periods occur only following hormone (for example, estrogen) administration.

Restricting Type: During the current episode of anorexia nervosa, the person has not regularly engaged in binge eating or purging behavior (for example, self-induced vomiting or the misuse of laxatives, diuretics, or enemas).

Binge Eating/Purging Type: During the current episode of anorexia nervosa, the person has regularly engaged in binge eating or purging behavior (for example, self-induced vomiting or the misuse of laxatives, diuretics, or enemas).

The case of anorexia nervosa most often cited as the earliest in the literature was of a twenty-year-old girl treated in 1686 by Richard Morton and described in his work, *Phthisiologia: or a Treatise of Consumption's.* Morton's description of what he termed "nervous consumption" sounds eerily familiar: "I do not remember that I did ever in my entire Practice see one, that was so conversant with the Living so much wasted with the greatest degree of Consumption, (like a Skeleton only clad with Skin) yet there was no Fever, but on the contrary a Coldness of the whole Body. . .Only her Appetite was diminished, and Digestion uneasy, with Fainting Fitts, (sic) which did frequently return upon her."

The first case study where we have descriptive detail from the patient's perspective is that of a woman known as Ellen West (1900–1933) who at age thirty-three committed suicide to end her desperate struggle that had manifested itself through an obsession with thinness and with food. Ellen kept a diary which contains perhaps the earliest record of the inner world of the eating disordered person:

Everything agitates me and I experience every agitation as a sensation of hunger, even if I have just eaten.

I am afraid of myself. I am afraid of the feelings to which I am defenselessly delivered over every minute.

I am in prison and cannot get out. It does no good for the analyst to tell me that I myself place the armed men there, that they are theatrical figments and not real. To me they are very real.

The woman of today suffering from an eating disorder, like Ellen West, appears to exhibit rigid control of her "out of controlness," making an effort to purge herself of yearnings, ambitions, and sensual pleasures. Emotions are feared and translated into somatic (body) experiences and eating disorder behaviors, which serve to eliminate the feeling aspect of self. Through their struggle with their bodies, anorexics are striving for mind over matter, perfection, and mastery of self, all of the things for which unfortunately their peers and our society in general willingly praise and applaud them. This, of course, entrenches the patterns into the very fabric of each individual's identity. Persons with anorexia nervosa seem not to have this disorder but to become it.

Quotes like Ellen's are repeated by patients today with amazing similarity.

I am in my own prison. No matter what anyone says, I have sentenced myself to thinness for life. I will die here. Judy, 1994, anorexic

It does not matter if everyone else tells me that I am not fat, that it is all in my head. Even if it is in my head I placed the thoughts there. They are mine. I know my therapist thinks I am making a bad choice but it's my choice and I do not want to eat. Andrea, 1995, anorexic

When I eat I feel. It is better if I don't feel, I am too afraid.

Ellen West was given several different diagnoses throughout her lifetime including manic depression and schizophrenia, but reading back through her diaries and studying the case, it is clear that she suffered at different times from both anorexia nervosa and bulimia nervosa and that her desperate battle with these eating disorders drove her to take her own life. Ellen West, Judy, and Andrea are not suffering from a loss of hunger, but a hunger they cannot explain.

The term *anorexia* is of Greek origin: *an* (privation, lack of) and *orexis* (appetite), thus meaning a lack of desire to eat. It was originally used to describe the loss of appetite caused by some other ailment such as headaches, depression, or cancer, where the person actually doesn't feel hungry. Normally, appetite is like the response to pain, beyond the individual's control. The term *anorexia* alone is an insufficient label for the eating disorder known commonly by that name. Persons afflicted with this disorder have not just lost their appetites; in fact they long to eat, obsess and dream about it, and some of them even break down and eat uncontrollably. Patients report spending 70 to 85 percent of each day thinking about food, creating menus, baking, feeding others, worrying about what to eat, bingeing on food, and purging to get rid of food eaten. The full clinical term, *anorexia nervosa* (lack of desire to eat due to a mental disorder) is a more appropriate name for the illness. This now commonly known term was not used until 1874 when a British physician, Sir William Gull, used it to describe several patients he had seen who exhibited all the familiar signs we associate with this disorder today: refusal to eat, extreme weight loss, amenorrhea, low pulse rate, constipation, and hyperactivity, all of which he thought resulted from a "morbid mental state." There were other early researchers who pointed out individuals with these symptoms and began to develop theories about why they would behave in such a fashion. Pierre Janet, from France, described the syndrome most succinctly when he concluded that "it is due to a deep psychological disturbance, of which the refusal of food is but the outer expression."

Individuals with anorexia nervosa may eventually develop a true lack of appetite, but for the most part it is not a loss of appetite but rather a strong desire to control it that is a cardinal feature. Rather than lose their desire to eat, anorexics, while suffering from the disorder, deny their bodies even when driven by hunger pangs, and they obsess about food all day long. They often want to eat so badly that they cook for and feed others, study menus, read and concoct recipes, go to bed thinking about food, dream about food, and wake up thinking about food. They simply don't allow themselves to have it and, if they do, they relentlessly pursue any means to get rid of it.

Anorexics are afraid of food and afraid of themselves. What begins as a determination to lose weight continues and progresses to be a morbid fear of gaining any lost weight back, and becomes a relentless pursuit of thinness. These individuals are literally dying to be thin. Being thin, which translates to "being in control," becomes the most important thing in the world.

In the throes of the disorder, anorexics are terrified of losing control, terrified of what might happen if they allowed themselves to eat. This would mean a lack of willpower, a complete "giving in," and they fear that once they let up on the control they have imposed on themselves, they will never get "in control" again. They are afraid that, if they allow themselves to eat, they will not stop, and if they gain one pound today or even this week, that they are now "gaining." A pound today means another pound later and then another and another until they are obese. Physiologically speaking, there is a good reason for this feeling. When a person is starving, the brain is constantly sending impulses to eat. The strength of these impulses to eat is such that the feeling that one may not be able to stop is powerful. Self-induced starvation goes against normal bodily instincts and can rarely be maintained. This is one reason why many anorexics ultimately end up binge eating and purging food to the point where approximately 50 percent develop bulimia nervosa.

Anorexics fear, as crazy as it may seem when looking at them, that they are or will become fat, weak, undisciplined, and unworthy. To them, losing weight is good and gaining weight is bad, period. With the progression of the illness, eventually there are no longer fattening foods but simply the dictum that "food is fattening." The anorexic mind-set seems useful at the beginning of a diet when the goal is to lose a few unwanted pounds, but when the dieting itself becomes the goal, there is no way out. The dieting becomes a purpose and what can be referred to as "a safe place to go." It's a world created to help cope with feelings of meaninglessness, of low self-esteem, of failure, of dissatisfaction, of the need to be unique, the desire to be special, to be a success, to be in control. Anorexics create a world where they can feel/be "successful," "good," and "safe" if they can deny food, making it through the day eating little if anything at all. They consider it a threat and failure if they break down and eat too much, which for them can be as little as six hundred calories or even less. In fact, for some anorexics, eating anything over one hundred calories in one item usually causes great anxiety. Anorexics seem to prefer two-digit numbers when it comes to eating and to weight. This kind of overcontrol and exertion of mind over matter goes against our understanding of all normal physiological impulses and instincts for survival. Of the eating disorders, anorexia nervosa is the most rare.

The following describes a more common manifestation of disordered eating, bulimia nervosa.

BULIMIA NERVOSA

A. Recurrent episodes of binge eating. An episode of binge eating is characterized by both of the following:

   1. Eating, in a discreet period of time (for example, within any two-hour period), an amount of food that is definitely larger than most people would eat during a similar period of time and under similar circumstances.

   2. A sense of lack of control over eating during the episode (for example, a feeling that one cannot stop eating or control what or how much one is eating).

B. Recurrent inappropriate compensatory behavior in order to prevent weight gain, such as self-induced vomiting, misuse of laxatives, diuretics, enemas, or other medications; fasting; or excessive exercise.

C. The binge eating and other compensatory behaviors both occur, on the average, at least twice a week for three months.

D. Self-evaluation is unduly influenced by body shape and weight.

E. The disturbance does not occur exclusively during episodes of anorexia nervosa.

Purging Type: During the current episode of bulimia nervosa, the person has regularly engaged in self-induced vomiting or the misuse of laxatives, diuretics, or enemas.

Nonpurging Type: During the current episode of bulimia nervosa, the person has used other inappropriate compensatory behaviors, such as fasting or excessive exercise, but has not regularly engaged in self-induced vomiting or the misuse of laxatives, diuretics, or enemas.

The term _bulimia_ is derived from Latin and means "hunger of an ox." It is commonly known that the Romans engaged in binge eating and vomiting rituals, but it was first described in medical terms in 1903 in _Obsessions et la Psychasthenie_, where the author, Pierre Janet, describes Nadia, a woman who engaged in compulsive binges in secret.

It is the bingeing that separates anorexics from bulimics, even though both populations will restrict food consumption and many anorexics also purge. Anorexics who purge and normal-weight individuals who do not binge but vomit whenever they eat food they consider "too fattening" are often improperly diagnosed with bulimia nervosa. Without binge eating, a diagnosis of bulimia is not correct. The disorders do seem to cross over into each other. Most people with bulimia have thought patterns and experience symptoms similar to those of anorexics. The drive for thinness and the fear of being fat appear in both disorders and while body image distortion is present in bulimia, it is usually not to the same degree as in anorexia nervosa.

Most people with bulimia restrict caloric intake such that they try to keep a weight that is too low for them to maintain without experiencing many of the symptoms of semi-starvation. Some bulimics are at or above normal weight but nevertheless experience starvation symptoms due to the restriction of food intake when not binge eating. Bulimics live in a world between compulsive, or binge eating, and anorexia, pulled in both directions. Bulimics are often referred to as failed anorexics—they have repeatedly tried to control their weight by restricting intake and have been unable to do so. These individuals end up bingeing and, out of anxiety and desperation, then purge through self-induced vomiting, laxatives, or diuretics, or use other compensatory behaviors to make up for their binges, such as fasting, exercise, saunas, or other similar means. On the other hand, many bulimics describe themselves as binge eaters first who then resort to purging after other dieting fail.

Purging and other compensatory behaviors actually calm bulimics down and ease their guilt and anxiousness about having consumed too much food or gained weight. As the disorder progresses, bulimics will purge or compensate for eating even normal or small amounts of anything they consider "bad" or "fattening" and, eventually, any food at all. Binges can eventually be quite extreme. For example, binges of up to 50,000 calories a day have been recorded. A major university even claimed it had to put signs up in its dormitory bathrooms pleading, "Please stop throwing up, you're ruining our plumbing!" The acid from vomiting was ruining the pipes.

Overall, it is important to understand that bulimia nervosa, which appears in the beginning to be related to dieting and weight control, eventually becomes a means of mood regulation in general. A bulimic finds solace in food and often in the purging itself. The act of purging becomes powerfully addictive, not just because it controls weight, but because it is calming, or serves as a way of expressing anger, or in some other way helps the individual cope, albeit destructively.

In fact, bulimics seem to be individuals who need help regulating or modulating mood states and therefore are more prone to use a variety of coping mechanisms such as drugs, alcohol, and even sex. Families of patients with bulimia nervosa also have increased rates of substance abuse, mood disorders, and obesity.

Social functioning and adjustment among bulimics vary. For one thing, unlike anorexics, bulimics are not easily identified and are able to be successful at work, in school, and in relationships, while keeping the bulimia a secret. Patients have disclosed their bulimia to therapists after successfully hiding it from everyone, including their spouses, for sometimes for as long as twenty years. Some bulimics become so entrenched in the disorder, bingeing and purging eighteen or more times per day, that they have little or no ability to perform on the job or in school and have marked difficulty with relationships.

Bulimics are almost always distressed by their behaviors and at the same time are amazed, surprised, and even horrified at their own inability to control them. They often talk about their bulimia as though they were not in control of it, as if they were possessed by something, or as if monsters were inside of them. They are alarmed at the things they hear themselves saying or what they have written. Below are quotes taken from patients' journals.

I sometimes find myself in the middle of a binge not knowing how I got there, it is like something is in control of me someone or some thing I don't even know.

I never eat bran muffins or cereal or any kind of dessert during the day, only at night. And then I binge on it. I actually go to the store during the night and get it. I keep telling myself I'm not going to do it, but I find myself at the store . . . and later eating and throwing up. Afterwards I say I won't do it again, but I always do. This is so sick.

Dinner time so I went and got a bowl of salad with tortilla chips. Then I had a corn muffin that I had bought that day. The corn muffin led to some cereal, then I just stopped and went to my room to go to sleep. Fell asleep for a while, woke up and had a corn muffin, bagel and some more cereal. Oh so full and bummed that I blew it again with bingeing. Hadn't thrown up yet, But I knew it was inevitable. I tried putting it off, I went onto the couch in the family room and tried sleeping there but that didn't work. I was too uncomfortable. I wish I was afraid to throw-up. I am tired of this whole thing. I don't like to throw-up, I don't even like bingeing as much as I use to. It doesn't feel the same now, as it use to feel, and it doesn't leave me feeling the way it use to. Then why do I keep doing it? I don't want to binge tonight, but I am afraid of what might become of me, if I don't! God, I wish I were with somebody right now. I keep trying to have this dialogue with myself.

I have been thinking about it lately in terms of license plates. Seven digits of synopsis; a Reader's Digest of my soul; and I came up with a few options. Monster, perhaps, will win the day. . . .Monster for the disgust it inspires. We could fault our narcissistic culture; we could point to a dysfunctional upbringing; and yet none of these alibis could redeem me of

*my status. To be a bulimic, a dumpster-snacking, bum-rolling,
gutter variety bulimic, is to have transposed into such a state
of Monsterdom. Perfect as a license plate, saying as it does all
that really needs to be understood of me. . . . being a Monster
is expensive. Monster math looks like this: assume, conserva-
tively speaking, you have purged 5 times a day for the last
four years. That is 35 times a week, 140 times a month,
1,680 times a year, 6,720 times in the four years. At each
occasion, you purged 30,000 calories worth of food (sometimes much more, sometimes less) for a total of 20,160,000
calories purged. Here we have a small African village. The
experts at UNICEF have agreed that a subsistence diet for
each of the villagers would be 1,500 a day. One African
man, on the 20,160,000 calories I either flushed down the
toilet, left in a back alley, or concealed in plastic bags for
later dumping, could live for almost 37 years. 500 villagers
could eat for 27 days. A new twist on the "starving people in
Africa" scenario, for which we clean our plates as children.
This is being a Monster.*

Because they feel ashamed of their behavior, out of control, taken over, and even possessed, bulimics often come into treatment seemingly more motivated than anorexics to have their eating disorders taken away. Goals have to be carefully explored due to the fact that motivation to seek help may be generated only by the desire to stop bingeing and become a better anorexic. Bulimics believe that bingeing is the root of their problem, the thing to be ashamed of and to control. It is common for bulimics to express their desire to stop bingeing but their reluctance to give up restrictive dieting. Furthermore, bulimics believe that, if they could just stop bingeing, the purging would stop, so they assert their efforts toward controlling their eating, thus setting themselves up again for a binge which is almost always secondary to the restricting.

Unlike in bulimia nervosa, there are individuals for whom bingeing is the primary problem, and the compulsive consumption of food is due to causes other than restricting. These individuals, if they do not resort to some form of purging or restricting, suffer from binge eating disorder, described in the following section.

BINGE EATING DISORDER

The term *binge eating disorder (BED)*, was officially introduced in 1992 at an International Eating Disorders Conference. The term was developed to describe individuals who binge eat but do not use extreme compensatory behaviors such as fasting or purging to lose weight. In the past, these individuals were often referred to as compulsive overeaters, emotional overeaters, or food addicts. Many of these individuals suffer from debilitating patterns of eating for self-soothing rather than following physiological cues to eat. This nonhunger eating, when done on a regular basis, produces weight gain and even obesity. Physicians, dietitians, and other health professionals often focus on the individual's overweight state without inquiring about possible eating disorder behaviors such as binge eating patterns or other forms of overeating done for the purposes of psychological self-medicating.

Some professionals are of the opinion that there are two distinct subcategories of binge eating: deprivation-sensitive binge eating and addictive or dissociative binge eating. Deprivation-sensitive binge eating appears to be the result of weight loss diets or periods of restrictive eating, both of which result in binge eating episodes. Addictive or dissociative binge eating is the practice of self-medicating or self-soothing with food unrelated to prior restricting. Many individuals report feelings of numbness, dissociation, calmness, or regaining of inner equilibrium after binge eating. More research is necessary to prevent the ongoing inappropriate treatment of binge eating disorders solely with weight loss diets and exercise programs. These types of recommendations may exacerbate the eating disorder and tragically fail individuals needing more extensive help to recover.

Although the research is scarce, it suggests that approximately one-fifth of the people who present for the treatment of obesity meet the criteria for BED. In the DSM IV, binge eating disorder is not an officially recognized eating disorder but is included in the category titled, "Eating Disorder Not Otherwise Specified," which will be discussed later. However, BED is also listed in the DSM IV in a category for proposed diagnoses and includes diagnostic criteria to aid further study.

DSM IV RESEARCH CRITERIA FOR BINGE EATING DISORDER

A. Recurrent episodes of binge eating. An episode of binge eating is characterized by both of the following:

    1. eating, in a discrete period of time (for example, within any two-hour period), an amount of food that is definitely larger than most people would eat in a similar period of time under similar circumstances; and

    2. a sense of lack of control over eating during the episode (for example, a feeling that one cannot stop eating or control what or how much one is eating).

B. The binge eating episodes are associated with three (or more) of the following:

    1. eating much more rapidly than normal,

    2. eating until feeling uncomfortably full,

    3. eating large amounts of food when not feeling physically hungry,

    4. eating alone because of being embarrassed by how much one is eating,

    5. feeling disgusted with oneself, depressed, or very guilty after overeating.

C. Marked distress regarding binge eating is present.

D. The binge eating occurs, on average, at least two days a week for six months. Note: The method of determining frequency differs from that used for bulimia nervosa; future research should address whether the preferred method of setting a frequency

---

> threshold is counting the number of days on which binges occur or counting the number of episodes of binge eating.
>
> E. The binge eating is not associated with the regular use of inappropriate compensatory behaviors (for example, purging, fasting, excessive exercise) and does not occur exclusively during the course of anorexia nervosa or bulimia nervosa.

Binge eating has been described as part of the diagnostic criteria of bulimia nervosa but is the central feature in binge eating disorder, which has surely existed as long as the other primary eating disorders even without its own official DSM category.

To distinguish simple overeating from binge eating, as in distinguishing dieting from anorexia, we need to look at definition and degree. According to the *Oxford English Dictionary*, the term *binge* refers to "a heavy drinking bout, hence a spree." For several years bingeing or binge drinking were terms commonly used in Alcoholics Anonymous meetings. But according to one definition in *Webster's Collegiate Dictionary, Tenth Edition*, the word *binge* can be applied to anything where there is "an unrestrained or excessive indulgence." In binge eating disorder, the food is binged on in a discrete period of time with the individual reporting an inability to stop or to control the behavior. According to the book *Overcoming Binge Eating*, by Dr. Christopher Fairburn, one in five young women today report this experience with food.

Binge eating was first observed and reported in studies on obesity in the late 1950s by Dr. Albert Stunkard of the University of Pennsylvania. In the 1980s, additional studies on obesity and bulimia nervosa showed that many people in both populations have binge eating problems without the other criteria for bulimia nervosa. A research group headed by Dr. Robert Spitzer of Columbia University proposed that a new disorder called "pathological overeating syndrome" be used to describe these individuals. Then in 1992, the term "binge eating disorder" was adopted at the International Eating Disorders Conference.

Binge eating disorder seems to affect a more diverse population than the other eating disorders; for example, men and African Americans appear to be equally at risk as women and Caucasians, and the age group is broader.

It is a common misconception that all people with binge eating disorder are overweight. It is also very important to clarify that being overweight or even obese is not enough to warrant the diagnosis of binge eating disorder. There are a variety of causes for obesity. Some overweight individuals graze on food all day long or eat foods with high caloric density but do not binge. Researchers in weight control and obesity are increasingly discovering evidence that biological and biochemical predispositions play a role.

The focus of treatment for this disorder is the individual's binge eating, compulsivity with food, inability to control food intake, and using food as a method of coping with anxiety or other underlying issues. Attempting to lose weight before resolving any psychological, emotional, or relational issues will most likely result in failure.

The following are excerpts from the diaries of binge eaters.

When I start eating I can't stop. I don't know when I'm hungry or when I'm full anymore. I really don't know, I can't remember what it was like to know. Once I start, I just keep eating until I literally can't take another bite.

I like to eat when I'm tired because I don't have enough energy to enjoy doing something more active. I'd like some nachos right now a lot of nachos right now. A lot of nachos with lots of cheese—super nachos with guacamole and jalapenos, plus everything and then I could go for some toast and cinnamon toast with lots of butter, cinnamon, and sugar. Then I wish we had some cheesecake that would be good with crunchy graham cracker crust and creamy filling. Then I would like something with chocolate such as, chocolate ice cream or soft brownies with vanilla ice cream and magic shell or magic shell on coffee ice cream or Swiss almond or oatmeal cookies and vanilla Haagen Daz with magic shell! Nuked rice cakes—popcorn rice

*cakes, still warm. Also I would like a whole bowl full of
granola; really good granola with milk. I want granola on ice
cream with magic shell! GRUB! Haagen Daz bar; vanilla with
chocolate cover and almonds or coffee toffee crunch. Then I
would like toast with butter and spun honey. Yum! Then soft
bread biscuits with butter and spun honey. Yum! Hot, soft biscuits with butter and honey; big ones, crusty on the outside and
soft on the inside. Then butter and honey melted together.
Food—different taste combinations new experiences—old familiar comforts like pancakes and toast are comforting. The
experiments with ice cream are new experiences—breakfast
foods seem to be more comforting—toast, cereal, pancakes, etc.
. . . They comfort—a reminder of safety and security. Having
breakfast in the comfort of your home before embarking on the
rigors of the day. It is a reminder that safety and security are
tangibly accessible—symbolized in breakfast foods.*

EATING DISORDERS NOT OTHERWISE SPECIFIED

Aside from binge eating disorder, there are several other variants of
disordered eating that do not meet the diagnostic criteria for anorexia
nervosa or bulimia nervosa, but nevertheless are eating disorders
requiring treatment. In fact, according to Christopher Fairburn and
Timothy Walsh, in their chapter titled "Atypical Eating Disorders"
from the book *Eating Disorders and Obesity* (1995), roughly one-third
of those who present for treatment of an "eating disorder" fall into this
category. The DSM IV places the atypical eating disorders into a
category commonly referred to as EDNOS, which stands for
"Eating Disorders Not Otherwise Specified." In this category are
syndromes that resemble anorexia nervosa or bulimia nervosa but
fall short of an essential feature or are not of the required severity,
thus precluding either diagnosis. Also in this category are eating disorders that may present quite differently from anorexia or bulimia
nervosa, such as binge eating disorder, described above. The diagnosis of EDNOS is used for chronic dieters who purge what is
considered by them to be "fattening" foods, even though they seldom

or never binge and do not restrict their eating to the point of severe weight loss.

EDNOS INCLUDES:

- anorexics with menses
- anorexics who despite significant weight loss are in the normal weight range
- bulimics who don't meet the frequency or duration requirement for symptoms
- purgers who don't binge
- individuals who chew and spit out food
- those with binge eating disorder

Even without meeting the full diagnostic criteria for one of the major eating disorders, it is clear that individuals with some form of EDNOS also need help. The people described in this book, no matter how varied and unique, are all suffering from disordered eating, a disordered society, and a disordered self.

EATING DISORDER STATISTICS—HOW BAD IS IT?

The following statistics were gathered from several resources, including the American Psychiatric Association Practice Guidelines for Eating Disorders, a ten-year study conducted by the National Association of Anorexia Nervosa and Associated Disorders, and the research of Walter Kaye, M.D. from the University of Pittsburgh.

FREQUENCY AND ONSET OF ILLNESS

The prevalence of anorexia nervosa and bulimia nervosa seems to be increasing and may range from 1 to 4 percent of adolescent and young adult women in predominantly white upper-middle and middle-class student groups. Even though the prevalence of these disorders is lower in other populations, increasing numbers of eating disorder cases are seen in males, minorities, and other age groups. A ten-year study conducted by ANAD (The National Association of

Anorexia Nervosa and Associated Disorders) found that seven million women and one million men suffer from anorexia nervosa and bulimia nervosa in the United States, with approximately 86 percent reporting onset by the age of twenty. The breakdown regarding onset reported by ANAD is as follows:

- 10 percent report onset at ten years or younger,
- 33 percent report onset between the ages of eleven and fifteen,
- 43 percent report onset between the ages of one and twenty.

DURATION OF ILLNESS

- 77 percent report duration of illness from one to fifteen years with the following breakdown:
- 30 percent report duration from one to five years,
- 31 percent report duration from six to ten years,
- 16 percent report duration from eleven to fifteen years.

Approximately 50 percent of anorexics develop bulimia nervosa, which is the more common illness of the two. Studies on bulimia nervosa have indicated that 25 to 35 percent of college-aged women are engaging in bingeing and purging as a weight management technique. Nearly a third of female college athletes have reported practicing diet abuses such as self-induced vomiting, bingeing, and taking laxatives, diuretics, and diet pills. There are fewer studies, particularly long term, on bulimia nervosa than anorexia nervosa. Bulimia nervosa has only been recognized in the *Diagnostic and Statistical Manual of Mental Disorders* as a separate diagnosis from anorexia nervosa since the mid-1980s.

Eating disorders are often seen in higher numbers in psychiatric populations suffering from various types and degrees of psychological illness. In the last few years there has been increasing attention paid to the relationship between eating disorders and sexual abuse, with a range of studies indicating that anywhere from 20 to 85 percent of those with eating disorders have suffered from sexual abuse. The variations in these studies are in part due to the definition of sexual abuse used and the populations surveyed; for example, inpatient versus outpatient populations.

19

PROGNOSIS AND MORTALITY RATE

Eating disorder patients can fully recover. It is important for clinicians, patients, and loved ones to understand that recovery can take many years and that it is not possible to predict at the outset who will be successful. We do know that there are some features that seem to improve the chances of recovery, such as early intervention, less coexisting psychological diagnoses, infrequent or no purging behavior, and supportive families or loved ones. As far as the medical consequences of eating disorders, most are reversible. However, there are some conditions that may be permanent, such as osteoporosis, endocrine abnormalities, ovarian failure, and, of course, death.

The mortality rate for anorexia nervosa is higher than that of any other psychiatric disorder, and it is the leading cause of death in young women, according to information provided at a lecture by Walter Kaye, M.D., given at the International Association of Eating Disorder Professionals Conference in 1995. The American Psychiatric Association guidelines for the treatment of eating disorders report that hospitalized or third-stage referral populations of anorexics show that at least four years after the onset of illness, about 44 percent have "good" outcomes (weight restored within 15 percent of recommended guidelines and menstruation was regular). "Poor" outcomes were reported for 24 percent, whose weight never approached 15 percent of that recommended and whose menstruation remained absent or sporadic. Intermediate outcomes were reported for 28 percent of the anorexics, whose results were somewhere between the "good" and "poor" groups. The ANAD study reported that 5 to 10 percent of anorexics die within ten years after contracting the disorder. Eighteen to 20 percent of anorexics will be dead after twenty years, and only 30 to 40 percent ever fully recover, while 20 percent bounce in and out of hospitals. Only 50 percent report being cured. However with out increasing knowledge, experience, and expertise in working with these patients, we can expect these statistics to improve.

The long-term outcome for bulimia has still not been sufficiently studied, but many clinicians believe that the mortality rate for bulimia will prove to be as high, if not higher, than that for anorexia. Treatment outcome is often reported in terms of reduction of symptoms and the average reduction in bingeing and purging for those who complete treatment is somewhere around 70 percent. For bulimics who have been hospitalized, three-year follow-up studies show that about 27 percent binge and purge less than once a month, which is considered a good outcome; 33 percent have poor outcomes, bingeing and purging/restricting daily; and 40 percent have intermediate outcomes, somewhere between the two.

STATISTICS ON BINGE EATING DISORDER

Since binge eating disorder is newly recognized, statistics are hard to come by. There are numerous statistics on obesity but, as previously mentioned, not all binge eaters are overweight. Studies on binge eating disorder indicate that only somewhere around 50 percent of patients are overweight. In *Overcoming Binge Eating*, Dr. Christopher Fairburn reports that in obese individuals, approximately 5 to 10 percent overall and 20 to 40 percent who participate in weight loss programs, have binge eating habits. The continuing research on binge eating disorder will provide further insight into this syndrome.

Most of our knowledge and understanding of eating disorders comes from information gathered on females diagnosed with these illnesses. Since males do have eating disorders and the number of such cases has been steadily increasing, we now have information available to help us understand the origins of these disorders in males, what part gender plays in these disorders, and how males with eating disorders differ from and are similar to their female counterparts. The next chapter will discuss this issue in detail.

2

NOT FOR FEMALES ONLY

It is generally assumed that only women develop eating disorders because, after all, appearance, weight, and dieting are feminine preoccupations. Magazine articles, television shows, movies, books, and even treatment literature dealing with eating disorders focus almost exclusively on females. Males do develop eating disorders and, rather than being a new phenomenon, this was observed over three hundred years ago. Among the first well-documented accounts of anorexia nervosa, reported in the 1600s by Dr. Richard Morton, and the 1800s by the British physician William Gull, are cases of males suffering from the disorder. Since these early times, eating disorders in males have been overlooked, understudied, and underreported. Worse still, eating disordered males seeking treatment are turned down when requesting admission to most of the programs in the country because they treat females only.

The number of females suffering from eating disorders far exceeds that of males, but in the last few years reported cases of males with anorexia nervosa and bulimia nervosa have been steadily increasing. Media and professional attention has followed suit. An article in the *Los Angeles Times* (1995) on this subject entitled, "Silence and Guilt," stated that roughly one million males in the United States suffer from eating disorders. A 1996 article in the *San Jose Mercury News* shocked readers by reporting that Dennis Brown, a twenty-seven-year-old Super Bowl defensive end, revealed that he used laxatives, diuretics, and self-induced vomiting to control his weight and even underwent surgery to repair bleeding ulcers made worse by his years of bingeing and purging. "It's always been the weight thing," said Brown. "They used to get on me for being too big." In the article, Brown reported that after making such statements in an NFL-sponsored interview session, he was pulled aside and reprimanded by coaches and team officials for ". . . embarrassing the organization."

The increase in articles and media reports on males with eating disorders is reminiscent of the early years when eating disorders in females first began to get public attention. One wonders if this is our early warning of how frequently the problem with males really occurs.

Studies indicate that somewhere between 5 and 15 percent of eating disorder cases are males, but there are problems in determining frequency and thus these figures are unreliable. Identifying males with eating disorders has been difficult for several reasons, including how these disorders are defined. Consider that until DSM IV, the diagnostic criteria for anorexia nervosa included amenorrhea, and since originally bulimia nervosa was not a separate illness but rather absorbed into the diagnosis of anorexia nervosa, a gender bias existed for both of these disorders such that patients and clinicians held the belief that males do not develop eating disorders. Walter Vandereycken reported that in a 1979 study, 40 percent of internists and 25 percent of psychiatrists surveyed believed that anorexia nervosa only occurs in females, and that in a 1983 survey 25 percent of psychiatrists and psychologists considered femaleness fundamental to anorexia nervosa. Being overweight and overeating are culturally more acceptable and less noticed in males; therefore, binge eating disorder also tends to go underrecognized.

As it now stands, the three essential requirements for the diagnosis of anorexia nervosa—substantial self-induced weight loss, a morbid fear of becoming fat, and an abnormality of reproductive hormone functioning—can be applied to males as well as females. (Testosterone levels in males decrease as a result of this disorder, and in 10 to 20 percent of cases, males remain with features of testicular abnormality.) The essential diagnostic features for bulimia nervosa—compulsive binge eating, a fear of fatness, and compensatory behaviors used to avoid weight gain—can also be equally applied to males and females. For binge eating disorder, both males and females binge eat and feel distress and out of control over their eating. However, the problem of identification continues. Males with eating disorders have been so rarely acknowledged or encountered that the diagnostic possibility of anorexia nervosa, bulimia nervosa, or binge eating disorder is overlooked when males present with symptoms which would lead to a correct diagnosis if presented by a female.

Diagnostic criteria aside, the problem of identifying males with eating disorders is heightened by the fact that admitting to an eating disorder is difficult for anyone, but even more difficult for males due to the perceived notion that only females suffer from these illnesses. In fact, males with eating disorders commonly report fears of being suspected of homosexuality for having what is considered a "female problem."

As far as the sexuality issue goes, males with all variations of sexual orientations develop eating disorders, but studies have indicated a possible increase in gender identity conflict and sexual orientation issues among many males who do. In this culture dieting, thinness, and obsession about appearance are predominantly feminine preoccupations; therefore, it is not surprising that male eating disorder patients often present with gender identity and orientation issues including homosexuality and bisexuality. For example, male anorexia nervosa patients have scored as more feminine than most other men on personality inventories. One 1987 study found that 25 percent of eating disordered males had some degree of homosexuality. Other research reveals that homosexual students report a higher prevalence of binge eating, fat phobia, and diuretic abuse than do other male students. Homosexual men have also scored higher than heterosexual men on the Eating Disorders Inventory scales for drive for thinness, awareness of internal stimuli, bulimia, body dissatisfaction, maturity fears, and ineffectiveness.

One problem with eating disorder and gender studies is that what are often considered feminine traits, such as a drive for thinness, body image disturbance, and self-sacrifice, are the hallmarks of eating disorders in both males and females. Therefore, using these traits to determine degree of femininity in anyone with an eating disorder, male or female, is misleading. Furthermore, the problem with all of these studies is that they involve self-reporting and/or populations in treatment settings, both of which may provide unreliable results. Since many individuals find it difficult to admit they have an eating disorder, and since the admission of homosexuality is also a difficult matter, the actual incidence of homosexuality among males with eating disorders in the general population is an unclear and undetermined issue.

Since females identified with eating disorders outnumber males by a large margin and gender issues such as homosexuality or bisexuality seem prevalent in reported cases involving males, there has been much speculation on why this should be the case. According to Dr. Arnold Andersen, who edited the only book on this subject, *Males with Eating Disorders* (Brunner/Mazel, 1990), definitive answers are not available, but sociocultural influences appear to play a much bigger role than biological ones. Anderson and other researchers, such as George Hsu (1989), agree that the most important factor may be that there is less reinforcement for slimness and dieting for males than for females. Dieting and weight preoccupation are precursors for eating disorders and these behaviors are more prevalent in females. Andersen points out that by a ratio of 10.5 to 1, articles and advertisements concerning weight loss are more frequent in the ten most popular women's versus men's magazines. It is more than interesting that the 10.5 to 1 ratio parallels that of women to men with eating disorders. Furthermore, in subgroups of males where there is a great emphasis on weight loss— for example, wrestlers, jockeys, or football players (such as in the above-mentioned case of Super Bowl defensive end Dennis Brown), there is an increased incidence of eating disorders. In fact, whenever weight loss is required for a particular group of individuals, male or female, such as in ballerinas, models, and gymnasts, there is a greater likelihood that those individuals will develop eating disorders. From this it can be speculated that as our society increasingly places pressure on men to lose weight, we will see an increase in males with eating disorders. In fact, it is already happening. Men's bodies are more frequently the targets of advertising campaigns, leanness for men is increasingly being emphasized, and the number of male dieters and males reporting eating disorders continues to rise.

One final note is that eating disordered men differ from eating disordered women in a few ways that may be important for better understanding and treatment.

1. They tend to have genuine histories of pre-illness obesity.

2. They often report losing weight in order to avoid weight-related medical illnesses found in other family members.

3. They are likely to be intensely athletic and to have begun dieting in order to attain greater sports achievement or from fear of gaining weight because of a sports injury. In this respect, they resemble individuals referred to as "obligatory runners." In fact, many eating disordered men may fit another proposed but not yet accepted diagnostic category, referred to as compulsive exercise, compulsive athleticism, or a term coined by Alayne Yates, *activity disorder*. This syndrome is similar to but separate from the eating disorders and thus deserves its own chapter.

TREATMENT AND PROGNOSIS FOR MALES

Although more research needs to be done on the specific psychological and personality features of males with eating disorders, the basic principles for treatment currently promoted are similar to those for treating females and include: cessation of starvation, cessation of binge eating, weight normalization, interrupting binge and purge cycles, correcting body image disturbance, reducing dichotomous (black or white) thinking, and treating any coexisting mood disorders or personality disorders.

Short-term studies suggest that the prognosis for males in treatment is comparable to that for females, at least in the short term. Long-term studies are not available. However, empathetic informed professionals are necessary, due to the fact that males with eating disorders feel misunderstood and out of place in a society that still doesn't understand these disorders. Even worse, males with eating disorders are often made to feel uncomfortable and otherwise rejected by females similarly afflicted. Although it may turn out to be true, it is often mistakenly assumed that males with eating disorders, most particularly anorexia nervosa, are more severely disturbed and have a poorer prognosis than females with such disorders. There are good reasons why this may appear to be the case. First, since males often go undetected, only the most severe cases come into treatment and thus under scrutiny. Second, there seems to be a contingent of males with other serious psychological disorders, most notably obsessive-compulsive disorder, where food rituals, food phobias, food restriction, and food rejection are prominent features. These individuals end up in treatment mostly due to their underlying psychological illnesses, not for their eating behavior, and they tend to be complex, difficult-to-treat cases.

With more time and research devoted to analyzing and understanding the sociocultural, biochemical, and gender-related factors in the roots of the problems of males with eating disorders, optimal treatment protocols will be revealed.

3

ACTIVITY DISORDER: TOO MUCH/LITTLE OF A GOOD THING

A long with the steady increase in the number of people with eating disorders has been a rise in the number of people with exercise disorders; people who are controlling their bodies and defining themselves through their overinvolvement in exercise activity, to the point where instead of choosing to participate in their activity, they have become "addicted" to it, continuing to engage in it despite adverse consequences. If dieting taken to the extreme becomes an eating disorder, exercise activity taken to the same extreme may be viewed as an *activity disorder*, a term used by Alayne Yates in her book Compulsive Exercise and the Eating Disorders.

In our society exercise is increasingly being sought, less for the pursuit of fitness or pleasure and more for the means to a thinner body or sense of control and accomplishment. In the climate of thinness mania, female exercisers are particularly vulnerable to problems arising when restriction of food intake is combined with intense physical activity. A female who loses too much body fat will stop menstruating and ovulating and will become increasingly susceptible to stress fractures and osteoporosis. Yet, similar to individuals with eating disorders, those with an activity disorder are not deterred from their behaviors by medical complications and consequences. People who continue to overexercise in spite of medical and/or other consequences feel as if they can't stop and that participating in their activity is no longer an option. These people have been referred to as obligatory or compulsive exercisers because they seem unable to "not exercise," even when injured, exhausted, and begged or threatened by others to stop. The terms *pathogenic exercise* and *exercise addiction* have been used to describe individuals

29

who are consumed by the need for physical activity to the exclusion of everything else, and to the point of damage or danger to their lives. The term *anorexia athletica* has been used to describe a sub-clinical eating disorder for athletes who engage in at least one unhealthy method of weight control, including fasting, vomiting, diet pills, laxatives, or diuretics. For the rest of this chapter, the term *activity disorder* will be used to describe the over exercising syndrome as this term seems most appropriate for comparison with the more traditional eating disorders.

SIGNS AND SYMPTOMS OF ACTIVITY DISORDER

The signs and symptoms of activity disorder often, but not always, include those seen in anorexia nervosa and bulimia nervosa. Obsessive concerns about being fat, body dissatisfaction, binge eating, and a whole variety of dieting and purging behaviors are often present in activity disordered individuals. Furthermore, it is well established that obsessive exercise is a common feature seen in anorexics and bulimics; in fact, some studies have reported that as many as 75 percent use excessive exercise as a method of purging and/or reducing anxiety. Therefore, activity disorder can be found as a component of anorexia nervosa or bulimia nervosa or, although there is yet no DSM diagnosis for it, as a separate disorder altogether. There are many individuals with the salient features of an activity disorder who do not meet the diagnostic criteria for anorexia nervosa or bulimia nervosa. The overriding feature of an activity disorder is the presence of excessive, purposeless, physical activity which goes beyond any usual training regimen and ends up being a detriment rather than an asset to their health and well-being.

In her book, *Compulsive Exercise and the Eating Disorders*, Alayne Yates lists the proposed features of an activity disorder, a summary of which is listed below.

Features of an Activity Disorder

1. The person maintains a high level of activity and is uncomfortable with states of rest or relaxation.

2. The individual depends upon the activity for self-definition and mood stabilization.

3. There is an intense, driven quality to the activity which becomes self-perpetuating and resistant to change, compelling the person to continue while feeling the lack of ability to control or stop their behavior.

4. Only the overuse of the body can produce the physiologic effects of deprivation (secondary to exposure to the elements, extreme exertion, and rigid dietary restriction) which are an important component perpetuating the disorder.

5. Although activity disordered individuals may have coexisting personality disorders, there is no particular personality profile or disorder which underlies an activity disorder. These persons are apt to be physically healthy, high functioning individuals.

6. Activity disordered persons will use rationalizations and other defense mechanisms to protect their involvement in the activity. This may represent a preexisting personality disorder and/or be secondary to the physical deprivation.

7. Although there is no particular personality profile or disorder, the activity disordered person's achievement orientation, independence, self control, perfectionism, persistence, and well-developed mental strategies can foster significant academic and vocational accomplishments in such a way that they appear as healthy, high functioning individuals.

Activity disorders like eating disorders are expressions of and defenses against feelings and emotions and are used to soothe, organize, and maintain self-esteem. Individuals with the eating disorders (anorexia nervosa and bulimia nervosa) and those with activity disorders are similar to one another in many respects. Both groups attempt to control the body through exercise and/or diet and are overly conscious of input versus output equations. They are extremely committed individuals and pride themselves on putting mind over matter, valuing self-discipline, self-sacrifice, and the ability to persevere. They are generally hard-working, task-oriented, high-achieving individuals who have a tendency to be dissatisfied with themselves as if nothing is ever good enough. The emotional investment these individuals place on exercise and/or diet becomes more intense and significant than work, family, relationships, and, ironically, even health. Those with activity disorders lose control over exercise just as those with an eating disorder lose control over eating and dieting, and both experience withdrawal when prevented from engaging in their behaviors.

Individuals with anorexia nervosa and bulimia nervosa and those with activity disorders usually score high on the EDI subscales of perfectionism and asceticism and have similar distortions in their cognitive (thinking) styles. The following list includes examples of the thinking patterns of people with activity disorders that are similar to the mental distortions in those with eating disorders.

COGNITIVE DISTORTIONS IN ACTIVITY DISORDER

DICHOTOMOUS, BLACK/WHITE THINKING

If I don't run, I can't eat.
I either run an hour or it's not worth it to run at all.

OVERGENERALIZATION

Like my Mom, people who don't exercise are fat.
Not exercising means you are lazy.

MAGNIFICATION

If I can't exercise my life will be over.
If I don't work out today, I'll gain weight.

SELECTIVE ABSTRACTION

If I can go to the gym, I am happy.
I feel great when I exercise so if I exercise, I'll never be depressed.

SUPERSTITIOUS THINKING

I must run every morning or something bad will happen.
I must do 205 sit-ups every night.
I can't stop at 1 hour and 59 minutes, it has to be exactly 2 hours, so when the fire alarm went off I couldn't get off the Stairmaster, I had to keep going, even if the gym was burning down.

PERSONALIZATION

People are looking at me because I'm out of shape.
People admire runners.
I am a runner, it's who I am, I could never give it up.

ARBITRARY INFERENCE

People who exercise get better jobs, relationships, and so on.
People who exercise don't get sick as much.

DISCOUNTING

My doctor tells me not to run, but she is flabby so I don't listen to her.
No pain, no gain.
Nobody really knows the effects of not having a period anyway, so why should I worry.

PHYSICAL SYMPTOMS OF ACTIVITY DISORDER

A key in determining if a person is developing an activity disorder is if they have the symptoms of overtraining (listed below) yet persist with exercise anyway. Overtraining syndrome is a state of exhaustion in which individuals will continue to exercise while their performance and health diminish. Overtraining syndrome is caused by a prolonged period of energy output which depletes energy stores without sufficient replenishment.

SYMPTOMS OF OVERTRAINING

- Fatigue
- Reduction in performance
- Decreased concentration
- Inhibited lactic acid response
- Loss of emotional vigor
- Increased compulsivity
- Soreness, stiffness
- Decreased maximum oxygen uptake
- Decreased blood lactate
- Adrenal exhaustion
- Decreased heart rate response to exercise
- Hypothalamic dysfunction
- Decreased anabolic (testosterone) response
- Increased catabolic (cortisol) response (muscle wasting)

The only cure for the above symptoms is complete rest, which may take a few weeks to a few months. To a person with activity disorder, resting is like giving up or giving in. This is similar to an anorexic who feels like eating is "giving in." When giving up their exercise behaviors, those with activity disorder will go through psychological and physical withdrawal often crying, yelling, and making statements like,

> *I can't stand not exercising, it's driving me crazy.*
> *I don't care about the consequences, I have to work out or I'll turn into a fat blob.*

*This is worse torture than any effects of the exercise, I feel like
I'm dying inside.
I can't even stand being in my own skin, I hate myself and
everyone else.*

It is important to note that these feelings diminish over time but
need to be carefully attended to.

APPROACHING AN INDIVIDUAL WITH AN ACTIVITY DISORDER

In January 1986, the *Physician and Sports Medicine Journal* discussed
the subject of pathogenic (negative) exercise in athletes and listed recommendations for approaching athletes practicing one or more
pathogenic weight control techniques. The recommendations can be
reformulated and extended for use when approaching individuals with
activity disorders who are not necessarily considered athletes.

GUIDELINES FOR APPROACHING THE ACTIVITY DISORDERED INDIVIDUAL:

1. A person who has good rapport with the individual such as a
   coach, should arrange a private meeting with him or her to discuss the problem in a supportive style.

2. Without judgment, specific examples should be given regarding
   the behaviors that have been observed that arouse concern.

3. It is important to let the individual respond but do not argue
   with him or her.

4. Reassure the individual that the point is not to take away exercise but that participation in exercise will ultimately be curtailed
   through an injury or by necessity if evidence shows that the
   problem has compromised the individual's health.

5. Try to determine if the person feels that he or she is beyond the
   point of being able to voluntarily abstain from the problem
   behavior.

6. Do not stop at one meeting; these individuals will be resistant to admitting that they have a problem and it may take repeated attempts to get them to admit a problem and/or seek help.

7. If the individual continues to refuse to admit that a problem exists in the face of compelling evidence, consult a clinician with expertise in treating these disorders and/or find others who may be able to help. Remember that these individuals are very independent and success oriented. Admitting they have a problem they are unable to control will be very difficult for them.

8. Be sensitive to the factors that may have played a part in the development of this problem. Activity disordered individuals are often unduly influenced by significant others and/or coaches who suggest they lose weight, or who unwittingly praise them for excessive activity.

RISK FACTORS

One outstanding difference between the eating disorders and activity disorders seems to be that there are more males who develop activity disorders and more females who develop eating disorders. Exploring the reason for this may provide a better understanding of both. What are the causes that contribute to the development of an activity disorder? Why do only some individuals with eating disorders have this syndrome and others who have this syndrome don't have eating disorders at all? What we do know is that the risk factors for developing an activity disorder are varied, including sociocultural, family, individual, and biological factors, and are not necessarily the same ones which cause the disorder to persist.

SOCIOCULTURAL

In a society that places a high value on independence and achievement combined with being fit and thin, involvement in exercise provides a perfect means for fitting in, or gaining approval. Exercise serves to enhance self-worth, when that self-worth is based upon appearance, endurance, strength, and capability.

FAMILY

Child rearing practices and family values contribute to an individual choosing exercise as a means of self-development and recognition. If parents or other caregivers endorse the above sociocultural values and they themselves diet or exercise obsessively, children will adopt these values and expectations at an early age. Children who learn not only from society but from their parents that to be acceptable is to be fit and thin may be left with a narrow focus for self-development and self-esteem. A child reared with phrases such as "no pain no gain," may endorse this attitude wholeheartedly without the proper maturity or common sense to balance this notion with proper self-nurturing and self-care.

INDIVIDUAL

Certain individuals seem predisposed to need a high level of activity. Individuals who are perfectionists, achievement oriented, and have the capacity for self-deprivation will be more likely to seek out exercise, and become addicted to the feelings or other perceived benefits the exercise provides. Additionally, individuals who develop activity disorder seem outwardly independent, unstable in their view of themselves, and lacking in their ability to have fully satisfying relationships with others.

BIOLOGICAL

Just as with eating disorders, researchers are exploring what biological factors may contribute to activity disorders. We know that certain individuals have a biologically based predisposition to obsessive thoughts, compulsive behaviors, and in women, amenorrhea. We know that in animals the combination of food restriction and stress causes an increase in activity level and, furthermore, that food restriction with increased activity can cause the activity to become senseless and driven. Furthermore, parallel changes have been detected in the brain chemicals and hormones of eating disordered females and long-distance runners that may explain how the anorexic tolerates starvation and the runner tolerates pain and exhaustion. In general, activity disordered men and women seem to be different biochemically than nondisordered individuals and are more easily led and trapped into a cycle of activity that is resistant to intervention.

TREATMENT FOR ACTIVITY DISORDER

The principles of treatment for individuals with activity disorders are similar to those with eating disorders. Medical issues must be handled and residential or inpatient treatment may be necessary for depression or suicidality, but most cases should be able to be treated on an outpatient basis unless the activity disorder and an eating disorder coexist. This combination can present a serious situation rather quickly. When lack of nutrition is combined with hours of exercise, the body gets broken down at a rapid pace and residential or inpatient treatment may be required. Sometimes hospitalization is encouraged to patients as a way to relieve the vicious cycle of nutrient deprivation combined with exercise before a breakdown occurs. Activity disordered individuals often recognize they need help to stop and know that they cannot do it with outpatient treatment alone. Eating disorder treatment programs are probably the best choice for hospitalizing those with activity disorder. An eating disorder facility that has a special program for athletes or compulsive exercisers would be ideal.

THERAPY FOR ACTIVITY DISORDER

It is important to keep in mind that activity disordered people tend to be highly intelligent, internally driven, independent individuals. They will most likely resist any kind of vulnerability such as going for treatment unless they become injured or face some kind of ultimatum. Excessive activity protects these individuals against desiring to get close, to take in something from another, or to depend on anyone. Therapists will have to maintain a calm, caring stance with the goal of helping the individual define what he or she needs, rather than focusing on taking things away. Another therapeutic task is to help the individual receive and internalize the soothing functions the therapist can provide, thus promoting relationships over activity.

THERAPEUTIC ISSUES TO DISCUSS IN THE TREATMENT OF ACTIVITY DISORDER

- Overactivity of mind or body
- Body image
- Overcontrol of the body
- Disconnection from the body
- Body care and self care
- Black and white thinking
- Unrealistic expectations
- Tension tolerance
- Communicating feelings
- Ruminations
- The meaning of rest
- Intimacy and separateness

The following section discusses the problem of the opposite of too much activity—exercise resistance, particularly seen in women.

EXERCISE RESISTANCE IN WOMEN

FRANCIE WHITE, M.S., R.D.

Just as binge eating disorder lies at the opposite end of the disordered eating spectrum from anorexia nervosa, exercise resistance is an activity disorder at the opposite end of the spectrum from addictive or compulsive exercise. As a dietitian specializing in eating disorders, I have noticed a common phenomenon in women with emotional overeating patterns, many of whom qualify as having binge eating disorder. These women often suffer from entrenched inactivity patterns that are resistant to intervention or treatment. Many professionals assume that inactivity is due to factors such as a harried lifestyle, industrialization, laziness, and in overweight individuals, the discouraging factor of physical difficulty or discomfort in moving. Behavior modification counseling programs, use of specialized personal trainers, and other types of motivational strategies to encourage a physically active lifestyle seem to be ineffective.

Over a three-year period, beginning in 1993, I began exploring what I call "exercise resistance" in a binge eating disordered population of six groups of ten to twenty women each. The following information is what emerged from studying these groups.

For many women with a history of body image problems, moderate to severe overeating histories, and/or a history of repeated attempts at weight loss, exercise resistance is a common syndrome which requires specialized treatment. Remaining inactive or physically passive appears to be an important aspect of the psychological defense system within the eating disorder itself, providing a balance of sorts from the psychological discomfort that accompanies exercising. This psychological discomfort varies from moderate to severe anxiety and is related to a profound sense of physical and emotional vulnerability.

Underactivity or physical passivity appears to offer a sense of control over body and feelings, just as disordered eating and overexercise do. Exercise resistance may simply be another component in the menu of options from which men and women find themselves suffering in this time of epidemic eating and body image problems. If we are to begin to look at exercise resistance as a separate syndrome worthy of specialized understanding and treatment, here are some factors to consider.

WHAT DIFFERENTIATES THE EXERCISE RESISTANT INDIVIDUAL FROM SOMEONE WITH SIMPLE LOW MOTIVATION OR POOR EXERCISE HABITS?

1. The individual strongly resists any suggestion to become more physically active (barring any physical impairments and given several workable options).

2. The individual reacts with anger, resentment, or anxiety to any suggestion to become more physically active.

3. The individual describes experiencing moderate to severe anxiety during physical activity.

RISK FACTORS FOR DEVELOPING EXERCISE RESISTANCE

1. A history of sexual abuse of any kind at any age.

2. A history of three or more weight loss diets.

3. Exercise used as a component of a weight loss regimen.

4. A larger body size as a boundary or defense against unwanted sexual attention or sexual intimacy (be it conscious or unconscious).

5. Parents who forced or overencouraged exercise, especially if the exercise was to compensate for perceived, or actual, overweight in the child.

6. Early puberty or development of large breasts and/or early significant weight gain.

THE MEANING OF EXERCISE RESISTANCE

To better understand exercise resistance, we can borrow from our understanding of how weight loss diets have affected eating behavior. We know that weight loss diets are a key aspect in the historical mistreatment of overweight individuals, actually contributing to binge eating, which increases over time. Responses from the women surveyed support the view that exercise resistance may be an unexpected, unconscious backlash against the current cultural emphasis on slimness and the overfocus on the symptom; for example, the weight, instead of the inner psychodynamic issues.

QUESTIONS TO ASK THE INDIVIDUAL WITH EXERCISE RESISTANCE

1. What feelings and associations emerge for you at hearing the term *exercise*? Why?

2. When did being physically active change for you from "playing" as a child to "exercise"? When did it shift from something natural, an activity you did spontaneously (for example, from an internal drive), to something you felt you should do?

3. Has physical activity ever been something that you did to control your weight? If so, how was that for you and how has it affected your motivation to exercise?

4. How did your exercise attitudes change during and after puberty?

5. Does being physically active relate in any way to your sexuality? If so, how?

A theme ran through the comments of the women studied that echoes the information in chapter 4, "Sociocultural Influences on Eating, Weight, and Shape." Most of the women expressed that they felt extremely degraded and vulnerable by their direct experiences of being encouraged to exercise as a means to achieve an acceptable body. Instead of being encouraged to exercise for fun, exercise for these women was connected to one thing; body image. Many of the women's stories included experiences of deep humiliation, public or otherwise, at being overweight and unable to achieve this illusive standard. Other women actually acquired a lean, thinner body and experienced unwanted sexual objectification by peers and adults. In a significant number of the women, rapes and other sexual abuse occurred after weight loss and for many, sexual abuse was connected to the onset of exercise resistance and binge eating.

Many women are confused as they experience the desire to be thinner while at the same time feeling anger and resentment at what they have been told they have to do to achieve it, for example, exercise. For some, exercise resistance and weight gain may be symbolic boundaries, expressing a rebellious refusal to patronize a system in which the playing field for women is not about sports, or even achievement, but about sexual attractiveness to men—"We'll play, you pose." This system is one in which women and men equally participate and perpetuate. Women objectify one another and themselves right along with men.

The above discussion of exercise resistance by Francie White is the only written information this author has found on the subject and was written specifically for inclusion in this book. It is important to understand this area as another disorder on the continuum of those being discussed. The understanding and treatment of exercise resistance is similar to that of eating disorders in that the therapist must impart an empathy for the need for the behaviors instead of trying to take them away. When working with an exercise resistant individual one must explore and resolve the source of the resistance, such as underlying anxiety, resentment, or anger. The goal of treatment is that the individual will be able to become physically active by choice not coercion. It is important to begin by validating the resistance and even in some cases prescribing it, making statements such as:

It is important that you don't exercise.
Resisting exercise serves a valuable function for you.
Continuing not to exercise is one way for you to keep saying no.

By making these comments, the therapist helps validate the need for the resistance and eliminates the obvious conflict.

It is important to clarify that the issue of addressing exercise resistance is to help individuals who are compelled to "not exercise" just as we try to help others who are compelled to do so, both of which leave the behavior out of the realm of choice. Little attention has been paid to exercise resistance, but it is clear that those who have it, like those with exercise obsession or disordered eating, appear to be in a love-hate relationship with their bodies; derive inner psychological or adaptive functions from their behavior; and are involved in a struggle not just with food or exercise but with the self.

For an examination of the struggle with self and other dynamics that result in eating disorders, the next three chapters will deal with the main areas in which the causes of eating disorders are understood, with a chapter devoted to each of the following:

SOCIOCULTURAL
A look at the cultural preference for thinness, and the current epidemic of body dissatisfaction and dieting, with an emphasis not only

on weight loss but the ability to control one's body as a means of gaining approval, acceptance, and self esteem.

PSYCHOLOGICAL

The exploration of underlying psychological problems, developmental deficits, and traumatic experiences such as sexual abuse, which contribute to the development of disordered eating or exercise behaviors as coping mechanisms or adaptive functions.

BIOLOGICAL

A review of the current information available on whether or not there is a genetic predisposition or biochemical status that is at least partly responsible for the development of an eating or activity disorder.

4

SOCIOCULTURAL INFLUENCES ON EATING, WEIGHT, AND SHAPE

What does it mean when studies show that 95 percent of American women report disgust or disappointment with their bodies? What is the cause and effect when our female fashion models are 23 percent below what is considered normal weight? What is the implication when adolescent girls are snorting cocaine, not to get high, but to lose weight, and 70 to 80 percent of fourth-grade girls report they are dieting, some claiming they would rather be dead than fat?

Since body image disturbance and episodes of dieting and weight preoccupation are seen in the histories of those with eating disorders, our culture's obsession with thinness has been offered as a leading cause. In today's culture, thinness represents not only attractiveness but self-sacrifice, virtue, success, and control. The pervasive attitude seems to be that the more fat one has on his or her body, the more unattractive, self-indulgent, lazy, and out of control one is. Culturally dictated definitions such as these are portrayed to us in various ways through the media.

In an advertisement featuring an extremely thin model and the slogan, "Just the Right Shape," one wonders what is being sold, the body or the outfit? Media advertisements like these both reflect and shape our perceptions and standards of beauty. Advertisements for taking off weight and keeping it off are found in every magazine and newspaper, on billboards, television commercials, and bumper stickers with messages such as, "Lose Weight Now, Ask Me How," "Lose 20 pounds, in 20 days," "Get the body that gets the guys," "Flatten your stomach," "Reduce those thighs." At least twenty million people respond to the propaganda and are on a diet at any given moment. Weight loss programs, diet books, and media advertisements for diet products have been steadily increasing, resulting in a multibillion dollar industry. As diet commercials have increased, the body size of *Playboy* centerfolds and Miss America contestants has decreased to the point where many of these individuals, according to recent studies, meet the weight criteria for anorexia nervosa! Is it any wonder that at the same time there has been a significant increase in the prevalence of eating disorders? As stated in *Eating Disorders, The Journal of Treatment and Prevention* in the spring of 1993, "It may be that the media pressure to diet is a major influence on the occurrence of eating disorders in otherwise vulnerable women and men." Since the culturally prescribed body weight is so unrealistically low and since mountains of evidence show that diets don't work (approximately 98 percent of those who lose weight gain it back), it follows that some individuals will resort to extreme measures such as starving or purging in order to deal with their dissatisfaction over their figures or sizes, striving to obtain "Just The Right Shape."

Most ads and diet products are directed toward females but males are no longer spared. Males are increasingly portrayed as ornamental objects and targeted for the purchase of beauty and weight loss products, as women have been since advertising began. (Is it a coincidence that the incidence of males with eating disorders is also increasing?) Still, eating disorders remain a predominantly female problem, with females accounting for approximately 90 to 95 percent of all known cases. In regard to this gender distribution, it may seem obvious, but cannot be minimized, that historically men are judged more for what they do and women for how they look. Women have always been taught that their value is associated with their appearance and their bodies.

Young girls or women who are disturbed by the way they experience their own body weight or shape have learned to do so only in context with what is acceptable and what is not. The current cultural standards and messages actually teach young women to have body image disturbance, therefore meeting the eating disorder criteria stated below. It is, after all, body image disturbance that distinguishes eating disorders from other psychological conditions that involve weight loss and eating abnormalities.

Body image disturbance is defined in the eating disorder section of *DSM IV* as:

FOR ANOREXIA NERVOSA

Disturbance in the way in which one's body weight or shape is experienced, undue influence of body weight or shape on self-evaluation, or denial of the seriousness of the current low body weight.

FOR BULIMIA NERVOSA

Self-evaluation is unduly influenced by body shape and weight.

It is our society, not any particular woman's psyche, which has brought about the undue influence that weight and shape play on self-esteem. Technological progress has fostered the obsession with women's bodies and overall appearance with the invention of items such as the compact mirror (so you can *always* know what you look like) and lipstick (so you can *always* improve what you look like). Technology has also given us the power to flash images across a screen in our homes and on billboards in our sky, constantly reminding us of what we are supposed to look like. It is interesting to note that although eating disorders are increasingly appearing in all cultures around the world, Western women seem to be at greater risk for developing them and the degree of Westernization seems to increase the risk (Dolan, 1991). Evidence suggests that anorexia nervosa is uncommon outside the Western world and in less affluent Western countries. Furthermore, when immigrants move from less industrialized countries to more industrialized countries they are more likely to develop eating disorders.

The requirement to be thin is just the latest version of torture used to mold women's bodies into a set criterion of beauty which changes over time and from culture to culture. In twelfth- and thirteenth-century China, stub feet were considered a desirable feminine characteristic; therefore, female babies would have their feet bound back (toe to heel) even though the resulting deformity meant hobbling or even crawling for life. In America in the nineteenth century, tiny waists, achieved by wearing painful whalebone corsets, were in vogue. During the 1920s, American women bound their breasts to make them flatter. And as odd as it may seem now, there were times, such as in the days of the artist Rubens, when large, soft bodies were considered more desirable and rounded bodies were considered fertile and more admired than thin ones.

Women have gone through fundamental changes in their place in society, both economically and politically, and thinness has come to symbolize not only control but wealth, independence, and freedom. Whereas at one time it was virtuous to abstain from sex, it has now become virtuous to abstain from food. Even thinness is no longer enough. The contemporary feminine ideal includes being thin and being physically fit. A young woman growing up and searching for her identity takes on these messages from her culture and her female role models. Therefore, at the same time that she is developing breasts and body fat to prepare for menstruation, pregnancy, and eventually childbirth and breast-feeding, she is compelled to fit in and to do so means being thin. Eating disorders need to be understood within the context of the current culture, where the idea that thinness is attractive and desirable for females is so commonly accepted that it is rarely even questioned.

Starving, stuffing, and purging women are trying desperately to gain acceptance, approval, control, and love through external validation of their bodies. Eating disorders are not about food or weight but about a disordered "sense of self" looking for approval and finding it, however temporarily, in the pursuit of thinness or the comfort of food. Eating disorders are the extreme of a continuum through which most women in our society, to some degree or another, are placed.

Here is what some women have to say about these cultural dictates:

You can't trust your body. It defies you and shows all your faults. I always thought I could do anything, but I can't look like the models on Madison Avenue, but I can try.

When no one else is there, food is there, food . . . exactly what I want, when I want. I need no one's approval and no one's involvement which might disappoint me. Why do I choose food to act out this need? . . . Because I'm not supposed to have it.

I will never allow myself to be fat. I saw what that did to my mother and my sister and if I have to die trying, I will stay thin.

I have accomplished something by being thin. Everyone tells me so, even those who want me to gain weight reinforce the idea that I have achieved an extreme that few people ever equal.

These women are all expressing a deeper struggle than thin versus fat. In essence, they are describing a struggle of mind over matter. We look up to people who can lose weight and keep it off even if they are unhealthy and unhappy. The ultimate power felt by anorexics is that they do without, punish their bodies, and make them obey. The increased incidence of eating disorders in certain subgroups of our population that stress these ideals along with thinness, such as ballerinas, models, gymnasts, and jockeys, lends even further credence to the cultural factor in the causes of eating disorders.

Although it would be easy to blame the current eating disorder epidemic solely on our society's standards of thinness, this is a far too simplistic and naive view. Eating disorders are highly complex and are the manifestation, not only of our culture, but of various underlying struggles in the core of the personality and even the biochemistry of each individual afflicted. After all, not every woman in our "thin-is-in" society has an eating disorder. Two young girls can grow up in the same household with the same parents and the same cultural influences, one becoming anorexic or bulimic while the other maintains a normal relationship with food and weight throughout her lifetime.

It is also important to acknowledge that there have been cases of anorexia nervosa and bulimia nervosa in a time when society's standards of thinness were very different. Richard Bell, the author of *Holy Anorexia,* makes a compelling and thought-provoking analogy between certain medieval Italian saints to whom he refers as having "holy anorexia," and individuals who fit the current diagnostic criteria for anorexia nervosa today. Bell tells us that in the service of purity and the search for perfect holiness, the saints starved themselves, were hyperactive and perfectionistic, and lost an excess of 25 percent of their normal body weight. These saints, like our present-day anorexics, believed that "to obliterate every human feeling of pain, fatigue, sexual desire, and hunger is to be master of oneself." The difference between "holy anorexia" and anorexia nervosa is the modifier "holy." This difference depends upon the cultural values and ideals present at the time in which the anorexia is used to gain a sense of mastery and control. In the twentieth century the ideals are bodily health, thinness, and self-control; in medieval Christendom, they were spiritual health, fasting, and self-denial. In both instances, the holy and the nervous, anorexics are the rare individuals that become champions of self-denial and mind over matter in the quest for the ideal and the perceived notion of perfection. (It's interesting to note that the Eating Disorder Inventory currently in widespread use to assess traits commonly seen in eating disorder patients includes, along with the drive for thinness, subscales for measuring asceticism and perfectionism.) For both the medieval "holy" anorexic and the individual with anorexia nervosa today, the behaviors and compulsive devotion that are initially rewarded and praised by their elders and their peers become self-destructive and life threatening to the point of demanding intervention.

The analogy made by Bell between "holy" and "nervous" anorexia is important in our search for cultural influences on anorexic behavior: "both states are characterized by an unwillingness to eat, but one is driven by the desire to be holy and the other by the desire to be thin. The point is that anorectics (sic) in the fourteenth century and those in the twentieth century do not want to eat because they abhor the consequences. And, whether in the service of holiness or thinness, they determinedly relish the effects of starvation." Even today, individuals with anorexia nervosa often report that starvation leads not only to thinness but to feelings of cleanliness, purity, and even holiness that are hard to give up. It is important to note that in the search for both holiness and thinness, the pursuit becomes the goal. The ability to be self-sacrificing, to be independent of needs, to nurture others while abstaining oneself, are ultimately sought in and of themselves.

An important aspect discussed in *Holy Anorexia* is the issue of gender conflict and the feminine pursuit of direct personal connectedness while striving for freedom from male authority in a patriarchal world. Bell repeatedly mentions that the anorexic saints had to battle with the Catholic male clergy and overcome patriarchal authority in order to attain their desired state of holiness, even though this seems to have been a by-product of their quest for holiness rather than a primary motivation; for example, nothing could stand in the way. Ideas involving gender conflict and female oppression compliment and support current feminist perspectives on the development, understanding, and treatment of eating disorders.

Perhaps most important, we learn from Bell's book that as the definition of holiness was altered such that self-starvation lost its purpose, the incidence of holy anorexia declined. This provides support for the notion that our real task and our true battle in the fight against eating disorders is to disconnect the cultural ideal of thinness from feminine beauty, acceptance, or esteem, so that self-starvation is again without a purpose. Meanwhile, it is important to keep in mind that although we cannot blame eating disorders solely on the cultural pressure to be thin, the current body image standards provide a perfect setting for a struggling will to do battle, an insecure feeling to have power, and a sense of despair to gain control.

5

EATING DISORDER BEHAVIORS ARE ADAPTIVE FUNCTIONS

A struggling will, an insecure feeling, and despair may manifest themselves in problems with the care and feeding of the body, but are fundamentally a problem with the care and feeding of the soul. In her aptly titled book, The Obsession, Kim Chernin has written, "The body holds meaning . . . when we probe beneath the surface of our obsession with weight, we will find that a woman obsessed with her body is also obsessed with the limitations of her emotional life. Through her concern with her body she is expressing a serious concern about the state of her soul."

What are the emotional limitations commonly seen in individuals with eating disorders? What is the state of their souls?

COMMON STATES OF BEING FOR THE EATING DISORDERED INDIVIDUAL

- Low Self-Esteem
- Diminished Self-Worth
- Belief in the Thinness Myth
- Need for Distraction
- Dichotomous (Black or White) Thinking
- Feelings of Emptiness
- Quest for Perfection
- Desire to Be Special/Unique
- Need to Be in Control
- Need for Power
- Desire for Respect and Admiration
- Difficulty Expressing Feelings

- Need for Escape or a Safe Place to Go
- Lack of Coping Skills
- Lack of Trust in Self and Others
- Terrified of not Measuring Up

A person in one or more of the above states of being will naturally seek comfort for, alleviation of, or distraction from their feelings. How and why a particular person turns to starving, bingeing, or purging as a way to cope is a matter of speculation and psychological theory.

The scope of this book does not allow a detailed analysis of every possible reason or theory that could explain the development of an eating disorder. What the reader will find is this author's overview explanation, which involves the discussion of common underlying issues observed in patients. Additional information on the development and treatment of eating disorders from varying theoretical viewpoints can be found in the chapter on treatment philosophies.

Eating disorder symptoms serve some kind of purpose that goes beyond weight loss, food as comfort, or an addiction, and beyond a need to be special or in control. Eating disorder symptoms can be seen as behavioral manifestations of a disordered self, and through understanding and working with this disordered self, the purpose or meaning of the behavioral symptoms can be discovered.

In trying to understand the meaning of someone's behavior, it is helpful to think of the behavior as serving a function or "doing a job." Once the function is discovered, it becomes easier to understand why it is so difficult to give it up and, furthermore, how to replace it. When exploring deep within the psyche of eating disordered individuals, one can find explanations for a whole series of adaptive functions serving as substitutes for the missing functions which should have been, but weren't, supplied in childhood. Paradoxically, then, an eating disorder, for all of the problems it creates, is an effort to cope, communicate, defend against, and even solve other problems. For some, starving may be in part an attempt to establish a sense of power, worth, strength and containment, and specialness because of inadequate mirroring responses, such as praise, from caregivers. Bingeing may be used to express comfort, or to numb pain, due to a developmental deficit in the ability to self-soothe. Purging may serve as an acceptable physiological and psychological release of anger or anxiety if expressing one's feelings in childhood led to ridicule or abuse. Eating disorder symptoms are an expression of and defense against feelings, needs, and the assertion of self, which has found no other way out.

Here are some examples of how these behaviors fill emotional needs:

1. An expression of and defense against early childhood needs and feelings.
   It's too scary to need anything, I try not to even need food.

2. Self-destructive and self-affirming attitudes.
   I will be the thinnest girl at my school, even if it kills me.

3. An assertion of self and a punishment of self.
   I love to eat whatever and whenever I want, but being fat is making me miserable.

4. Used as cohesive functions, psychologically holding the person together.
   If I don't purge I'm anxious and distracted. After I purge I can get things done.

The development of an eating disorder can begin early in life when childhood needs and mental states are not properly responded to by caregivers and thus get disowned, repressed, and shunted off into a separate part of a person's psyche. The child develops deficits in his or her capacities for self-cohesion and self-esteem regulation. At some point in time, the individual learns to create a system whereby disordered eating patterns, rather than people, are used to meet needs because previous attempts with caregivers have brought about disappointment, frustration, or even abuse. For example, caregivers who do not properly comfort and soothe their babies, allowing them to eventually learn how to comfort themselves, create lacks in their children's ability to self-soothe. These children grow up needing to seek abnormal amounts of external comfort or relief.

Caregivers who do not accurately listen, acknowledge, validate, and respond make it difficult for a child to learn how to validate him- or herself. Both of these examples could result in:

1. a distorted self-image (I am selfish, bad, stupid),

2. no self-image (I don't deserve to be heard or seen, I don't exist).

Disruptions or deficits in self-image and self-development make it increasingly difficult for people to function as they grow older. Adaptive measures are developed, the purpose of which is to make the individual feel whole, safe, and secure. With certain individuals, food, weight loss, and eating rituals are substituted for responsiveness from caregivers. Perhaps in other eras different means were sought as substitutes, but today turning to food or dieting for validation and acknowledgment is understandable in the context of the sociocultural factors described in the previous chapter. Personality development is disrupted in persons with eating disorders, as eating rituals are substituted for responsiveness and the usual developmental process is arrested. The early needs remain sequestered and cannot be integrated into the adult personality, thus remaining unavailable to awareness and operating on an unconscious level.

Some theorists, including this author, view this process as if, to a greater or lesser degree in each individual, a separate adaptive self is developed. The adaptive self operates from these old sequestered feelings and needs. The eating disorder symptoms are the behavioral component of this separate, split-off self, the "eating disorder self," which has a special set of needs, behaviors, feelings, and perceptions all dissociated from the individual's total self-experience. The eating disorder self functions to express, mitigate, or in some way meet underlying unmet needs and make up for the developmental deficits. The problem is that the eating disorder behaviors are only a temporary Band-Aid and the person needs to keep going back for more; that is, continuing the behaviors. Dependency is developed on these "external agents" to fill the unmet needs; thus, an addictive cycle is set up, not an addiction to food but an addiction to whatever function the eating disorder behavior is serving. There is no self-growth, and the underlying deficit in the self remains. To get beyond this, the adaptive function of an individual's eating and weight-related behaviors must be discovered and replaced with healthier alternatives. The following is a list of adaptive functions that eating disorder behaviors commonly serve.

ADAPTIVE FUNCTIONS OF EATING DISORDERS

1. Comfort, soothing, nurturance

2. Numbing, sedation, distraction

3. Attention, cry for help

4. Discharge tension, anger, rebellion

5. Predictability, structure, identity

6. Self-punishment or punishment of "the body"

7. Cleanse or purify self

8. Create small or large body for protection/safety

9. Avoidance of intimacy

10. Symptoms prove "I am bad" instead of blaming others (for example, abusers)

Treatment involves helping individuals get in touch with their unconscious, unresolved needs and providing or helping to provide in the present what the individual was missing in the past. One cannot do this without dealing directly with the eating disorder behaviors themselves, as they are the manifestation of and the windows into the unconscious unmet needs. For example, when a bulimic patient reveals that she binged and purged after a visit with her mother, it would be a mistake for the therapist, in discussing this incident, to focus solely on the relationship between mother and daughter. The therapist needs to explore the meaning of the binge- ing and purging. How did the patient feel before the binge? How did she feel before the purge? How did she feel during and after each?

When did she know she was going to binge? When did she know she was going to purge? What might have happened if she didn't binge? What might have happened if she didn't purge? Probing these feelings will provide rich information concerning the function the behaviors served.

When working with an anorexic who has been sexually abused, the therapist should explore in detail the food-restricting behaviors to uncover what the rejection of food means to the patient or what the acceptance of food would mean. How much is too much food? When does a food become fattening? How does it feel when you take food into your body? How does it feel to reject it? What would happen if you were forced to eat? Is there a part of you that would like to be able to eat and another part that won't allow it? What do they say to each other? Exploring how acceptance or rejection of food may be symbolic of controlling what goes in and out of the body is an important component of doing the necessary therapeutic work. Since sexual abuse is frequently encountered when dealing with eating disordered individuals, the whole area of sexual abuse and eating disorders warrants further discussion.

SEXUAL ABUSE

A controversy has long been brewing about the relationship between sexual abuse and eating disorders. Various researchers have presented evidence supporting or refuting the idea that sexual abuse is prevalent in those with eating disorders and can be considered a causal factor. Looking at the current information, one wonders if early male researchers overlooked, misinterpreted, or downplayed the figures. In David Garner and Paul Garfinkel's major work on treating eating disorders published in 1985, there were no references to abuse of any nature. H.G. Pope Jr. and J.I. Hudson (1992), concluded that evidence did not support the hypothesis that childhood sexual abuse is a risk factor for bulimia nervosa. However, on close examination, Susan Wooley (1994) called their data into question, referring to it as highly selective. The problem with Pope and Hudson, and many others who refute the relationship between sexual abuse and eating disorders, is that their conclusions have been based upon a cause-and-effect link. Looking only for a simple cause-and-effect relationship is like searching with blinders on. Many factors and variables interacting with one another play a role. For an individual who was sexually abused as a child, the nature and severity of the abuse, the functioning of the child prior to the abuse, and how the abuse was responded to will all factor in as to whether this individual will develop an eating disorder or other means of coping. Although other influences need to be present, it is absurd to say that just because the sexual abuse is not the only factor, it is not a factor at all.

As female clinicians and researchers increased on the scene, serious questions began to be raised regarding the gender-related nature of eating disorders and what possible relationship this might have with abuse and violence against women in general. As the studies increased in number and the investigators were increasingly female, the evidence grew to support the association between eating problems and early sexual trauma or abuse.

As reported in the book *Sexual Abuse and Eating Disorders,* edited by Mark Schwartz and Lee Cohen (1996), systematic inquiry into the occurrence of sexual trauma in eating disorder patients has resulted in alarming prevalence figures:

> *Oppenheimer, et al. (1985) reported sexual abuse during childhood and/or adolescence in 70 percent of 78 eating disorder patients. Kearney-Cooke (1988) found 58 percent with a history of sexual trauma of 75 bulimic patients. Root and Fallon (1988) reported that in a group of 172 eating disorder patients, 65 percent had been physically abused, 23 percent raped, 28 percent sexually abused in childhood, and 23 percent maltreated in actual relationships. Hall, et al. (1989) found 40 percent sexually abused women in a group of 158 eating disorder patients.*

Although researchers have used varying definitions of sexual abuse and methodologies in their studies, the above figures show that sexual trauma or abuse in childhood is a risk factor for developing eating disorders. Furthermore, clinicians across the country have experienced countless women who describe and interpret their eating disorder as connected to early sexual abuse. Anorexics have described trying to avoid sexuality and thus evade or escape potential perpetrators. Bulimics have described their symptoms as a way of purging the perpetrator, raging at the violator or oneself, and getting rid of the filth or dirtiness inside of them. Binge eaters have suggested that overeating numbs their feelings, distracts them from other bodily sensations, and results in weight gain which "armors" them and keeps them unattractive to potential perpetrators.

It is not important to know the exact prevalence of sexual trauma or abuse in the eating disorder population. When working with an eating disordered individual, it is important to inquire about and explore any abuse history and to discover its meaning and significance along with other factors contributing to the development of disordered eating or exercise behaviors.

With more women in the field of eating disorder research and treatment, the understanding of the origins of eating disorders is shifting. A feminist perspective considers sexual abuse and trauma of women as a social rather than an individual factor that is responsible for our current epidemic of disordered eating of all kinds. The subject calls for continued inquiry and closer scrutiny.

Considering the cultural and psychological contributions to the development of an eating disorder, one question remains: Why don't all people from the same cultural environment, with similar backgrounds, psychological problems, and even abuse histories, develop eating disorders? One further answer may be in genetic or biochemical individuality.

6

HEREDITY AND BIOCHEMICAL INDIVIDUALITY

Serious questions remain as to the precise nature of the relationship between those with anorexia nervosa and bulimia nervosa and those who fall somewhere else in the continuum of weight and shape preoccupation in the general population. Are some people more prone to develop an eating disorder because of a genetic predisposition? Do eating disorders run in families? Is there some biochemical predisposition that increases an individual's chance of developing an eating disorder? These questions are the topic of current research, which so far has provided some information but no definitive answers.

GENETIC CONTRIBUTIONS TO EATING DISORDERS

Despite varying methodologies, studies have consistently demonstrated elevated rates of anorexia nervosa and bulimia nervosa in families of individuals with these disorders compared to control populations. A simple genetic study consists of making observations about the relative occurrence of a certain condition in specific families and comparing the rate in these families with rates in known, comparable families. It is important to note the difference between "running in families" and genetic inheritability. The current evidence supports the notion that anorexia nervosa and bulimia nervosa have a strong familial component, but the degree to which this component is due to genetic rather than environmental influences is much less clear. For example, my mother was a schoolteacher and I also became a schoolteacher, but this does not mean that being a schoolteacher is a genetic condition. A mother who has anorexia nervosa may pass on her eating habits to her daughter rather than a genetic predisposition for developing the disorder. Evidence that supports a genetic component can be found in twin studies (Holland et al.) and to a lesser extent in family studies (Strober et al.), but research is still ongoing in this area. There is no clear suggestion as to what might be the genetic liability in anorexia nervosa or bulimia nervosa. However, examination of the nature of these illnesses suggests a number of possibilities, including defects in the regulation of satiety and hunger, mental and perceptual disturbances that may contribute to the ability to restrict eating in the face of hunger, or some variant of a genetic propensity for obsessive-compulsive behavior.

The relationship between anorexia nervosa and bulimia nervosa and other psychiatric syndromes, particularly mood, anxiety, obsessive-compulsive, and substance use disorders, is also of interest genetically. Due to the rates of the above syndromes found in family members of those with eating disorders, it has been the opinion of some that eating disorders are variants of these other syndromes. At this point in time, there is not enough data confirming whether this is the case, but a discussion of the coexisting conditions is warranted.

EATING DISORDERS AND AFFECTIVE DISORDERS

The relationship between eating and affective (mood) disorders has been intensively researched. Family studies have demonstrated elevated rates of depression in first-degree relatives of individuals with anorexia nervosa or bulimia nervosa compared to control populations (Strober et al., 1982). The available evidence suggests that coexisting depression exists in a high proportion of individuals with anorexia nervosa and bulimia nervosa but does not support the notion that eating and affective disorders are manifestations of a common underlying genetic vulnerability. The observation of Dr. Mike Strober and colleagues (1990) strongly suggests that the majority of cases of anorexia nervosa and bulimia nervosa cannot be explained by the assumption that they are due to shared liability to affective disorders. It remains possible, however, that there is a subgroup of such patients.

EATING DISORDERS AND OBSESSIVE-COMPULSIVE DISORDERS

Several researchers have explored the relationship between obsessive-compulsive disorder, anorexia nervosa, and bulimia nervosa. Obsessive-compulsive behavior is often part of the symptoms presented by individuals with these disorders. In fact, the positive response that bulimic individuals have to the medication fluoxetine, commonly known as Prozac, may in part be due to the same mechanism that occurs when fluoxetine is used for other obsessive-compulsive behaviors, such as sexual addiction rather than its antidepressant effect. Despite older research to the contrary, new studies are even confirming that fluoxetine is also useful in the treatment of anorexia nervosa, when given after weight restoration in order to prevent relapse. Studies are currently underway to determine if these disorders are variants of obsessive compusive disorders.

EATING DISORDERS AND SUBSTANCE USE DISORDERS

Researchers have suggested that substance use disorders might be related genetically to anorexia nervosa and bulimia nervosa. Studies have documented elevated rates, as high as 37 percent, of substance use disorder in the first-degree relatives of those with anorexia nervosa and bulimia nervosa, but the reason for this remains unclear and more investigation will have to be done.

DIRECTIONS FOR FUTURE RESEARCH

While there is evidence that eating disorders have a familial component and a genetic predisposition is likely in at least some patients, the nature and extent of this predisposition remains unknown. Further studies that demonstrate the familial nature of anorexia nervosa and bulimia nervosa will need to provide more detailed information on the precise mode of inheritance. Large sets of family data, gathered in a methodologically sophisticated fashion, could provide important insights. Present evidence would suggest focusing on patients with young-onset anorexia nervosa as a first step. Additionally, twin studies are a high priority, as they may clarify environmental and psychological factors that are both protective and predisposing for the development of eating disorders.

The next decade will bring a considerable increase in our knowledge about these factors through continued application of sophisticated genetic and biological techniques. For additional information on this topic the reader is referred to chapter 14, where biochemical, genetic, and neurological individuality are discussed in relation to the use of medication. Additional sources of information are listed in the bibliography.

7

ASSESSING THE SITUATION

O nce it is suspected that someone has an eating disorder, there are several ways of assessing the situation further, from a personal as well as professional level. This chapter will review assessment techniques that can be used by loved ones and significant others, in addition to those used in professional settings. Advances in our understanding and treatment of anorexia nervosa and bulimia nervosa have resulted in improvements in assessment tools and techniques for these disorders. Standard assessments for binge eating disorder are still being developed because less is known about the clinical features involved in this disorder. An overall assessment should ultimately include three general areas: behavioral, psychological, and medical. A thorough assessment should provide information on the following: history of body weight, history of dieting, all weight loss–related behaviors, body image perception and dissatisfaction, current and past psychological, family, social, and vocational functioning, and past or present stressors.

ASSESSING THE SITUATION IF YOU ARE A SIGNIFICANT OTHER

If you suspect that a friend, relative, student, or colleague has an eating disorder and you want to help, first you need to gather information in order to substantiate your concerns. You can use the checklist below as a guide.

Checklist of Observable and Nonobservable Signs of an Eating Disorder

____ Does anything to avoid hunger and avoids eating even when hungry

____ Is terrified about being overweight, or gaining weight

____ Obsessive and preoccupied with food

____ Eats large quantities of food secretly

____ Counts calories in all foods eaten

____ Disappears into the bathroom after eating

____ Vomits and either tries to hide it or is not concerned about it

____ Feels guilty after eating

____ Is preoccupied with a desire to lose weight

____ Must earn food through exercising

____ Uses exercise as punishment for overeating

____ Is preoccupied with fat in food and on the body

____ Increasingly avoids more and more food groups

____ Eats only nonfat or "diet" foods

____ Becomes a vegetarian (in some cases will not eat beans, cheese, nuts, and other vegetarian protein)

____ Displays rigid control around food: in the type, quantity, and timing of food eaten (food may be missing later)

____ Complains of being pressured by others to eat more or eat less

____ Weighs obsessively and panics without a scale available

____ Complains of being too fat even when normal weight or thin, and at times isolates socially because of this

____ Always eats when upset

____ Goes on and off diets (often gains more weight each time)

____ Forgoes nutritious food on a regular basis for sweets or alcohol

____ Complains about specific body parts and asks for constant reassurance regarding appearance

____ Constantly checks the fitting of belt, ring, and "thin" clothes to see if any fit too tightly

____ Checks the circumference of thighs particularly when sitting and space between thighs when standing

Is found using substances that could affect or control weight such as:

____ Laxatives

____ Diuretics

____ Diet pills

____ Caffeine pills or large amounts of caffeine

____ Other amphetamines or stimulants

____ Herbs or herbal teas with diuretic, stimulant, or laxative effects

____ Enemas

____ Ipecac syrup (household item which induces vomiting for poison control)

____ Other (_____)

If the person you care about displays even a few of the behaviors on the checklist, you have reason to be concerned. After you have assessed the situation and are reasonably sure there is a problem, you will need help deciding what to do next. You can refer to the rest of this chapter and chapter 8 "Guidelines for Significant Others," for more information.

ASSESSING THE SITUATION IF YOU ARE A PROFESSIONAL

Assessment is the first important step in the treatment process. After a thorough assessment, a treatment plan can be formulated. Since the treatment of eating disorders takes place on three simultaneous levels, the assessment process must take all three into consideration:

1. Physical correction of any medical problem.

2. Resolving underlying psychological, family, and social problems.

3. Normalizing weight and establishing healthy eating and exercise habits.

There are several avenues the professional can use for assessing an individual with disordered eating, including face-to-face interviews, inventories, detailed history questionnaires, and mental measurement testing. The following is a list of specific topics that should be explored.

ASSESSMENT TOPICS

- Eating behaviors and attitudes
- History of dieting
- Depression
- Cognitions (thought patterns)
- Self-esteem
- Hopelessness and suicidality
- Anxiety
- Interpersonal skills
- Body image, shape, and weight concerns
- Sexual or other trauma
- Perfectionism and obsessive-compulsive behavior
- General personality
- Family history and family symptoms
- Relationship patterns
- Other behaviors (for example, drug or alcohol abuse)

ASSESSMENT STRATEGIES AND GUIDELINES

It is important to get necessary information from clients while at the same time establishing rapport and creating a trusting, supportive environment. If less information is gathered in the first interview because of this, that is acceptable, as long as the information is eventually obtained. It is of primary importance that the client knows that you are there to help and that you understand what he or she is going through. The following guidelines for gathering information will help:

1. *Data:* Gather all the identifying data—age, name, address, occupation, spouse, and so on.

2. *Presentation:* How does the client look, act, present herself or himself.

3. *Reason for seeking treatment:* What is his/her reason for coming for help? Don't assume that you know. Some bulimics are coming because they want to be better anorexics. Some clients are coming for their depression or relationship problems. Some come because they think you have a magic answer or a magic diet to help them lose weight. Find out from the client's own words!

4. *Family information:* Find out information about the parents and/or any other family members. Find out this information from the client and, if possible, from the family members, too. How do they get along? How do they see the problem? How have they, or do they, attempt to deal with the client and the problem?

5. *Support systems:* Who does the client usually go to for help? From whom does the client get her/his normal support (not necessarily regarding the eating disorder)? With whom does she/he feel comfortable sharing things, who does he/she feel really cares? It is important to have a support system in recovery other than the treating professionals. The support system can be the family or a romantic partner but doesn't have to be. It may turn out that members of a therapy or support group and/or a teacher, friend, or coach provide the needed support. I have found that clients with a good support system recover much faster and more thoroughly than those without.

6. *Personal goals:* What are the client's goals regarding recovery? It is important to determine these, as they may be different from those of the clinician. To the client, recovery may mean, being able to stay 95 pounds, or gaining 20 pounds because "my parents won't buy me a car unless I weigh 100 pounds." The client may want to learn how to lose more weight without throwing up, even though only weighing 105 at a height of 5′8″. You must try to find out the client's true goals, but don't be surprised if she or he really doesn't have any. It may be that the only reason some clients come for treatment is that they were forced to be there or they are trying to get everyone to stop nagging them. However, usually underneath, all clients want to stop hurting, stop torturing themselves, stop feeling trapped. If they don't have any goals, suggest some—ask them if they wouldn't like to be less obsessed and even if they want to be thin, wouldn't they also like to be healthy.

Even if clients suggest an unrealistic weight, try not to argue with them about it. This does no good and scares them into thinking you are going to try to make them fat. You might respond that the client's weight goal is an unhealthy one or that she or he would have to be sick to reach or maintain it, but at this point it is important to establish understanding without judgment. It is fine to tell clients the truth, but important that they know the choice for how to deal with that truth is theirs. As an example, when Sheila first came in weighing 85 pounds, she was still on a losing weight pattern. There was no way I could have asked her to start gaining weight for me or for herself; that would have been premature and would have ruined our relationship. So instead, I got her to agree to remain at 85 pounds and not lose any more weight and to explore with me how much she could eat and still stay that weight. I had to show her, help her to do that. Only after time was I able to gain her trust and alleviate her anxiety in order for her to gain weight. Clients, whether anorexic, bulimic, or binge eaters, don't have any idea how much they can eat just to maintain their weight. Later, when they trust the therapist and are feeling safer, another goal can be established.

7. *Chief complaint:* You want to know what's wrong from the client's perspective. This will depend on whether they were forced in or came in voluntarily, but either way the chief complaint usually changes the safer the client feels with the clinician. Ask the client, "What are you doing with food that you would like to stop doing?" "What can't you do with food that you would like to be able to do?" "What do others want you to do or stop doing?" Ask what physical symptoms the client has and what thoughts or feelings get in her or his way.

8. *Interference:* Find out how much the disordered eating, body image, or weight control behaviors are interfering with the client's life. For example: Do they skip school because they feel sick or fat? Do they avoid people? Are they spending a lot of money on their habits? Are they having a hard time concentrating? How much time do they spend on weighing themselves? How much time do they spend buying food, thinking about food, or cooking food? How much time do they spend exercising, purging, buying laxatives, reading about weight loss, or worrying about their bodies?

9. *Psychiatric history:* Has the client ever had any other mental problems or disorders? Have any family members or relatives had any mental disorders? The clinician needs to know if the client has other psychiatric conditions, such as obsessive-compulsive disorder or depression, that would complicate treatment or indicate a different form of treatment (for example, signs of depression and a family history of depression which might warrant antidepressant medication sooner than later in the course of treatment).

Symptoms of depression are a common underlying issue in eating disorders. It is important to explore this and see how persistent or bad the symptoms are. Many times clients are depressed because of the eating disorder and their unsuccessful attempts to deal with it, thus increasing low self-esteem. Clients also get depressed because their relationships often fall apart over the eating disorder. Furthermore, depression can be caused by nutritional inadequacies. However, depression may exist in the family history and in the client before the onset of the eating disorder. Sometimes these details are hard to sort out. The same is often true for other conditions such as obsessive-compulsive disorder. A psychiatrist experienced in eating disorders can provide a thorough psychiatric evaluation and recommendation regarding these issues. It is important to note that antidepressant medication has been shown to be effective in bulimia nervosa even if the individual does not have symptoms of depression.

10. *Medical history:* The clinician (other than a physician) doesn't have to go into great specifics here because one can get all the details from the physician. However, it is important to ask questions in this area to get an overall picture and because clients don't always tell their doctors everything. In fact, many individuals do not tell their doctors about their eating disorder. It is valuable to know if the client is often sickly or has some current or past problems that could have affected or have been related to their eating behaviors. For example, it is important to distinguish between true anorexia (loss of appetite) and anorexia nervosa. It is important to determine if a person is genetically obese with fairly normal food intake or is a binge eater. It is critical to discover if vomiting is spontaneous and not willed or self-induced. Food refusal can have other meanings than those found in the clinical eating disorders. An eight-year-old was brought in for anorexia nervosa and during my assessment I discovered she was afraid of gagging due to sexual abuse. She had no fear of weight gain or body image disturbance and had been inappropriately diagnosed.

11. *Family patterns of health, food, weight, and exercise:* This may have a great bearing on the cause of the eating disorder and/or the forces that sustain it. For example, clients with overweight parents who have struggled with their own weight unsuccessfully over the years may provoke their children into early weight loss regimens, causing in them a fierce determination not to follow the same pattern. Eating disorder behaviors may have become

the only successful diet plan. Also, if a parent pushes exercise, some children may develop unrealistic expectations of themselves and become compulsive and perfectionistic exercisers.

If there is no nutrition or exercise knowledge in the family or there is misinformation, the clinician may be up against unhealthy but long-held family patterns. I'll never forget the time I told the parents of a sixteen-year-old binge eater that she was eating too many hamburgers, french fries, burritos, hot dogs, and malts. She had expressed to me that she wanted to have family meals and not be sent for fast food all the time. Her parents didn't supply anything nutritious in the house and my client wanted help and wanted me to talk to them. When I approached the subject, the father got upset with me because he owned a fast-food drive-through stand where the whole family worked and ate. It was good enough for him and his wife and it was good enough for his daughter, too. These parents had their daughter working there and eating there all day, providing no other alternative. They had brought her into treatment when she had tried to kill herself because she was "miserable and fat" and they wanted me to "fix" her weight problem.

12. *Weight, eating, diet history:* Get a detailed history of all weight issues and concerns. How has the client's weight changed over the years? What was her or his weight and eating like when she or he was little? Ask clients what was the most they ever weighed and the least? How did they feel about their weight then? When did they first start feeling bad about their weight? What kind of eater were they? When did they first diet? How did they try to diet? Did they take pills, when, how long, what happened? What different diets have they tried? What are all the ways they tried to lose weight and why do they think these ways haven't worked? What, if anything, has worked? These questions will reveal healthy or unhealthy weight loss, they also tell how chronic the problem is. Find out about each client's current dieting practices: What kind of diet are they on? Do they binge, throw up, take laxatives, enemas, diet pills, or diuretics?

Are they currently taking any drugs? Find out how much of these things they take and how often. How well do they eat now and how much do they know about nutrition? What is an example of what they consider a good day of eating and a bad one? I may even give them a mini–nutrition quiz to see how much they really know and to "open their eyes" a little bit if they are misinformed. However, a thorough dietary assessment should be performed by a registered dietitian who specializes in eating disorders. (See chapter 13, "Nutrition Education and Therapy.")

13. *Substance abuse:* Often, these clients, especially bulimics, abuse other substances besides food and diet-related pills or items. Be careful when asking about these matters so clients do not think you are categorizing them or just deciding they are hopeless addicts. They often see no connection between their eating disorders and their use or abuse of alcohol, marijuana, cocaine, and so on. Sometimes they do see a connection; for example, "I did snorting coke because it made me lose my appetite. I wouldn't eat so I lost weight, but now I really like the coke all the time and I eat anyway."

Clinicians need to know about other substance abuse which will complicate treatment and may give further clues into the client's personality (for example, that they are a more addictive personality type or the type of person who needs some form of escape or relaxation, or they are destructive to themselves for an unconscious or subconscious reason, and so on).

14. *Any other physical or mental symptoms:* Make sure you explore this area fully, not just as it pertains to the eating disorder. For example, eating disorder clients often suffer from insomnia. They often do not connect this to their eating disorders and neglect to mention it. To varying degrees, insomnia has an effect on the eating disorder behavior. Another example is that some anorexics, when questioned often report a history of past obsessive-compulsive behavior such as having to have their clothes in the closet arranged perfectly and according to colors or they had to have their socks on a certain way every day, or they may pull

out leg hairs one by one. Clients may not have any idea that these types of behaviors are important to divulge or will shed any light on their eating disorder. Any physical or mental symptom is important to know. Keep in your mind, and let the client know as well, that you are treating the person and not just the eating disorder.

15. *Insight:* How aware is the client about her or his problem? How deeply does the client understand what is going on both symptomatically and psychologically? How aware is she or he of needing help and of being out of control? Does the client have any understanding of the underlying causes of their disorder?

16. *Motivation:* How motivated and/or committed is the client to get treatment and to get well?

These are all things that the clinician needs to assess during the early stages of treatment. It may take a few sessions or even longer to get information in each of these areas. In some sense, assessment actually continues to take place throughout therapy. It may actually take months of therapy for a client to divulge certain information and for the clinician to get a clear picture of all the issues outlined above and to sort them out as they relate to the eating disorder. Assessment and treatment are ongoing processes tied together.

STANDARDIZED TESTS

A variety of questionnaires for mental measurement have been devised to help professionals assess behaviors and underlying issues commonly involved in eating disorders. A brief review of a few of these assessments follows.

EAT (EATING ATTITUDES TEST)
One assessment tool is the Eating Attitudes Test (EAT). EAT is a rating scale which is designed to distinguish patients with anorexia nervosa from weight-preoccupied, but otherwise healthy, female college students, which these days is a formidable task. The twenty-

six-item questionnaire is broken down into three subscales: dieting, bulimia and food preoccupation, and oral control.

The EAT can be useful in measuring pathology in underweight girls but caution is required when interpreting the EAT results of average weight or overweight girls. The EAT also shows a high false-positive rate in distinguishing eating disorders from disturbed eating behaviors in college women. The EAT has a child version, which researchers have already used to gather data. It has shown that almost 7 percent of eight- to thirteen-year-old children score in the anorexic category, a percentage which closely matches that found among adolescents and young adults.

There are advantages to the self-report format of the EAT, but there are also limitations. Subjects, particularly those with anorexia nervosa, are not always honest or accurate when self-reporting. However, the EAT has been shown to be useful in detecting cases of anorexia nervosa, and the assessor can use whatever information is gained from this assessment combined with other assessment procedures to make a diagnosis.

EDI (Eating Disorder Inventory)

The most popular and influential of the available assessment tools is the Eating Disorder Inventory, or EDI, developed by David Garner and colleagues. The EDI is a self-report measure of symptoms. Although the intent of the EDI was originally more limited, it is being used to assess the thinking patterns and behavioral characteristics of anorexia nervosa and bulimia nervosa. The EDI is easy to administer and provides standardized subscale scores on several dimensions that are clinically relevant to eating disorders. Originally there were eight subscales. Three of the subscales assess attitudes and behaviors concerning eating, weight, and shape. These are drive for thinness, bulimia, and body dissatisfaction. Five of the scales measure more general psychological traits relevant to eating disorders. These are ineffectiveness, perfectionism, interpersonal distrust, awareness of internal stimuli, and maturity fears. The EDI 2 is a follow-up to the original EDI and includes three new subscales: asceticism, impulse control, and social insecurity.

The EDI can provide information to clinicians that is helpful in understanding the unique experience of each patient and in guiding treatment planning. The easy-to-interpret graphed profiles can be compared to norms and to other eating disorder patients and can be used to track progress of the patient during the course of treatment. The EAT and the EDI were developed to assess the female population who most likely have or are susceptible to developing an eating disorder. However, both of these assessment tools have been used with males with eating problems or compulsive exercise behaviors.

In nonclinical settings the EDI provides a means of identifying individuals who have eating problems or those at risk for developing eating disorders. The body dissatisfaction scale has been successfully used to predict the emergence of eating disorders in high-risk populations.

There is a twenty-eight-item, multiple-choice, self-report measure for bulimia nervosa known as BULIT-R which was based on the DSM III-R criteria for bulimia nervosa and is a mental measurement tool to assess the severity of this disorder.

BODY IMAGE ASSESSMENTS

Body image disturbance has been found to be a dominant characteristic of eating disordered individuals, a significant predictor of who might develop an eating disorder, and an indicator of those individuals having received or still receiving treatment who might relapse. As Hilda Bruch, a pioneer in eating disorder research and treatment, pointed out, "Body image disturbance distinguishes the eating disorders, anorexia nervosa and bulimia nervosa, from other psychological conditions that involve weight loss and eating abnormalities and its reversal is essential to recovery." This being true, it is important to assess body image disturbance in those with disordered eating. One way to measure body image disturbance is the Body Dissatisfaction subscale of the EDI mentioned above. Another assessment method is the PBIS, Perceived Body Image Scale, developed at British Columbia's Children's Hospital.

The PBIS provides an evaluation of body image dissatisfaction and distortion in eating disordered patients. The PBIS is a visual rating scale consisting of eleven cards containing figure drawings of bodies ranging from emaciated to obese. Subjects are given the cards and asked four different questions which represent different aspects of body image. Subjects are asked to pick which of the figure cards best represents their answers to the following four questions:

1. Which body best represents the way you *think you look?*

2. Which body best represents the way you *feel you are?*

3. Which body best represents the way you *see yourself in the mirror?*

4. Which body best represents the way you *would like to look?*

The PBIS was developed for easy and rapid administration to determine which components of body image are disturbed and to what degree. The PBIS is useful not only as an assessment tool but as an interactive experience facilitating the therapy.

There are other assessment tools available. In assessing body image it is important to keep in mind that body image is a multifaceted phenomenon with three main components: perception, attitude, and behavior. Each of these components needs to be considered.

Other assessments can be done to gather information in the above-listed domains, such as the "Beck Depression Inventory" to assess depression, or assessments designed specifically for dissociation or obsessive-compulsive behavior. A thorough psychosocial evaluation should be done to gather information on family, job, work, relationship, and any trauma or abuse history. Additionally, other professionals can perform assessments as part of a treatment team approach. A dietitian can do a nutrition assessment and a psychiatrist can perform a psychiatric evaluation. Integrating the results of various assessments allows the clinician, patient, and treatment team to develop an appropriate, individualized treatment plan. One of the most important assessments of all that needs to be obtained and maintained is the one performed by a medical doctor, to evaluate the individual's medical status.

Medical Assessment

Eating disorders are often referred to as psychosomatic disorders, not because the physical symptoms associated with them are "all in the person's head," but because they are illnesses where a disturbed psyche directly contributes to a disturbed soma (body). Aside from the social stigma and psychological turmoil that an eating disorder causes in an individual's life, the medical complications are numerous, ranging all the way from dry skin to cardiac arrest. In fact, anorexia nervosa and bulimia nervosa are two of the most life-threatening of all psychiatric illnesses. Below is a summary of the various sources from which complications arise.

Sources of Medical Symptoms in Patients with Eating Disorders

1. Self-starvation

2. Self-induced vomiting

3. Laxative abuse

4. Diuretic abuse

5. Ipecac abuse

6. Compulsive exercise

7. Bingeing

8. Exacerbation of preexisting diseases (for example, insulin-dependent diabetes mellitus)

9. Treatment effects of nutritional rehabilitation and psychopharmacological agents (drugs prescribed to alter mental functioning).

The medical complications that arise vary with each individual. Two persons with the same behaviors may develop completely different symptoms or the same symptoms within different time frames. Some patients who self-induce vomiting have low electrolytes and a bleeding esophagus; others can vomit for years without ever developing these symptoms. People have died from ipecac abuse, poisoning, or excessive pressure on their diaphragms from a binge, while others have performed these same behaviors with no evidence of medical complications. It is critical to keep this in mind. A bulimic woman, bingeing and vomiting eighteen times a day or a 79-pound anorexic can both have normal lab results. It is necessary to have a well-trained and experienced physician as part of the treatment of an eating disorder patient. Not only do these physicians have to treat symptoms that they find, they have to anticipate what is to come, and discuss what is not revealed by medical lab data.

A physician treating a patient with an eating disorder needs to know what to look for and what laboratory or other tests to perform. The physician must have some empathy and understanding of the overall picture involved in an eating disorder to avoid minimizing symptoms, misunderstanding, or giving conflicting advice. Unfortunately, physicians with special training and/or experience in diagnosing and treating eating disorders are not very common and furthermore patients who seek psychotherapy for an eating disorder often have their own family doctors they may prefer to use rather than one the therapist refers them to. Physicians not trained in eating disorders may overlook or disregard certain findings to the detriment of the patient. In fact, eating disorders often go undetected for long periods of time even when the individual has been to a physician. Weight loss of unknown origin, failure to grow at a normal rate, unexplained amenorrhea, or high cholesterol can all be signs of undiagnosed anorexia nervosa that physicians too often fail to act upon or attribute to other causes. Patients have been known to have loss of dental enamel, parotid gland enlargement, damaged esophagi, high serum amylase levels, and scars on the back of the hand from self-induced vomiting, and yet still be undiagnosed with bulimia nervosa!

A THOROUGH MEDICAL ASSESSMENT INCLUDES:

1. A physical exam,

2. Laboratory and other diagnostic tests,

3. A nutritional assessment/evaluation,

4. A written or oral interview of weight, dieting, and eating behavior,

5. Continued monitoring by a physician. The physician must treat any medical or biochemical cause for the eating disorder, treat the medical symptoms that arise as a result of the eating disorder, and must rule out any other possible explanations for symptoms such as malabsorption states, primary thyroid disease, or severe depression resulting in loss of appetite. Additionally, medical complications may arise as consequences of the treatment itself; for example, refeeding edema (swelling that results from the starved body's reaction to eating again—see chapter 15), or complications from mind-altering medications prescribed,

6. Assessment and treatment of any needed medication (most often referred to a psychiatrist).

THE PHYSICAL EXAM

Physicians should include a variety of assessments in their medical examination and evaluation of eating disorder patients:

PHYSICAL EXAM OF EASILY OBSERVED SYMPTOMS

- Emaciated body
- Hypotension (low blood pressure)
- Slow heart rate
- Edema (fluid retention, particularly of the lower extremities)
- Dry skin
- Cold extremities
- Thinning hair
- Increased lanugo hair (fine body hair)
- Swollen or puffy cheeks, glands
- Brittle hair and nails
- Lesions on the back of the hand, (scars, callouses, hyperpigmentaion or ulcers)
- Broken blood vessel in the eyes

LABORATORY TESTS

Recommended:

- Complete blood count
- Electrolytes (sodium, potassium, chloride, and Co^2)
- Chemistry panel
- Liver function tests
- Total protein and albumin
- Calcium
- Sedementation rate
- Hormones
    Thyroid function tests
    Follicle-stimulating hormone
    Luteinizing hormone
    Estrogen (females)
    Testosterone (males)
- Electrocardiogram

Selectively Performed:

- Chest X ray
- Abdominal X ray for severe bloating
- Lower esophageal sphincter pressure studies for reflux
- Lactose deficiency tests for dairy intolerance
- Total bowel transit time for severe constipation
- Dual photon absorptiometry (bone density test for amenorrheic or emaciated patient)

It is important for the physician not only to check for any medical complications that must be attended to but to establish a baseline for future comparisons. It must always be kept in mind that medical tests often fall short of revealing problems until the more advanced stages of the illness. Patients engaging in ultimately dangerous behaviors whose laboratory tests come back normal may get the wrong message. It must be explained to them that the body finds ways to compensate for starvation; for example, decreasing the metabolic rate to conserve energy. It usually takes a long time for the body to break down to the point of serious, life-threatening danger.

Most eating disorder complaints, like headaches, stomachaches, insomnia, fatigue, weakness, dizzy spells, and even fainting do not show up on lab results. Parents, therapists, and doctors too often make the mistake of expecting to scare patients into improving their behaviors by having them get a physical exam in order to discover whatever damage has been done. For one thing, patients are rarely motivated by medical consequences and often have the attitude that being thin is more important than being healthy, or nothing bad is really going to happen to them, or they don't care if it does. Furthermore, patients can appear to be healthy and receive normal lab results even though they have been starving, bingeing, or vomiting for months and in some cases years. The following journal entries from patients reveal how disturbing this can be.

When I first was dragged into the doctor's office by my mother when my weight had dropped from 135 to 90 pounds, all my lab tests came back fine! I felt vindicated. I just felt like, "See, I told you so, I'm fine, so leave me alone." My doctor told me then, "You may seem healthy now but these things will show up later. You are doing damage to your body that may not show itself for years." I didn't believe it and even if I did, I felt helpless to do anything about it.

When I went for an exam and lab work I was bingeing and vomiting up to twelve times daily and was also smoking marijuana and snorting cocaine regularly. I was very worried about my health! On the way to the doctor's office I snorted cocaine. When my lab test came back normal, I felt excited thinking, "I can get away with this." In some ways I wish the tests had been worse, I wish they would have scared me, maybe it would have helped me to stop. Now, I feel like since it hasn't done any damage, why stop. I know I am damaging myself, my voice is raspy and my salivary glands are swollen from the constant acid wash of the vomit. My skin is grayish and my hair is falling out, but . . . my lab tests were fine!

It is clear that a normal lab report is not a guarantee of good health and physicians need to explain this to their patients. In some cases at the indiscretion of the physician, more invasive tests like an MRI for brain atrophy or bone marrow test may have to be performed to show abnormality. If lab tests are even slightly abnormal, the physician should discuss these with the eating disorder patient and show concern. Physicians are unaccustomed to discussing abnormal lab values unless they are extremely out of range, but with eating disorder patients this may be a very useful treatment tool.

Detailed information regarding the ongoing medical management of eating disorders is provided by Dr. Philip Mehler in chapter 15, "Medical Management of Anorexia Nervosa and Bulimia Nervosa."

Once it is determined or likely that an individual has a problem that needs attention, it is important to get help not only for the person with the disorder but for those significant others who are also affected. Significant others not only need assistance in understanding eating disorders and in getting their loved ones help but in getting help for themselves as well.

Those who have tried to help know all too well how easy it is to say the wrong thing, feel like they are getting nowhere, lose patience and hope and become increasingly frustrated, angry, and depressed themselves. For these reasons and more the following chapter offers guidelines for family members and significant others of individuals with eating disorders.

8

GUIDELINES FOR SIGNIFICANT OTHERS

Friends and family members are often the forgotten victims of eating disorders. If someone you care about has an eating disorder, it is difficult to know what to do for the person or for yourself. No matter what effort might be taken, such as helping find a therapist, sitting up all night talking, taking away laxatives, and so on, ultimately you have no power over another person's behavior. You do have power over what you choose to do about the situation, and the more knowledgeable and prepared you are, the better chance you have for success. Even when you don't know how your friend or loved one will react to your concern, it is important that you express it and offer to help. Even if your concern or help is received poorly, don't give up. It is difficult but important that friends and family members keep trying to reach out to a suffering loved one in order to facilitate the person getting help and to support her or him during her or his struggle. Your efforts, love, and encouragement may be crucial to your loved one's recovery. People who have recovered from eating disorders often cite being loved, believed in, and not given up on as crucial factors in their getting help and getting well.

If you have observed behaviors in friends or loved ones and are concerned that they have a problem with food or weight, that is enough reason to say something to them. You do not need to wait until you have signs or proof of a full-blown eating disorder. The sooner you discuss things the better, for your sake and for theirs.

HOW TO APPROACH AND TALK TO SOMEONE YOU SUSPECT HAS A PROBLEM

PICK A TIME AND PLACE WHERE THERE WILL BE NO INTERRUPTIONS AND NO NEED TO HURRY

You must allow for privacy and plenty of time for both you and your friend or loved one to say everything that needs to be said.

BE EMPATHIC AND UNDERSTANDING

The first step, and most important thing to remember throughout your experience with a loved one who suffers from an eating disorder, is to have empathy. The best way to describe empathy is that it is like standing in someone else's shoes. Empathy is an effort to understand someone's experience as he or she experiences it and to convey that understanding. The only way to do this is to not be invested in changing the person or in getting her (or him) to change her or his perspective; that can come later. Before a loved one is going to be able to see another perspective, she or he will need to know that someone recognizes the legitimacy and importance of their own.

Don't worry that empathizing is not enough and that you need to do something or get your loved one to take action. It is true that if you stop at empathy you can "love and understand someone with an eating disorder to death," but empathy is a necessary first step and must be continually maintained. Once a person knows you understand and are not going to try and take over or take the eating disorder away, then you can begin helping in other ways, such as getting information, finding specialists, making appointments, reassuring, and even confronting. Just remember that all of this needs to take place after a person first feels understood and accepted.

Asking for help is usually one of the hardest things for those suffering from eating disorders to do. They need to learn that asking for and receiving help is not a weakness and they do not need to handle everything alone. Ultimately this helps them to learn that they can reach out to people instead of their eating disorder behaviors to escape from their pain. Even if there are limits to what you can do, they need to know you can help.

EXPRESS YOUR CONCERN ABOUT WHAT YOU HAVE OBSERVED AND SPEAK FROM YOUR OWN EXPERIENCE

It is important to stay calm and keep to specific personal examples. It is best to use "I" statements rather than "You" statements. Using "I" statements means that it is only in your opinion or from your own perspective that you are speaking. Using "You" statements sounds judgmental and is apt to create a defensive reaction.

Instead of saying:

You're too thin, say, *I look at you and see you wasting away and I'm scared.*

You have to stop throwing up, say, *I heard you throwing up and I'm worried about your health.*

You are ruining our relationship, say, *I'm concerned for you and felt like I had to say something or we would both run the risk of being dishonest with each other.*

You must get help, say, *I'd like to help you to find help.*

Be careful not to use "You" statements that are disguised as "I" statements (for example, "I think you are just trying to get attention.") Don't focus all of your discussion on food, weight, exercise, or other behaviors. It is easy to get caught up and stuck in discussing your loved one's behaviors, such as eating too little, not weighing enough, bingeing too much, purging, and so on. These are valid concerns and important to comment on, but focusing on behaviors alone can be counterproductive. For example, a person with anorexia nervosa will be pleased rather than alarmed to hear that she is painfully thin. Remember, those are the underlying issues, not just the behaviors, which are important. Finally, loved ones may be less defensive when approached with the idea that they seem sad, not "themselves," or unhappy. They are likely to be less threatened about discussing these problems.

PROVIDE INFORMATION ABOUT RESOURCES FOR TREATMENT

It is wise to be prepared with helpful information and suggestions in case your friend or loved one is ready and willing to receive them. Try to have the name of a doctor and/or therapist, the fees they charge, and how to make an appointment. If a treatment program is needed, have that information as well. Ask your loved one to consider going to at least one appointment and offer to go together. Of course, if you are a parent of a minor you will have to go at least to the first appointment and you should be included on some level, but it is important that it is your loved one's session, not yours. You don't need to be in the room the whole time when they are being seen.

DO NOT ARGUE OR GET INTO A POWER STRUGGLE

Expect to be rejected in the beginning and don't give up. It is very likely that the person you are concerned about will deny the problem, become angry, or refuse to get help. It does no good to argue. Stick to your feelings, how you experience the situation, and your hope that the person will get help. Parents may eventually have to use their authority over a child and force them to go to treatment. In this situation let the therapist help negotiate power struggles.

ACCEPT YOUR LIMITATIONS

There is a limit to what you can do for another person. It is easy to fall into the trap of believing that if you said or did the right thing, then your friend or loved one would be helped and you would not feel powerless. There is a lot you can do, but ultimately you alone cannot change the problem or make it go away. You must learn to accept your own helplessness and limitations as to what you can and cannot do—but don't give up. Keep in mind that people often need to hear something several times before they act on it.

It is important to remember that your friend or loved one has a right to refuse treatment. Even minors forced to go can sit silently refusing to get help. If you believe that his/her life is in danger, you must get immediate help from a professional. Go to the appointment yourself even if your loved one refuses. A professional can help you deal with a person who is in denial or resisting treatment. It is possible that an intervention (discussed next) can be set up that may facilitate your loved one agreeing to get help.

INTERVENTIONS—GETTING HELP FOR A PERSON WHO IS IN DENIAL OR REFUSES IT

If you are concerned that someone you care about has an eating disorder that is severe or life threatening, and you have tried to talk to her or him or get her or him into treatment without success, an intervention may be in order. Interventions are well known in the field of drug and alcohol abuse, but not for eating disorders. An intervention is a carefully orchestrated event planned in secret by significant others with the help of a professional for the purpose of confronting a loved one in order to discuss concerns and compel the person to get help for his/her problem.

Interventions should be carefully planned or they may do more harm than good. The professional involved should have experience in eating disorders and in interventions. The timing, the people involved, the structuring of what is said, getting the person there, and the treatment plan options are all critical for a successful intervention.

If you want to do an intervention for a loved one, you need to enlist the help of a professional and a few people (try for six or so) who are significant in your loved one's life, such as relatives, friends, coaches, coworkers, teachers, and so on. These people will all need to meet together and carefully plan the intervention. A summary of an intervention follows.

On the day of the intervention a plan will be carried out regarding how to get the person to the intervention or to bring the intervention to her/him. Presenting a united front, the participants will tell the loved one in a caring, compassionate, and straightforward way what they have personally observed and what their concerns are. The examples should include health and functioning, not just weight or eating behaviors. Each person should give specific examples and express the desire that the loved one be healthy and happy. How the eating disorder has affected the person physically, emotionally, psychologically, and in relationships should be discussed. Although the intervention is planned in advance, it is important to be natural and informal enough to help the loved one be as comfortable as possible.

Expect that the person with the eating disorder will feel set up and become angry. Try to understand the anger and reassure the individual that you are not trying to control her/him but that you could not go on without doing something about the situation. Encourage your loved one to express whatever feelings he or she has and listen in a nonjudgmental manner. Do not argue about whether there is a problem. Validate anything the person says and then reiterate your worries and what you have observed.

Provide information regarding the plan or options for treatment. Explain that arrangements have been made and are ready to be carried out, and execute the plan if the person agrees. If your loved one persists in denying the problem and refusing to get treatment, you will have to accept it. Remind yourself that the eating disorder is serving a purpose in her or his life and you cannot force her/him to let it go. Don't give up; the issue may have to be addressed repeatedly before a person agrees to get help.

Every individual involved in the intervention will then have to decide what the next step is and what course the relationship with the loved one will take. For example, husbands have actually threatened to divorce their wives unless they get help. This may sound extreme and unfair but, when there are children involved who suffer from the caretaking of an anorexic mother, this drastic measure is easier to understand and can turn out to be the motivation that initiates treatment and even recovery.

GUIDELINES FOR OTHERS WHEN A LOVED ONE IS IN TREATMENT

Aside from the above suggestions for approaching and talking to a person with an eating disorder, there are additional considerations listed below for parents or significant others who live with and/or love someone who is in treatment for an eating disorder. Remember, each case is unique and warrants special individualized attention. The guidelines listed should be discussed and followed with the assistance of professional help.

Be Patient—There Are No Quick Solutions

Eating disorder treatment usually takes two to five years. Even if you are aware of this, you may still be inclined to think that your loved one should be improving faster and that more progress should be made. Long-term thinking and endless patience are necessary.

Avoid Power Struggles

As much as possible, find alternatives to power struggles, especially when it comes to eating and to weight. Don't make mealtimes or eating a battle of wills. Don't try to force or restrict eating. Leave these issues up to the therapist or other treating professional unless your involvement is discussed, requested, and worked out with help from a therapist or other helping professional.

Avoid Blaming or Demanding

Don't try to find causes or someone to blame for the eating disorder, and don't plead or demand that your loved one stop his or her behaviors. Neither of these will help; they will only serve to oversimplify the situation and will cause even more shame and guilt. It is easy for your loved one to feel responsible for your or anyone else's feelings. You can help prevent this by avoiding blame or making demands.

Don't Ask Your Loved One How You Can Help—Ask a Professional

Your loved one will not know how you can help and may feel worse if you ask. A professional is in a better position to give you advice.

Deal with Feelings of All Family Members

Family members are often the forgotten victims, especially other children. They need to talk about their feelings. It doesn't help to keep feelings bottled up inside; therefore, it is useful for all family members to express themselves in journals, letters, or verbally as a way of getting their feelings out and communicating.

SHOW AFFECTION AND APPRECIATION VERBALLY AND PHYSICALLY

A little unconditional love goes a long way. There are many ways to show affection and support besides talking; for example, hugging a lot or spending special time together.

DO NOT COMMENT ABOUT WEIGHT AND LOOKS

Avoid making appearance a focus. Don't comment about your loved one's or other people's looks. Physical appearance has become too important in our society and especially in the eating disordered person's life. It is best to stay away from the topic of weight altogether. It is a trap to answer questions like, "Do I look fat?" If you say no, you won't be believed and if you say yes or even hesitate for a moment, your reaction may be used as an excuse to engage in eating disorder behavior. Telling someone with anorexia they look too thin is a mistake because chances are that is what he/she wants to hear. Telling a bulimic she looks good on a particular day may reinforce her binge/purge behaviors if she believes that they are responsible for the compliment.

DO NOT USE BRIBES, REWARDS, OR PUNISHMENTS TO CONTROL YOUR LOVED ONE'S EATING BEHAVIOR

Bribing, if it works at all, is only temporary and postpones the person's dealing with internal means of controlling her or his behaviors.

DON'T GO UNREASONABLY OUT OF YOUR WAY TO PURCHASE OR PREPARE SPECIAL FOODS

It is fine to help out by buying foods your loved one likes and feels safe eating—to a point. Don't drive all the way to the frozen yogurt store because that is all the individual will eat. Don't be pushed into any action by the threat, "I won't eat unless . . . " If a person refuses to eat unless very strict circumstances are adhered to, they may ultimately need inpatient treatment. Giving in to every whim will only postpone the inevitable.

DO NOT MONITOR SOMEONE ELSE'S BEHAVIOR FOR THEM, EVEN WHEN ASKED

Do not become the food or bathroom police. Often loved ones will ask you to stop them if you see them eating too much or tell them when you see they have gained too much weight. They may seek your praise for the amount of food they are eating. Monitoring your loved one's behaviors may work for a short time, but always ends up backfiring in the end. People with eating disorder need to monitor themselves with a professional's guidance and help until such time as the professional requests otherwise.

DON'T ALLOW YOUR LOVED ONE TO DOMINATE THE REST OF THE FAMILY'S EATING PATTERNS

While nurturing others, individuals with eating disorders deny their own needs for food. As much as possible, the family's normal eating patterns should be maintained unless they also are in need of altering. Don't let the person with the eating disorder shop, cook for, or feed the family unless she/he also eats the items bought, prepared, and served.

ACCEPT YOUR LIMITATIONS

Accepting your feelings and your limitations means learning to set rules or say "No" in a caring and reasonable but firm and consistent manner. For example, you may have to discuss cleaning the bathroom, limiting the amount of food your loved one goes through, or charging him/her for binged food. You may have to tell your loved one that you can't always be there when she/he needs to talk and that calling you at work is not acceptable. You may want to establish certain rules, for example, that laxatives or ipecac syrup aren't allowed in the house. If the illness progresses, you may have to add many more rules and reevaluate your own limitations. Do not get overinvolved and try to become a substitute for professional care. Eating disorders are very complicated and difficult to treat; getting professional help is necessary.

GETTING HELP AND SUPPORT FOR YOURSELF

If you care about someone who has an eating disorder, it can be painful, frustrating, and confusing. You need knowledge, guidance, and support in dealing with the situation. The more knowledge you have about the causes of eating disorders and what to expect in regard to treatment, the easier it will be for you. Check the resource section in the back of this book for reading material and other resource suggestions.

You are going to experience a range of emotions from helplessness and anger, to despair. You may find yourself losing control of your feelings and actions. You may even become preoccupied with your own and other family members' eating and weight. It is important to get help for yourself.

You need to talk about your own feelings as well as getting guidance in how to deal with your loved one. Good friends are important, but a therapist or support group may also be necessary. There are support groups and therapy groups you can attend that include your loved one and groups for parents and significant others only. These groups are hard to find, and it may be worth your while to start a support group yourself and let local hospital programs, therapists, and doctors know about it. You will find information about support groups in the resource section. An individual therapist may also be important, so you can discuss in detail your particular situation, your feelings, and your specific needs.

Whether your significant other or loved one with the eating disorder gets help, let him/her know that you are getting help for yourself. This may help your loved one take the situation more seriously, but even if it does not, you must take care of yourself. If you do not stay healthy and strong, you will not be able to help someone else. Remember the instructions on an airline flight to first put on your own oxygen mask, then to put one on your child? With your own "oxygen mask" on, you can safely explore, pursue, and participate in helping and supporting those you care about and love.

9

TREATMENT PHILOSOPHY AND APPROACHES

This chapter provides a summary of the three main philosophical approaches to the treatment of eating disorders. These approaches are used alone or in combination with one another according to the treating professional's knowledge and preference as well as the needs of the individual receiving care. Medical treatment and treatment with drugs that are used to affect mental functioning are both discussed in other chapters and not included here. However, it is important to note that medication, medical stabilization, and ongoing medical monitoring and treatment are necessary in conjunction with other approaches. Depending on how clinicians view the nature of eating disorders, they will most likely approach treatment from one or more of the following perspectives:

- Psychodynamic
- Cognitive behavioral
- Disease/addiction

It is important when choosing a therapist that patients and significant others understand that there are different theories and treatment approaches. Admittedly, patients may not know whether or not a certain theory or treatment approach is suitable for them, and they may need to rely on instinct when choosing a therapist. Many patients know when a certain approach is not appropriate for them. For example, I often have patients elect to go into individual treatment with me or choose my treatment program over others because they have previously tried and do not want a Twelve Step or addiction based approach. Getting a referral from a trustworthy individual is one way to find an appropriate professional or treatment program.

PSYCHODYNAMIC MODEL

A psychodynamic view of behavior emphasizes internal conflicts, motives, and unconscious forces. Within the psychodynamic realm there are many theories on the development of psychological disorders in general and on the sources and origins of eating disorders in particular. Describing each psychodynamic theory and the resulting treatment approach, such as object relations or self psychology, is beyond the scope of this book, but an overview is provided below.

The common feature of all psychodynamic theories is the belief that without addressing and resolving the underlying cause for disordered behaviors, they may subside for a time but will all too often return. The early pioneering and still relevant work of Hilde Bruch on treating eating disorders made it clear that using behavior modification techniques to get people to gain weight may accomplish short term improvement but not much in the long run. Like Bruch, therapists with a psychodynamic perspective believe that the essential treatment for full recovery from an eating disorder involves understanding and treating the cause, adaptive function, or purpose that the eating disorder serves.

In human development when needs are not met, adaptive functions arise. These adaptive functions serve as substitutes for developmental deficits that protect against the resulting anger and pain. The problem is that the adaptive functions can never be internalized. They can never fully replace what was originally needed and furthermore they have consequences that threaten long-term health and functioning. For example, an individual who never learned the ability to self soothe may use food as a means of comfort and thus binge eat when she is upset. Binge eating will never help her internalize the ability to soothe herself and will most likely lead to negative consequences such as weight gain or social withdrawal. Understanding and working through the adaptive functions of eating disorder behaviors is important in helping patients internalize the ability to attain and maintain recovery.

In all of the psychodynamic theories, symptoms are seen as expressions of a struggling inner self that uses the disordered eating and weight control behaviors as a way of communicating or expressing underlying issues. The symptoms are viewed as useful for the patient and attempts to directly try to take them away are avoided. In a strict psychodynamic approach the premise is that, when the underlying issues are able to be expressed, worked through and resolved, the disordered eating behaviors will no longer be necessary. Chapter 5, "Eating Disorder Behaviors Are Adaptive Functions," explains this in some detail.

Psychodynamic treatment usually consists of frequent psychotherapy sessions using interpretation and management of the transference relationship, or in other words, the patient's experience of the therapist and vice versa. Whatever the particular psychodynamic theory, the essential goal of this treatment approach is to help patients understand the connections between their pasts, their personalities, and their personal relationships and how all this relates to their eating disorders.

The problem with the psychodynamic approach to treating eating disorders is twofold. First, many times patients are in such a state of starvation, depression, or compulsivity that psychotherapy cannot effectively take place. Therefore, starvation, tendency toward suicide, compulsive bingeing and purging, or serious medical abnormalities may need to be addressed before psychodynamic work can be effective. Second, patients can spend years doing psychodynamic therapy gaining insight while still engaging in destructive symptomatic behaviors. To continue this kind of therapy for too long without symptom change seems unnecessary and unfair.

Psychodynamic therapy can offer a lot to eating disordered individuals, and may be an important factor in treatment, but a strict psychodynamic approach alone has not been shown to be effective in achieving high rates of full recovery. At some point, dealing directly with the disordered behaviors is important. The most well-known and studied technique or treatment approach currently used to challenge, manage, and transform specific food and weight-related behaviors is known as cognitive behavioral therapy.

COGNITIVE BEHAVIORAL MODEL

The term cognitive refers to mental perception and awareness. Cognitive distortions in the thinking of eating disorder patients that influence behavior are well recognized. A disturbed or distorted body image, paranoia about food itself being fattening, and binges being blamed on the fact that one cookie has already destroyed a perfect day of dieting, are common unrealistic assumptions and distortions. Cognitive distortions are held sacred by patients who rely on them as guidelines for behavior in order to gain a sense of safety, control, identity, and containment. Cognitive distortions have to be challenged in an educational and empathetic way in order to avoid unnecessary power struggles. Patients will need to know that their behaviors are ultimately their choice but that currently they are choosing to act on false, incorrect, or misleading information and faulty assumptions.

Cognitive behavioral therapy (CBT) was originally developed in the late 1970s by Aaron Beck as a technique for treating depression. The essence of cognitive behavioral therapy is that feelings and behaviors are created by cognitions (thoughts). The clinician's job is to help individuals learn to recognize cognitive distortions and either choose not to act on them or, better still, to replace them with more realistic and positive ways of thinking. Common cognitive distortions can be put into categories such as all-or-nothing thinking, over generalizing, assuming, magnifying or minimizing, magical thinking, and personalizing.

Those familiar with eating disorders will recognize the same or similar cognitive distortions repeatedly being expressed by eating disordered individuals seen in treatment. Disordered eating or weight-related behaviors such as obsessive weighing, use of laxatives, restricting all sugar, and binge eating after one forbidden food item passes the lips, all arise from a set of beliefs, attitudes, and assumptions about the meaning of eating and body weight. Regardless of theoretical orientation, most clinicians will eventually need to address and challenge their patients' distorted attitudes and beliefs in order to interrupt the behaviors that flow from them. If not addressed, the distortions and symptomatic behaviors are likely to persist or return.

1. *They provide a sense of safety and control.*

Example: All-or-nothing thinking provides a strict system of rules for an individual to follow when he or she has no self-trust in making decisions. Karen, a twenty-two-year-old bulimic, does not know how much fat she can eat without gaining weight so she makes a simple rule and allows herself none. If she does happen to eat something forbidden she binges on as many fatty foods as she can get because, as she puts it, "As long as I have blown it I might as well go the whole way and have all those foods I don't allow myself to eat."

2. *They reinforce the eating disorder as a part of the individual's identity.*

Example: Eating, exercise, and weight become factors that make the person feel special and unique. Keri, a twenty-one-year-old bulimic, told me, "I don't know who I will be without this illness," and Jenny, a fifteen-year-old anorexic, said, "I am the person known for not eating."

3. *They enable patients to replace reality with a system that supports their behaviors.*

Eating disorder patients use their rules and beliefs rather than reality to guide their behaviors. Magically thinking that being thin will solve all of one's problems or minimizing the significance of weighing as little as 79 pounds are ways that patients mentally allow themselves to continue their behavior. As long as John holds the belief that, "If I stop taking laxatives I will get fat," it is difficult to get him to discontinue his behavior.

4. *They help provide an explanation or justification of behaviors to other people.*

Cognitive distortions help people explain or justify their behavior to others. Stacey, a forty-five-year-old anorexic, would always complain, "If I eat more I feel bloated and miserable." Barbara, a binge eater, would restrict eating sweets only to end up bingeing on them later, justifying this by telling everyone, "I'm allergic to sugar." Both of these claims are more difficult to argue with than, "I'm afraid to eat more food," or "I set myself up to binge because I don't allow myself to eat sugar." Patients will justify their continued starving or purging by minimizing negative lab test results, hair loss, and even poor bone density scans. Magical thinking allows patients to believe and try to convince others to believe that electrolyte problems, heart failure, and death are things that happen to other people who are worse off.

Treating patients with cognitive behavioral therapy is considered by many top professionals in the field of eating disorders to be the "gold standard" of treatment, especially for bulimia nervosa. At the April 1996 International Eating Disorder Conference, several researchers such as Christopher Fairburn and Tim Walsh presented findings reiterating that cognitive behavioral therapy combined with medication produces better results than psychodynamic therapy combined with medication, either of these modalities combined with a placebo, or medication alone. Even though these findings are promising, the researchers themselves concede that the results show only that in these studies, one approach works better than others tried, and not that we have found a form of treatment that will help most patients. Many patients are not helped by the cognitive behavioral approach and we are not sure which ones will be. More research needs to be done. A prudent course of action in treating eating disorder patients would be to utilize cognitive behavioral therapy at least as a part of an integrated multidimensional approach.

DISEASE/ADDICTION MODEL

The disease or addiction model of treatment for eating disorders, sometimes referred to as the abstinence model, was originally taken from the disease model of alcoholism. Alcoholism is considered an addiction and alcoholics are considered powerless over alcohol because they have a disease that causes their bodies to react in an abnormal and addictive way to the consumption of alcohol. The Twelve Step program of Alcoholics Anonymous (AA) was designed to treat the disease of alcoholism based upon this principle. When this model was applied to eating disorders, and Overeater's Anonymous (OA) was originated, the word alcohol was substituted with the word food in the Twelve Step OA literature and at Twelve Step OA meetings. The basic OA text explains, "The OA recovery program is identical with that of Alcoholics Anonymous. We use AA's twelve steps and twelve traditions, changing only the words "alcohol" and "alcoholic" to "food" and "compulsive overeater" (Overeaters Anonymous, 1980). In this model, food is often referred to as a drug over which those with eating disorders are powerless. The Twelve Step program of Overeaters Anonymous was originally designed to help people who felt out of control with food: "The major objective of the program is to achieve abstinence, defined as freedom from compulsive overeating" (Malenbaum & Herzog et al., 1988). The original treatment approach involved abstaining from certain foods considered binge foods or addictive foods, namely sugar and white flour, and following the Twelve Steps of OA which are as follows:

TWELVE STEPS OF OA

Step I: We admitted we were powerless over food—that our lives had become unmanageable.

Step II: Came to believe that a Power greater than ourselves could restore us to sanity.

Step III: Made a decision to turn our will and our lives over to the care of God *as we understood Him.*

Step IV: Made a searching and fearless moral inventory of ourselves.

Step V: Admitted to God, to ourselves, and to another human being the exact nature of our wrongs.

Step VI: Were entirely ready to have God remove all these defects of character.

Step VII: Humbly asked Him to remove our shortcomings.

Step VIII: Made a list of all persons we had harmed, and became willing to make amends to them all.

Step IX: Made direct amends to such people wherever possible, except when to do so would injure them or others.

Step X: Continued to take personal inventory and when we were wrong, promptly admitted it.

Step XI: Sought through prayer and meditation to improve our conscious contact with God as we understood Him, praying only for knowledge of His will for us and the power to carry that out.

Step XII: Having had a spiritual awakening as the result of these steps, we tried to carry this message to compulsive overeaters and to practice these principles in all our affairs.

The addiction analogy and abstinence approach makes some sense in relationship to its original application to compulsive overeating. It was reasoned that if addiction to alcohol causes binge drinking, then addiction to certain foods could cause binge eating; therefore, abstinence from those foods should be the goal. This analogy and supposition is itself debatable. To this day we have found no scientific proof of a person being addicted to a certain food, much less masses of people to the same food. Nor has there been any proof that an addiction or Twelve Step approach is successful in treating eating disorders. However, making the analogy that compulsive overeating was fundamentally the same illness as bulimia nervosa and anorexia nervosa and thus all were addictions made a leap based on faith, or hope, or desperation. In an effort to find a way to treat the growing number and severity of eating disorder cases, the

OA approach began to be loosely applied to all forms of eating disorders. The use of the addiction model was readily adopted due to the lack of guidelines for treatment and the similarities that eating disorder symptoms seemed to have with other addictions (Hatsukami, 1982). Twelve Step recovery programs sprung up everywhere as a model that could be immediately adapted for use with eating disorder "addictions." This was happening even though one of OA's own pamphlets, entitled "Questions & Answers," tried to clarify that "OA publishes literature about its program and compulsive overeating, not about specific eating disorders such as bulimia and anorexia" (Overeaters Anonymous, 1979).

The American Psychiatric Association (APA) recognized a problem with Twelve Step treatment for anorexia nervosa and bulimia nervosa in their treatment guidelines established in February 1993. In summary, the APA's position is that Twelve Step based programs are not recommended as the sole treatment approach for anorexia nervosa or the initial sole approach for bulimia nervosa. The guidelines suggest that for bulimia nervosa Twelve Step programs such as OA may be helpful as an adjunct to other treatment and for subsequent relapse prevention. In determining these guidelines the members of the APA expressed concerns that due to "the great variability of knowledge, attitudes, beliefs, and practices from chapter to chapter and from sponsor to sponsor regarding eating disorders and their medical and psychotherapeutic treatment and because of the great variability of patients' personality structures, clinical conditions, and susceptibility to potentially counter therapeutic practices, clinicians should carefully monitor patients' experiences with Twelve Step programs."

Some clinicians feel strongly that eating disorders are addictions; for example, according to Kay Sheppard, in her 1989 book, *Food Addiction, The Body Knows*, "the signs and symptoms of bulimia nervosa are the same as those of food addiction." Others acknowledge that although there is an attractiveness to this analogy, there are many potential problems in assuming that eating disorders are addictions. In the *International Journal of Eating Disorders*, Walter Vandereycken, M.D., a leading figure in the field of eating disorders from Belgium, wrote, "The interpretative 'translating' of bulimia into a known disorder supplies both the patient and therapist with a reassuring point of reference . . . . Although the use of a common language can be a basic factor as to further therapeutic cooperation, it may be at the same time a diagnostic trap by which some more essential, challenging, or threatening elements of the problem (and hence the related treatment) are avoided." What did Vandereycken mean by a diagnostic trap? What essential or challenging elements might be avoided?

One of the criticisms of the addiction or disease model is the idea that people can never be recovered. Eating disorders are thought to be lifelong diseases that can be controlled into a state of remission by working through the twelve steps and maintaining abstinence on a daily basis. According to this viewpoint, eating disordered individuals can be "in recovery" or "recovering" but never "recovered." If the symptoms go away, the person is only in abstinence or remission but still has the disease. A "recovering" bulimic is supposed to continue referring to him/herself as a bulimic and continue attending Twelve Step meetings indefinitely with the goal of remaining abstinent from sugar, flour, or other binge or trigger foods or bingeing itself. Most readers will be reminded of the alcoholic in Alcoholics Anonymous (AA), who says, "Hi. I'm John and I am a recovering alcoholic," even though he may not have had a drink for ten years. Labeling eating disorders as addictions may not only be a diagnostic trap but a self-fulfilling prophecy.

There are other problems applying the abstinence model for use with anorexics and bulimics. For example, the last thing one wants to promote in an anorexic is abstinence from food, whatever that food might be. Anorexics are already masters at abstinence. They need help knowing it's okay to eat any food, particularly "scary" foods, which often contain sugar and white flour; the very ones that were originally forbidden in OA. Even though the idea of restricting sugar and white flour is fading in OA groups and individuals are allowed to choose their own form of abstinence, these groups can still present problems with their absolute standards, such as promoting restrictive eating and black or white thinking. In fact, treating anorexia patients in mixed groups such as OA may be extremely counterproductive. According to Vandereycken, when others are mixed with anorexics "They envy the abstaining anorexic whose willpower and self-mastery represent an almost utopian ideal for the bulimic, while binge eating is the most horrifying disaster any anorexic can think of. This, in fact, constitutes the greatest danger of treatment according to the addiction model (or the Overeaters Anonymous philosophy). Regardless if one calls it partial abstinence or controlled eating, simply teaching the patient to abstain from binge eating and purging means 'anorexic skills training'!" To resolve this issue it has even been argued that anorexics can use "abstinence from abstinence" as a goal, but this is not clearly definable and, at least, considered pushing the point. All of this adjusting just tends to water down the Twelve Step program as it was originally conceived and well utilized.

Furthermore, behavior abstinence, such as refraining from binge eating, is different from substance abstinence. When does eating become overeating and overeating become binge eating? Who decides? The line is fuzzy and unclear. One would not say to an alcoholic, "You can drink, but you must learn how to control it; in other words, you must not binge drink." Drug addicts and alcoholics don't have to learn how to control the consumption of drugs or alcohol. Abstinence from these substances can be a black and white issue and, in fact, is supposed to be. Addicts and alcoholics give up drugs and alcohol completely and forever. A person with an eating disorder has to deal with food every day. Full recovery for a person with an eating disorder is to be able to deal with food in a normal, healthy way.

As has been previously mentioned, bulimics and binge eaters could abstain from sugar, white flour, and other "binge foods," but in most cases, these individuals will ultimately binge on any food. In fact, labeling a food as a "binge food" is another self-fulfilling prophecy, actually counterproductive to the cognitive behavioral approach of restructuring dichotomous (black or white) thinking which is so common in eating disorder patients.

Although I have concerns and criticisms of the addiction approach, I recognize that the Twelve Step philosophy has a lot to offer. However, I strongly believe that if it is to be used with eating disorder patients, it must be used with caution and adapted to the

105

uniqueness of eating disorders. Craig Johnson has discussed this adaptation in his article published in 1993 in the *Eating Disorder Review*, "Integrating the Twelve Step Approach." The article suggests how an adapted version of the Twelve Step approach can be useful with a certain population of patients and discusses criteria that can be used to identify these patients. Occasionally, I encourage certain patients to attend OA meetings when I feel it is appropriate. I am especially grateful to their sponsors when those sponsors respond to my patients' calls at 3:00 AM. It's nice to see this commitment from someone out of genuine comradery and caring. If patients who begin treatment with me already have sponsors, I try to work with these sponsors, so as to provide a consistent treatment philosophy. I am moved by the devotion, dedication, and support that I have seen in sponsors who give so much to anyone wishing help. I have also been concerned at the many occasions where I have seen "the blind leading the blind."

In summary, based on my experience and my recovered patients themselves, I urge clinicians who use the Twelve Steps with eating disorder patients to:

1. Adapt them for the uniqueness of eating disorders and of each individual.

2. Monitor patients' experiences closely.

3. Allow that every patient has the potential to become recovered.

The belief that one will not have a disease called an eating disorder for life but can be "recovered" is a very important issue. How a treating professional views the illness and the treatment will not only affect the nature of the treatment, but the actual outcome itself. Consider these quotes taken from a book about Overeaters Anonymous: "It is that first bite that gets us into trouble. The first bite may be as 'harmless' as a piece of lettuce, but when eaten between meals and not as part of our daily plan, it invariably leads to another bite. And another, and another. And we have lost control. And there is no stopping" (Overeaters Anonymous, 1980). "It is the experience of recovering compulsive overeaters that the illness is progressive. The disease does not get better, it gets worse. Even while we abstain, the illness progresses. If we were to break our abstinence, we would find that we had even less control over our eating than before" (Overeaters Anonymous, 1980).

I think most clinicians will find these statements troubling. Whatever the original intention, they might more often than not be setting up the person for relapse and creating a self-fulfilling prophecy of failure and doom.

Tony Robbins, an international lecturer, says in his seminars, "When you believe something is true, you literally go into the state of it being true . . . . Changed behavior starts with belief, even at the level of physiology" (Robbins, 1993). And Norman Cousins, who learned firsthand the power of belief in eliminating his own illness, concluded in his book *Anatomy of an Illness*, "Drugs are not always necessary. Belief in recovery always is." If patients believe they can be more powerful than food and can be recovered, they have a better chance of it. I believe all patients and clinicians will benefit if they begin and involve themselves in treatment with that end in mind.

SUMMARY

The three main philosophical approaches to the treatment of eating disorders do not have to be considered exclusively when deciding on a treatment approach. Some combination of these approaches seems to be the best. There are psychological, behavioral, addictive, and biochemical aspects in all cases of eating disorders, and therefore it seems logical that treatment be drawn from various disciplines or approaches even if one is emphasized more than the others. Individuals who treat eating disorders will have to decide on their own treatment approach based on the literature in the field and their own experience. The most important thing to keep in mind is that the treating professional must always make the treatment fit the patient rather than the other way around.

10

Individual Therapy: Putting the Eating Disorder Out of a Job

Writing this chapter on individual therapy was different from the rest, since it is impossible to ignore the quantity and quality of information that comes directly from my personal experience. My own battle and subsequent recovery from anorexia nervosa during the ages of fifteen to twenty-one and my experiences as an eating disorder therapist since 1979 add a strong personal influence to this chapter. In treating eating disorder patients I use a very informal approach going by my first name and sharing information about myself and my own recovery. I work from a psychodynamic and cognitive behavioral perspective intermittently and at times simultaneously. I believe that the nature of an eating disorder makes tending to specific behavioral change important and the attention I give in treatment to this aspect varies in degree depending upon how healthy the patient is. Early on in my career I realized that if treatment were left to typical psychoanalysis, patients could take years explaining their childhoods, how they get along with their parents, their inability to control their anger, or any number of past experiences, all the while continuing to exist on frozen yogurt and salad, or bingeing all day, or purging their dinner every night. Eating disorder patients can starve to death or have heart failure while trying to figure out "why" they are doing this to themselves. Therefore, my individual sessions with patients vary greatly in nature because along with an ongoing exploration of developmental deficits and underlying issues, I deal directly with thinking patterns, behaviors, and symptom management.

HOW DOES THERAPY CURE?

Every experienced, effective therapist comes to his or her own understanding of how therapy cures and then works from that understanding, even if he/she does not consciously recognize it. To do justice in describing, not just the technique but the art of individual therapy with eating disorder patients, I have drawn not only from the literature but from the knowledge and experience I have gained and utilized with success over the last sixteen years. For simplicity's sake, the term "patient" is used in this chapter to denote an eating disordered individual who is in treatment, and the word "therapy" is used instead of the more proper term, psychotherapy.

Therapy with eating disorder patients involves providing education, insight, and a corrective emotional experience, allowing the patient to rectify faulty thought patterns, fill in developmental deficits, and internalize missing psychological functions. In individual therapy it is the relationship between the therapist and patient, rather than any certain technique, that is the most curative aspect. In essence, the therapist uses his or her training and the therapeutic relationship to put the eating disorder "out of a job." Until patients can "do it on their own," the therapist lends her/his ego and self-organization, capacity to anticipate, to delay gratification, to use sound judgment, to relate to another, to regulate tension and moods, and to integrate feelings, thoughts, and behavior. Once patients have internalized these abilities into their self-structure, they no longer need to use substitute or self-destructive measures (eating disorder behaviors) to meet needs or provide important psychological functions.

CONTACTING AND TRANSFORMING THE EATING DISORDER SELF

Anyone who works closely with eating disordered individuals realizes that in each patient, to a greater or lesser degree, there is a separate adaptive, disordered self (the eating disorder self) with a separate set of perceptions, thoughts, needs and behaviors. (The eating disorder self is also described in chapter 5.) Therapists must help each individual discover how and why his or her eating disorder self developed and how its specific behaviors have served a function and helped the patient adapt. An important goal of therapy is getting the patient to contact, transform, and ultimately integrate the eating disorder self. Many techniques can be used for this process. Having patients journal, particularly before engaging in one of their eating disorder behaviors, for example, immediately before binge eating, is often an effective way for both patient and therapist to contact and eventually learn about the eating disorder self.

Examples of journal entries:

Right now I feel like there is a monster inside of me, controlling me and telling me to binge and I can't make it go away.

I wake up and tell myself that I'm not going to binge and purge today and then, even when I don't want to, I find myself doing it again. It's like there are two of me. At some point one of us goes away and the other takes over.

Another technique is to have patients write dialogues between the eating disorder self and what I call their healthy self. This can be done anytime but is particularly helpful right before the person engages in some sort of disordered behavior, for example, before a binge or purge. Dialoguing with the eating disorder self helps patients discover what's going on inside of them and bring it to their conscious awareness.

Here is an example of such a dialogue:

Healthy Self: *I don't want to binge tonight, I don't need you.*

Bulimic Self: *Yes, you do.*

Healthy Self: *Why?*

Bulimic Self: *Because you don't want to get fat.*

Healthy Self: *Yeah, that's true, but I exercise enough, I am not going to get fat. I kind of believe that, my therapist believes it, and I believe her.*

Bulimic Self: *Baloney, you two don't know anything, I know.*

Healthy Self: *You know what? All you've done for me is screw me up. You know nothing. You are confusion, hatred, madness, guilt, humiliation, and more. You drain my brain and my body and I am tired of you.*

Bulimic Self: *Well, what are you going to do? I am not going to leave. You need me and I still think you want me.*

Healthy Self: *No, I don't want you but I am confused as to why I need you. I can't see it, except I am afraid to let you go, in a strange way I like that I can count on you.*

Bulimic Self: *That is right. We can't count on you because you never speak up. I am the one who can say, No, no way, no more, or leave her alone. You never do it. If I relied on you, where would we be?*

Healthy Self: *But I know more now, I want to try again. I need you to let me try, even if I am scared and mess up some.*

Bulimic Self: *It scares me to let you be in charge as it has never worked, but I might. But I'm not going anywhere, in case you need me.*

It is important to discuss patients' dialogues and the feelings they had writing them. This helps the patient discover what the eating disorder self is trying to express, what it wants, and how to get it constructively. The ultimate goal is the integration of the eating disorder self into the person's total self-structure so that it is not acting unconsciously and operating at odds with the person's best interest.

Summary of How the Therapist Works

1. The therapist needs to help each patient discover the adaptive function or purpose their eating disorder behaviors serve.

2. With genuine empathy the therapist experiences past and present with the patient as though both of them were "in the trenches together." The therapist serves as parent, guide, teacher, and coach.

3. It is the therapist's task to uncover what developmental arrests or deficits exist for each patient and help "re-parent" the patient so he or she gains the needed functions for self growth.

4. Through modeling as well as through analyzing and managing the transference relationship, the therapist assists the patient in internalizing missing psychological functions such as the ability to express feelings, the ability to self soothe, and the ability to internally validate oneself.

5. As strange as it might seem, a therapeutic task in treating eating disorder patients is to get the patients dependent on the therapist instead of on their eating disorder. The next step is to wean them off the therapist and onto other relationships in order to meet their needs. Weaning patients off the eating disorder is much harder than transferring their relationship with the therapist to healthy relationships with others.

Critical Techniques for Successful Treatment

- Alliance with the patient
- Sustained empathy
- Patience and long term thinking
- Limiting control battles
- Making behavioral agreements
- Challenging cognitive distortions
- Balance between nurturing and being authoritative

ALLIANCE AND EMPATHY

The most important thing for a therapist to remember when treating a person with an eating disorder is to establish an alliance and maintain consistent empathy with the patient throughout the course of treatment. Therapists should always strive to know what it is like to be "in their patients' shoes." Empathic failure leads to treatment failure. Therapists should continually check for understanding. Patients need to be reminded that the therapist is there to help them reach their goals in a healthy rather than a destructive way. In the very beginning of treatment I tell patients, "I cannot take this away from you. You and I both know I can't do that. I can't make you give up your eating disorder, but by working with me you might want to give it up. Once you really want to, you will be far more than half of the way there."

In the first session I let patients know that I recovered after struggling with anorexia nervosa for several years. Patients are reassured that not only will I understand them, but there is hope that they can be recovered, too. It is common for patients to come into therapy with the experience of constantly being misunderstood and with the idea that they have a disease from which they will never recover. I let them know that what they are doing makes some sense and fulfills some purpose in a way that together we will work to understand. I let them know that they can get out of the vicious cycle of their eating disorders and to do so does not mean getting fat or losing weight.

Individual therapy should empower patients with the belief that they can be fully recovered. Not everyone holds this view. The debate on whether individuals with eating disorders can ever be fully "recovered," rather than always in a state of "recovering," is discussed in chapter 9, "Treatment Philosophy and Approaches."

PATIENCE AND LONG-TERM THINKING

Therapy for an eating disorder is usually long term, two to five years. I have had a handful of patients recover in three or four months but this is very rare. Therapists who treat eating disorders need to have patience and be willing and capable of hanging in for the long haul, through thick and thin, both literally and figuratively. It is important

114

to remember that the patient is in the driver's seat and the therapist has the road map; both are in for a lengthy, challenging, sometimes painful, but rewarding road to recovery.

Additionally, it is important to remind all involved that seeing a patient once a week is not much time devoted to recovery. When a parent once suggested displeasure and frustration that his anorexic daughter was not better after four months of therapy I responded by saying, "I have only seen her for sixteen hours, not four months!"

LIMITING CONTROL BATTLES

From the beginning I establish with patients that I will, as much as possible, avoid control battles. I explain the general idea that "The fight will not be between you and me, it will be between you and your eating disorder self. I am here to help strengthen your healthy self so that your healthy self will take care of the eating disorder self." If a patient says she likes her behaviors and is not ready to give them up I reply that I am not interested in taking them away from her. This is tricky with an emaciated anorexic who is unwilling to gain weight. In this case I am careful to pick and choose my battles wisely. For example, I may not take issue with a vegetarian or fat free meal plan but I will not allow the patient to lose weight to a dangerous level without intervention. If this happens I inform the patient that since he or she has become incapable of fighting off the eating disorder self that is killing him or her, I now have to step in and take over. (What "take over" means depends on the age of the patient and the strength of the therapeutic alliance.)

There are some issues that I will strongly "fight" over. For example, I feel strongly that the scale is a weapon that eating disorder patients use against themselves. Therefore, I usually only agree to weigh patients because they want me to and/or it is the only way I can get them to agree to stop weighing themselves (except in the case of anorexia nervosa where we have agreed to a certain weight gain protocol, the individual is at risk and hospitalization may be necessary). If I do weigh patients I do it in a way as to not reveal the number to them and I will not tell them their weight. If appropriate, I may give them indications about what their weight is doing, or I may set with them a goal weight which I agree to share with them once they have reached it. I believe that knowing the number on the scale serves no purpose and I usually stand firm in not revealing it, even though I realize that they can go anywhere else and weigh themselves. (This is where alliance and empathy come in handy.) Part of my work involves getting my patients to give up the scale as a measure of evaluating their self worth or evaluating their progress in treatment. Each therapist will naturally develop his or her own "battlegrounds" and will decide on a case by case basis how far to "hold the line."

MAKING BEHAVIORAL AGREEMENTS

Behavior goals can be simple or complex, easy or challenging. The importance of setting behavior goals is to give patients an increasing ability to gain control so that eventually they can commit to and keep healthy goals they set for themselves. Sometimes patients are so out of control that what seems like a small step, like writing in their journals one night prior to bingeing, or eating a piece of fruit, is a great step and the beginning of regaining control. Patients must be told and consistently reminded of how these tiny behavioral steps are going to help them recover from an overwhelming illness which can involve hundreds or more behaviors a day. It must be explained to them that a) it is not the specific behavior but the ability to do it that's important, and b) once the function of the behavior is discovered, healthy substitutes can serve the same purpose. Both "a" and "b" often take place in therapy with no conscious recognition of what is happening, only that the patient is getting better. Once certain abilities are internalized and needs can be met in healthy ways, patients are no longer dependent on the therapist to sustain the cure.

Making contracts with patients is a useful technique for working on specific behaviors. The following are examples of behavioral agreements therapists can make with patients.

Patient agrees to:

1. Call therapist's office or pager before self-inducing vomiting

2. Write down everything eaten and feelings about eating it

3. Do at least three other activities to relieve anxiety before purging

4. Write down thoughts and feelings before a binge

5. Reduce laxative intake by five per day

6. Write an angry letter to anyone appropriate and bring to session

7. Eat fresh fruit at lunch this week

8. Set a timer to delay a binge

Through exploration, execution, or even resistance, these agreements can help lead patient and therapist to deeper psychodynamic issues.

CHALLENGING COGNITIVE DISTORTIONS

In challenging cognitive distortions (false and incorrect beliefs) about food, eating, and weight-related behaviors, considerable resistance should be expected. Allow the resistance or justification to be verbalized and try to understand it, pushing for further and deeper explanation from the patient after each response. For example, if an emaciated anorexic patient says that her stomach is fat, ask her to show you. If she shows you where she sees it sticking out, provide a reality check by telling her that you don't see it that way at all but you understand that she does. Don't stop here! Continue to search for understanding from the patients' perspective by saying something to the patient such as, "Even if your stomach did stick out, what would that mean?" This will cause the patient to have to search further into the meaning her stomach size has for her. At this point, patients often resort to, "Well, I just like it better when it doesn't stick out." The therapist must not give up but continue probing by asking, "Why is that?" or "Do you like other people better when their stomachs don't stick out?" This kind of dialogue should continue as long as possible and will often lead into a sort of stalemate. This is not a bad result and the therapist should not be discouraged. He or she should ask the patient to write in a journal about the issue and should gear up to have the same or similar conversations with the patient for a long time to come. Patients need to have things repeated over and over and patience on the part of the therapist is not only a virtue but a necessity.

To avoid power struggles and the development of a winner-loser mentality, it is important for patients to understand that the therapist is not overly invested in the idea that they will change to the therapist's set of beliefs, way of thinking, or point of view. The therapist does best when maintaining a collaborative, caring, and empathic approach expressing a desire to help patients get better by helping them understand their behaviors and discover the truth which will allow them to make more appropriate and healthy decisions for themselves.

NURTURANT/AUTHORITATIVE THERAPY

In his book, *Treating and Overcoming Anorexia Nervosa and Related Disorders*, Steve Levenkron described his style of treatment as nurturant/authoritative therapy. I believe this concept is vital in the treatment of eating disorders. Patients need so much comfort and caretaking that those treating them must go beyond the traditional roles of a psychotherapist. Patients need to learn how to be needy and how to ask for help. They need to learn the difference between self-care and selfishness and how to be less rigid and demanding of themselves. On the other hand, they are lost and confused and often need a strong but compassionate authority figure to help them out of their self-imposed prison. The therapist needs to let patients know that they will not be allowed to self-destruct and that they can lean on the therapist for support and direction. This kind of role puts the therapist in a more authoritative and directive stance. Interpretations and even advice must be forthcoming and long silences avoided. The therapeutic stance of being a blank slate or of waiting for the patient to speak can be frightening to eating disorder patients who desperately need to feel that someone who cares is in charge and knows what he/she is doing and can help others do the same.

The line between nurturing and being authoritative with a patient is a constantly fluid one. In some sessions I am a passive recipient while patients cry, telling them I know how hard it is, reassuring them that things will be okay. The therapy sometimes serves as a container for emotions. Other times, I challenge the patient and ask the patient to take a risk that unsettles him or her. I'll challenge patients for not trying hard enough. I'll challenge them to add a can of tuna to their daily diets or to call me before purging. I'll explain what I think some of their recent behaviors have meant. The therapist has to know when to challenge and how far to push a patient, and then be clear that working through the patient's response is the key. Whether the patient does or does not meet the challenge is not the most important therapeutic issue. It is the meaning the challenge has for the patients and the meaning of their responses that is important. Working through why the patient responded the way he/she did, what the challenge meant to him/her, how he/she felt about the challenge and about accomplishing it or not accomplishing it are the important issues in the therapy. Nothing will be accomplished by pushing and challenging, unless a certain bond in the therapeutic relationship has been established and a high level of trust exists.

EXAMPLES OF TOPICS DEALT WITH IN INDIVIDUAL THERAPY SESSIONS

POOR SELF-ESTEEM/DIMINISHED SELF-WORTH

Nothing I do ever seems enough, I don't think there is a thin enough I can get to.

It is interesting that on the surface many patients present a self to others that looks very together and self-confident but in therapy admit that there is an emptiness in them and they feel insignificant or unworthy. This brings up an important difference between self-esteem and self-worth. Someone can seemingly have a good measure of self-esteem, allowing him or her to be on the debate team, go to modeling school, or perform to live audiences. Yet, whatever the person does, it is not good enough. There is an ongoing conflict between "I'm worthy" and "I'm not." These patients set high and unrealistic requirements for themselves just to be acceptable, hence, five more miles, one more hour of exercise, and nothing less than straight A's are common mantras. No matter how successful the individual is, the accomplishments never seem to be internalized.

Discovering and working through all the reasons why and how individuals developed their poor self-esteem and requirements for self-worth are important and helpful, but not critical for recovery. The therapist can deal with these issues from a here-and-now perspective as long as he/she understands the nature of the underlying problem.

BELIEF IN THE THINNESS MYTH

I will be happy and successful if I am thin.

Society presents advertising and other media that perpetuate the myth of thinness. If people are confused, lonely, or struggling and think thinness will solve their problems, then why not go for it? The problem is that thinness alone doesn't do the trick, and if individuals have to give up their health and even their souls just to get it, what do they have in the long run? They may gain thinness but they lose themselves. They may feel happy or successful about their thinness, but nothing else.

In individual therapy, where there should be no consequences for telling the truth, patients can explore what the struggle for thinness does for them. For some patients, being thin has brought them the most attention they have ever received. If this is true, they will need to discuss, "Is it worth it?" and "Is there a healthy way?" For others, being thin does not measure up to the myth, but they fear that letting go would mean defeat or some fate worse than the one in which they find themselves.

FEELINGS OF EMPTINESS/NEED FOR DISTRACTION

Eating helps me forget my problems.

In this respect, eating disorders are similar to drug and alcohol addictions. Bulimics and binge eaters describe how they can tune out the world and their problems when bingeing and/or purging. Individual therapy can help patients learn that when the original problems are addressed and dealt with, the need to binge, purge, or starve is no longer necessary. However, it is often the case that the underlying problems may be worked on and greatly improved with no reduction in eating behavior symptoms. Patients may change many aspects of their lives that contribute to the eating disorder but still be unable to stop their negative behaviors. This is why cognitive behavioral therapy, symptom management, and psychodynamic therapy dealing with the underlying issues all need to be used concurrently.

DICHOTOMOUS (BLACK/WHITE) THINKING

I am perfect or a failure. I am thin or fat. I starve or binge.

Dichotomous thinking, leaving no room for the in-between, is a common feature of eating disordered individuals. A goal in individual therapy is to help the patients see how and why they may have developed this way of looking at the world and how their dichotomous thinking sets them up for continued problems and pain. For example, helping a young anorexic woman uncover why she has such a need to please, to be the best at everything, to be perfect is important. Exposing her faulty thought patterns is important as well. She may not be aware of the impossibility of the task she has set for herself by thinking, "If I work hard enough, I will not make a mistake" or "If I eat fat I'll be fat, if I don't eat fat, I'll be thin."

DESIRE FOR ATTENTION AND TO BE SPECIAL/UNIQUE

If I give up my eating disorder I won't be special anymore, I have nothing else that is unique.

The symptoms become the goal when patients don't know what they would have without their eating disorder, and giving it up makes them feel as if they would have nothing to take its place. The ability to pursue the goal, do the behaviors, and follow the self-imposed rules becomes a unique special way of behaving and getting attention. A patient who said, "If I get better, people will think I'm okay," was telling her therapist that her eating disorder was getting her the attention she needed but was unable to ask for. Another very young patient once asked, "If I get better does that mean I can't see you anymore?" Understanding developmental needs and deficits and how to correct them are important in this area. Every therapist's task is to help patients find a way to be special, unique, and get attention in some other way.

NEED FOR POWER AND CONTROL

I know I purged often to get back at my dad. It would be the only thing that got him really mad, that he could do nothing about.

If there is one consistent feature seen in all eating disorders that causes and perpetuates their existence, it is the need for control and power. Eating disorder behaviors can make certain individuals feel in control and powerful. These people will not give up the behaviors to become out of control and powerless. The therapist can help the patient resolve old issues which result in the need for control. In the above example, working on the father-daughter relationship may help alleviate symptoms. The therapist should also help the patient find a sense of control and personal power in other ways, while showing that eventually the eating disorder leaves him/her out of control and powerless.

Therapists need to be assertive in convincing patients that, in fact, they are out of control with their symptoms and not in control as they desperately want to be. The therapist will need to ask questions such as:

Is it really control to not even be able to eat?

Is it control to run every day or weigh five times per day or are you compelled to do so?

Is it control to avoid going to a party because there will be food or throw food away because you are afraid of it?

CHOOSING A THERAPIST

Qualified therapists have varying degrees and training. Psychiatrists, as well as nonmedical therapists such as psychologists, social workers, marriage-family-child counselors, and other licensed counselors are all called therapists. It is important that the therapist is licensed and has training and experience in treating eating disorders. Non medical therapists will usually have one or more psychiatrists or other physicians whom they refer to for medication assessment and treatment. The psychiatrist's role and medication will be discussed in chapter 14.

To find a qualified therapist, ask your family doctor, a nearby university or college counseling center, any women's organization or resource center, or an employee assistance counselor. Another way is to call one of the eating disorder organizations or treatment centers listed in the appendix and ask for a professional in your area.

Once you have a name or several names, call and, either on the phone or in the first session, be prepared to ask a variety of questions and find out more information using the guidelines that follow:

GUIDELINES FOR INTERVIEWING A THERAPIST

1. Find out the extent of the therapist's training and/or experience treating eating disorders.

2. With what other treating professionals such as physicians and dietitians does the therapist work?

3. What are the therapist's policies and procedures (for example, frequency of sessions, length of sessions, fees, insurance coverage, billing practices, and so on)?

4. What are the therapist's thoughts or beliefs regarding medication?

5. What is the availability of medical/hospital backup if needed?

6. What is the therapist's treatment approach or philosophy?

The most important thing is the comfort level and the relationship the patient has with the therapist. If the patient is a minor, the parents should be comfortable with the therapist as well, but the patient-therapist relationship is the more important one. It should be a goal to find a therapist on whom both patient and parents can agree. If you do not feel comfortable with the relationship or the treatment plan, seek more information or consult another therapist, but avoid unnecessarily postponing treatment.

When selecting a therapist expect treatment to be long term, as much as two to five years. This means matters must be carefully planned and cost must be considered. Health insurance companies may provide coverage and even resources for treatment, but do not give up hope if your resources are limited. Free or low-fee support groups are available in many areas. Community or college counseling centers often provide therapy on a sliding fee scale.

THE THERAPIST AND NUTRITION KNOWLEDGE

Dealing with eating disorders involves talking about food, nutrition, weight, body fat, dieting, and calories, or risking empathic failure. Therapists may need or choose to work with a dietitian who can be a useful adjunct to outpatient therapy and is a given in inpatient settings. Nevertheless, therapists should also have knowledge in these matters. Certainly, a degree in nutrition is not necessary, but therapists should be well read in these areas, especially as they apply to eating disorders. Therapists should also keep up with current periodicals and medical findings in this field. Knowledge of nutrition, dieting, and weight control will help the therapist to better understand and educate the patient. Therapists with little or no knowledge in this domain may frustrate or alienate the patient, since this is an area of importance to her/him. Even when using a dietitian, therapists cannot expect patients to reserve all discussion regarding food and weight for someone else. Eating disorder patient's feelings and food are enmeshed. Therapeutic work involves working directly with the food and weight-related issues, uncovering specific and personal meanings for various patients. In this way therapists are like detectives, exploring and uncovering clues that will eventually help solve a mystery.

Here are some examples of statements relating to nutrition but needing to be responded to and discussed in a therapy session:

I didn't eat the cheese because it would make me fat.

I needed to burn off the calories I ate so I went back to the gym for two hours last night.

We don't eat bread at our house, my mom has always said bread makes you fat.

I read in a magazine that a 1,200-calorie diet was fine, so that is what I'm willing to do.

I always throw up when I eat sugar, sugar turns to fat.

Responding to the nutritional aspect of these statements is important to establish expertise and to relate directly to the topic brought up by the patient. However, after asking for clarification and providing correct nutritional information (if possible), the therapist needs to go beyond to a deeper level of responding such as "And what would that mean if you didn't burn off the calories?" or "What will happen if you gain some weight?"

INSIDE AN INDIVIDUAL THERAPY SESSION

The following dialogue is taken directly from two therapy sessions with a twenty-six-year-old female patient who had recently been hospitalized for bulimia nervosa. She had gone for approximately five therapy sessions with another therapist a few months prior to her hospitalization but had ended therapy, telling her therapist that she was "Just not ready for treatment." After a few months went by, her problem became more severe and upon realizing that it was well beyond her control, to the point of interfering with work and her relationship with her boyfriend, she decided she needed serious help. She called an eating disorder treatment program where she was admitted and we met. She was a very attractive, athletic, bright, responsible and hard working individual who was beside herself that she could not get a handle on her binge eating and purging. We began a course of therapy after her discharge from the hospital and the following two excerpts were taken from approximately the fourth and fifth sessions we had after she was out of the hospital, back home, and back at work.

SESSION 4

Patient: *Since the hospital, you had said there would probably be a change and there has been a change. It's not, I don't use it as comfort it is more like a punishment now. It is an addiction but not as big an addiction all the time. It seems more controllable. Like yesterday, I did it, I didn't need to, I didn't want to, but I did it anyway.*

Carolyn: *That is an interesting thing to say, isn't it. "I didn't need to." I get that, "I didn't want to," that's a little weirder, so why would you do something you didn't need or want to do?*

Patient: *I've had that feeling many times where I think, "No I don't want to do this, I don't want to do it" and then I do it anyway.*

Carolyn: *So why would you do something you didn't want to do?*

Patient: *Habit.*

Carolyn: *So let's think of something other than the word habit. I get habit, I really do, but even habits are usually things you're getting something out of, like smoking. There is something you get out of it. So that's the time when I say that there are two parts of you. The one that wants to and the one that doesn't want to.*

Patient: *I'm sure part of it is the addiction part. The eating disorder part of me doesn't want to give it up. I know that. Because it is the black and white thinking again. Because once I stop, I'm stopping for good and it's never coming back.*

Carolyn: *Oh wow I see, that's big.*

Patient: *That's a long time, and that goes through my head all the time, I mean I think, "This is the first day of the rest of my life," it's not like, "Let's see how far I can go," it is more like, "This is forever, and that's a long time" and without, that's a big fear. I mean this is my safety net and well, can I make it without my safety net? Can I let it go, well, I don't know.*

Carolyn: *Well you know, you aren't ready to do that. You don't have the underlying stuff solved like, "How do I get my needs met and get off this perfectionism thing and learn to accept myself better and not have to live by rules?" All of that has to feel a little bit better for you to give this up just like that.*

Patient: *Oh, definitely.*

Carolyn: *Well, how about this? How about the concept that you say to yourself, "I'm going to put it up on the shelf, I'm going to put it up there like in a box, and it can be up there and get dusty . . . . and if I really need it I can bring it back down.*

Patient: *I always try to say, "I'll deal with it tomorrow," that's what I always used to think.*

Carolyn: *Well, that's what the one-day-at-a-time concept is supposed to be, you know. Don't think of it as forever, think of it as one day at a time. Unfortunately, they say that in OA but then there is this whole thing of the chips and the days and the starting over.*

Patient: *I can't count days, it drives me nuts. I mean I know I will, I mean, I can't help it now. I look at the calendar and think, okay on April 16th I started again.*

Carolyn: *Why will you do that, stop that (laughs). Oh what am I going to do with you?*

Patient: *Well, I really don't want to go back to OA and get stinking chips because that's gonna be hard.*

Carolyn: *I thought you liked it.*

Patient: *To a point. It's great when you are doing good and get recognition, but it's also a lot of reverse pressure that some of us can't handle.*

Carolyn: *Yes, I know. Besides, this is yours, it's a part of you, there shouldn't be an audience to give it up for or keep it for. It just really has to be known inside of you, all the parts of you that it is yours to give up when you are darn good and ready. And there is no reason. I mean, what do I need you to give it up for? I have no agenda here, I really don't, I mean I want you to be happy. I want you to be well, but it's not going to affect my life if you do or don't give it up or throw up today or tomorrow or you know, it's the long haul, I'm in it for the long haul. If I waited for everyone to be ready, really ready to give it up before they entered into treatment, I don't think I would have any patients.*

Patient: *Probably not.*

Carolyn: *But something happened to you when you went to the hospital program, something snapped and you were ready to give it up and that's OK but it was the executive part of you that went in and did treatment, not the eating disorder part.*

Patient: *Yeah I remember, my eating disorder part was not really there.*

Carolyn: *The executive self was and you know that part of you is useful. You just have to put it to its proper usefulness. You get a lot from it; your grades and determination and accomplishments and all those things, you get a lot for that. But in some areas it can be a problem if it is just acting blindly and not in touch with anything else. Sometimes it's bad when things are taken to the extreme, even recovery.*

Patient: *Oh I know and it has always been that way.*

Carolyn: *Now that you are out of the hospital and it is back, I mean the bingeing and purging are back, now perhaps you can learn from it. We need to get in touch with that part of you. We need to know what she is feeling or wanting. One way to do this is through a journal. I want you to, when you feel like you want to go and binge, I want you to take a minute to write down what you are thinking and feeling.*

Patient: *I've tried that and I just think, "Forget it, I don't want to write, I want to binge."*

Carolyn: *Well, you get to go ahead and binge after you write. The writing isn't meant to stop you from bingeing or purging. Of course, you don't want to write if you think that it is supposed to be instead of bingeing. The goal of writing is to get access to the part of you that does the bingeing and purging because she doesn't come to therapy sessions. Neither you nor I are in touch with her. So, I just want her to be able to write down what is going on for her. But you have to make sure that she knows she can go ahead and binge and purge anyway, but to please just write first.*

Patient: *Wow, okay, I can't believe you are telling me this, but I think you are right.*

Carolyn: *So you're going to try to do it then?*

Patient: *Yeah, yes, I mean I will.*

Session continued untaped.

SESSION 5

Carolyn: *So what's right up there for you tonight?*

Patient: *Well, what's up there is the assignment you asked me to do last time, to write down what it is I'm thinking or feeling when I feel like I have to go binge.*

Carolyn: *Uh huh.*

Patient: *Well, I couldn't do that. I don't know why. I would just sit there with the piece of paper and the pen and I could not write down what it was. I could think of things in my head but.*

Carolyn: *Like what?*

Patient: *Oh general stuff, stress, fear, anxiety . . .*

Carolyn: *And what were you thinking sitting there with the pen?*

Patient: *That it's just words and it is not getting at what the problem really is. Because I can handle stress during the day at work, no problem. I get through the day, and I don't really feel stress when I leave there but for some reason I'll go binge. Even if it is a perfect, great day and nothing goes wrong at work I still go binge. So there is something else besides saying I'm stressed, because I don't feel stressed.*

Carolyn: *OK, so you're not stressed, so what else is it?*

Patient: *It's more like images, you know I'll think of food, I don't really think I want to go binge, I'll start thinking of food.*

Carolyn: *Yeah, I remember now that you told me that before. You start thinking of food, specific types of food that you consider what, fattening? off your diet plan? What is another way of describing them?*

Patient: *Well, I was thinking of bad, or junk food.*

Carolyn: *Anything else or why it is bad?*

Patient: *Because I was brought up that way. It was bad to have that kind of food around the house. We had family binges on that kind of food, so . . . .*

Carolyn: *I remember that but . . . .*

Patient: *Only on birthdays, we would get a big cake and a gallon of ice cream and between the four of us we would eat the whole thing that same night. And if there was anything left my brother and I would race to it in the morning and have it for breakfast.*

Carolyn: *Because you weren't going to be able to have it for awhile?*

Patient: *Oh yeah, we wouldn't see it again until someone else's birthday.*

Carolyn: *It was a very big deal. You'd race to it in the morning. I mean that is a very big deal.*

Patient: *Oh yeah, we'd get up extra early and it was insane.*

Carolyn: *Like Santa Claus had come. So you know when you are a kid your parents have control over it, so what does that tell you about this?*

Patient: *It's a rebellion thing, there is no one to tell me I can't, I can do whatever I want.*

Carolyn: *Yeah, I think you are making up for a lot of lost time.*

Patient: *Probably.*

Carolyn: *You say, "I didn't want to, but I did it." And to me it's like, remember I was telling you about putting it up on the shelf and taking it down when you need it because you can't give it up for me or for anybody else?*

Patient: *Well, I have tried that shelf thing and it's almost like there is a bungie cord hooked onto it because it keeps slapping me right back in the head. I mean it's like there is something attached to it and it won't stay up on the shelf, it hurls itself at me.*

Carolyn: *Okay, so it's not ready to be up there, so where is it then? Because you are not doing it like you used to.*

Patient: *It's just hovering around.*

Carolyn: *All right, so let's go back to this because it makes sense to me now that there is no way you are going to put it on the shelf and delay gratification and tell yourself that it is anywhere that you don't have immediate access to it.*

Patient: *Because that would be back to what it was when I was growing up.*

Carolyn: *Yeah, yeah. In the box and on the shelf is like when it was in your parent's control. You haven't quite got it yet that it is in your control. And all of a sudden thinking about all of those foods and wanting to go eat them is like your right to do it. And not only that, it is your right to do it and what else? There is something else besides that?*

Patient: *My desire.*

Carolyn: *Yes, it is your desire. There is a preference for sweet foods, it's natural in human beings and besides that it's natural to want it more if you are restricted from it. It made those things even more desirable. And when you were little you must have built up a great desire for all those things. So I don't think it is just about your right to do it, it's desire as well.*

Patient: *Yes.*

Carolyn: *I read about this experiment once where a psychologist put a bunch of toys in a room and had a one-way window where he could view kids in the room playing with the toys but they only could see a reflection on their side, so for them it was a mirror, not a window. One thing he did was to put kids in there one at a time and tell them they could play with anything but the green truck. Then he would leave and go watch in the one-way mirror. So, what do you think they did?*

Patient: *Well, I think they'd go for the green truck.*

Carolyn: *Do you get the analogy?*

Patient: *Yes, the more I think I'm not supposed to have those foods, the more I want them, or I think I want them.*

Carolyn: *Then after the hospital you were really strict with yourself, with a very strict food plan. How were you doing that?*

Patient: *I was just parenting myself all the time, saying "You can't have it." Oh no, I really see. I mean I never had dessert, maybe one or two bites of my boyfriend's. I guess it was the same old thing.*

Carolyn: *So could you . . .*

Patient: *It's hard to go back to that because it is that all-or-nothing thing again.*

Carolyn: *I don't want you to go back to that.*

Patient: *But that is how it is in my mind. If I stop bingeing and purging it means I can't have anything else, you know? I can't have those foods.*

Carolyn: *So you have to be bad and sick to have them?*

Patient: *Yes, it's an all or nothing thing.*

Carolyn: *So what is an alternative, to the all or nothing?*

Patient: *Well, I will try to let myself have it sometimes but I don't want to say whenever I want because I will have it every single day all day long.*

Carolyn: *Not necessarily, that is the point. But what's it?*

Patient: *Junk food.*

Carolyn: *Well, but why don't you pick an "it," like, "every day after work I'll go get something." Not a bunch of things, not, "okay, I'm going to let myself eat those things today and go crazy, all out, but rather, "Every day after work I'm going to go and get a treat."*

133

Patient: *I don't know if I can.*

Carolyn: *I'd just like you to try an experiment. Every day after work you have something, like, give me some ideas, what are some things that you would have? What would you go have?*

Patient: *Like a frozen yogurt or something.*

Carolyn: That *is a junk food? You mean you don't even allow yourself that?*

Patient: *No. But if I was going to keep it, it would still have to be something nonfat.*

Carolyn: (Holds up a chocolate chip cookie she has on her desk, left over from lunch)

Patient: *There's no way I could eat a chocolate chip cookie and keep it.*

Carolyn: *Because?*

Patient: *Because chocolate's full of fat.*

Carolyn: *Well, okay, and what's it going to do to you?*

Patient: *Eventually, it will make me fat.*

Carolyn: *A chocolate chip cookie is going to make you fat? That's like insane.*

Patient: *Well, it's like once in a great while, okay, that's fine. But if I have one every single day, you see the problem is stopping after one.*

Carolyn: *But the reason you have a problem stopping after one is the same reason that you rushed to the cake the next morning when you and your brother woke up.*

Patient: *Because, I'm not going to get it again.*

Carolyn: *So that's why I'm suggesting you start out by going and getting a cookie. I want you to acknowledge it. I don't want you to have to turn into this crazed rush-*

to-the-cake-in-the-morning kid. I want you to be able to say, "It's after work, I really feel like having something." Boy, am I so glad you said, "Well, I'd have frozen yogurt," it tells me a lot. I didn't know you couldn't even allow that. It's like that's not a big deal. I'm talking about . . . like for me my first thought would be to have a big treat, frozen yogurt is more of a standard thing.

Patient: *But I don't even let myself have frozen yogurt.*

Carolyn: *Well, for you, maybe we can start there. I'm okay to start there if you don't even let yourself have that, but good God.*

Patient: *Well, it's a dessert, to me.*

Carolyn: *A dessert, it's amazing. Why should you go through your life without dessert?*

Patient: *Because that's how my life started out.*

Carolyn: (Sighs) *Well, it doesn't have to be that way.*

Patient: *Yeah. Well, I'll try the one-thing-a-day idea.*

Carolyn: *So, at least one thing, and if you want to be safe, just drive someplace and get one thing.*

Patient: *Okay.*

Carolyn: *So on the way home you get whatever it is that is going to be your dessert. Then eat dinner and then have your dessert like normal.*

Patient: *Like a normal person? All right, I'll try.*

Carolyn: *So the requirement is that you have dinner. There is no requirement about anything else, just that you have dinner. And if you want to eat the cookie on the way home, fine, but the requirement is that you have dinner. The preference is that you have dinner and then see how you feel. Sometimes I have a bowl of cereal before I go to bed just because it is sweet and I like it. It's funny to say that now, as it used to be not okay and now it is. And you are going to be okay.*

Patient: *Uh, okay.*

Carolyn: *You don't believe it? Tell me your thoughts, what are they?*

Patient: *Well, mainly I'm afraid I won't control myself with just one. There was a time when you told me that if I binged just to try and keep it and that would kind of simmer things down. And I did that like half a binge and I did keep it but the next day I was even more crazed for sugar, so it concerns me that it will happen again really bad.*

Carolyn: *Well, there is a possibility that it will be like, like, "My parents are gone and we can have all the dessert we want." There is a possibility. And I think that is why we have to have that talk with the two parts of you. I think we have to talk with that little girl. Now I know why you told me in that session before that when you think you will get to eat something you feel like you have a little girl inside you skipping around. I didn't quite get why before, but now it seems obvious. And when you sit down to write now, think of it this way, whichever part of you feels the most present, write to the other part. Let me give you an example: If you are going to eat a cookie let's say, you need to reassure the little girl part that, "Hey, you get to have it tomorrow, too, you don't have to eat it all tonight, we can have it tomorrow, too." I think you need to reassure that part of you. That is the only reason you would have to go way off, craving and eating more. You have to tell her. It's not physical, it's not that you are addicted to certain foods and will never be able to control it. There is no proof that these foods are addictive. Well, you need to know that not everyone agrees with me. I think you already know that. Some people do think they are addictive. It's not that I don't think sugar ever does things to the body. Sugar is empty calories, and raises your blood sugar really high when eaten alone. That's why my preference is that you have dinner. Because when you eat high-sugar foods, what happens to your blood sugar, is that it goes really high and then there is the insulin release and then the crash, causing more craving for more sugar afterward. But this is mitigated by eating dinner first, you know with protein, because then insulin is released more slowly. It's really when you are eating those things instead of dinner that there is a problem. It's not just calories, you know, it's the way your body responds to and utilizes food.*

Patient: *You know, I really do know this.*

Carolyn: *Yes, but part of you doesn't know and she needs to be talked to.*

Patient: *I know, I'm seeing that.*

Carolyn: *Do you think you could write some reassuring thing to your little girl part? If you go and buy a box of animal cookies, or a chocolate chip cookie, or a muffin, or whatever it is and you go home and have your dinner and then you have it, then you start thinking "I want more, I want more." Do you think you could write, "It's okay, we get to have it tomorrow, too." Do you think you could write something like that?*

Patient: *Sometimes I can.*

Carolyn: *And the times you can't?*

Patient: *I'm mad.*

Carolyn: *At?*

Patient: *Probably just that I am being controlled.*

Carolyn: *By?*

Patient: *By me* (laughs).

Carolyn: *So have a fight with yourself, knock yourself out.*

Patient: *No, I mean it's like I end up having a temper tantrum, I want to have what I want and I'm not going to write on the stinking paper because that's what the parent in me wants and it's not going to happen.*

Carolyn: *It's the integration of those two that has to happen. It's the meeting of those two. So it can't be your kid and your parents fighting it in the past. You have to know that it's not like that anymore. You really have to be concentrating on "What is it that I want? Me, Nancy, what do I want?"*

Patient: *You're right. I need help figuring out what I really want. I need help at the moment I'm going through it.*

Carolyn: *Well, writing will help you get in touch with what you want, with what all of the parts of you want. I think that the kids playful, spontaneous part is pressed down and that is the one way that she can act out, because if you act out in other ways there are always other people to affect.*

Patient: *Yeah.*

Carolyn: *If you do it with your boyfriend, if you do it with your friends, if you do it with your boss or at work, there are other people at stake. But if you do it with the food, if she does it with the food, then it's only you.*

Patient: *Actually, I've noticed that since my boyfriend and I had that big confrontation and he let me know how hard it has been on him since I've been so down and hard on myself and stuff, well, ever since we had that talk I have been totally up and appearing self-confident but my bingeing has been worse. So it's going there and I can hide it from him all I want but, in fact, he's been gone all this week but he comes back tomorrow so tomorrow I'm probably going to be a total bitch because he comes back and we will be together and I can't binge.*

Carolyn: *No, no, no, what do you mean you can't binge? Stop talking like that.*

Patient: *Well, it won't be like it was.*

Carolyn: *Well, don't say I* can't. *Reframe it.*

Patient: *I'll try.*

Carolyn: *Say . . .*

Patient: *I can have my one cookie.*

Carolyn: *Well, yeah, and say, "I'm gonna be a bitch because I'm going to try to change my patterns, and that is going to be unfamiliar," but it's not that you can't binge. You can. I'm going to tell you again. You don't have to give it up for me or for anybody else. You can binge tomorrow. But what you are going to start doing tomorrow, I mean tonight, right after you leave here, is to get in touch with what you really want. You can do anything, you can jump off a bridge, you can stand on the freeway, but what do you want? You don't want to binge. You want your right to eat those things that everybody else seems to be able to eat. You want the right to be able to eat chocolate or cookies or whatever and not be fat and not feel like you can't have it. And if you do have it, you want for it not to turn into some sinister weird kind of obsessive race. So, you might have trouble tomorrow because you are changing and growing and accepting yourself and allowing yourself and that is new and it is uncomfortable. But you are not going to be a bitch because you can't binge, because you can.*

Patient : *Okay, I get it, but it's hard.*

Carolyn: *I know, so do you think I'm a nut case?*

Patient: *I think it could work.*

Carolyn: *It will work but I'm not saying it will work tomorrow. It will work and you are going to get better.*

Patient: *Actually, I've thought of trying to do something like that where eating the foods is more commonplace for me because most of my friends have grown up with having junk foods in their house and they are fine with it, they can have it or not.*

Carolyn: *Yeah, what do you mean by commonplace?*

Patient: *Well, you know there is always a bag of cookies around or something and it's not a big deal.*

Carolyn: *Uh huh.*

Patient: *That's what I want because when I have kids I don't want them to go through this. I don't want them to only have dessert once a year.*

Carolyn: *Good point.*

Patient: *There is another thing that has come to mind since we are talking about this and trying to get myself to come up with what "it is." Well, my most vulnerable time is right after I binge and get rid of the food. I'm like open for maybe two minutes, where I can really see into what's going on, and this week I was in the shower and I kept asking myself, "What it it? What is it?" So I went through ideas: fear, anxiety, blah, blah, blah, and I just started crying. And I said, "What the hell is this?" And then all I could picture was myself rocking back and forth in a fetal position and that was it. It was like a little kid, though, it wasn't me grown up, it was when I was little. And then the next thing that flashed into my mind was my mom and dad hugging me and then I was like a stone again and shut off to everything. And that was it, so I don't know if that means anything at all.*

Carolyn: *It means something.*

Patient: *It's comfort. I don't like being alone, feeling alone, and most of the time I am. Not so much physically but emotionally, I think. I am really isolated. A lot of times, like when I am at my mom and dad's, if I am there for a period of days and it is time for me to leave, I get very anxious because I don't want to go and I always think, "I wish I could stay here. I wish there was some way." And that scares me because I wonder with the different injuries I have had if they were some sort of, oh, I don't know. I forgot the word I was going to say.*

Carolyn: *You mean an excuse or justification?*

Patient: *Yeah, an excuse to go home.*

Carolyn: *I don't know but that is an interesting image.*

Patient: *It's not like everything is okay when I'm home because I binge there, too.*

Carolyn: *Well, I think there is something with your wanting to be home now when you can be with your parents and you can have the food, too, you know, because when you were a kid you couldn't.*

Patient: *Yeah, we sure are getting deeper in these sessions, it makes sense.*

Carolyn: *Yeah, and we have a long way to go.*

End of tape

11

SHARING THE PAIN AND THE PROMISE IN GROUP

G roup therapy is frequently mentioned as a useful treatment method for eating disorders. Group can be a crucial aspect of treatment for many eating disorder patients, yet contraindicated for others. For example, many anorexics seem to have poorer outcomes than bulimics with group therapy, partly due to the fact that they tend to be more rigid, withdrawn, and anxious, and also have extreme difficulty identifying and expressing feelings. However, many anorexics have had valuable group experiences which have indeed helped them overcome these obstacles. Although group is not appropriate for every person, those for whom it is seem to benefit greatly from it.

This chapter will serve as an overview and summary of the various issues involving group therapy in the treatment of eating disorders, from why it works to variations on group structure, philosophy, and settings.

WHY DOES GROUP THERAPY WORK?

EDUCATION
Group therapy can be a good forum to educate patients on important topics such as nutrition, medical consequences of laxative abuse, or assertiveness techniques. Educating patients in group saves individual therapy time for more personalized and deeper issues. Group members also educate each other from their varied experiences in identifying and solving problems. Each group session can be educational, psychodymanic, cognitive behavioral, or a mixture of all three.

UNIVERSALITY

By sharing with and listening to others, patients learn that they are not alone in their suffering, their feelings, and their experience of having an eating disorder. Even though individual stories vary and patients are all unique, a camaraderie exists among people who are suffering from eating disorders. It can enhance a person's self-esteem just to realize that she or he is neither crazy nor alone. Some patients handle certain issues better than others, and they help each other in this way. Furthermore, a common trait in individuals with eating disorders is the desire to be special and unique, and the eating disorder helps provide that. In a group of peers also with eating disorders, patients must explore and find other, more constructive ways to be unique.

SUPPORT AND ACCEPTANCE

All people benefit from being accepted and cared about, even if they need to make changes. Eating disorder patients often feel or have been rejected by their families and others and the only support system they feel they can count on is the therapy group. In a positive group therapy experience, group members provide acceptance while at the same time supporting and encouraging necessary changes.

INTERPERSONAL RELATIONS

Often patients have lost or never acquired the necessary trust or interpersonal skills to develop quality relationships. With the help of other group members, patients can learn what their feelings are and how to communicate them. Patients who otherwise have a hard time forming relationships can eventually learn to share, get close, trust, love, and be loved.

CONFRONTATION

If group therapy always consisted, session after session, of everyone being nice and encouraging, it would not only get boring, but very little growth would take place. Once an atmosphere of trust and caring is established, the therapist facilitates group members in confronting each other about inconsistencies, self-destructive behaviors, and issues of disagreement. The therapist's task is to help patients learn to challenge each other in a caring manner, so they learn that they can like or love someone and yet disagree or question them at the same time. Many eating disorder patients don't know that it is okay to get mad, discuss negative feelings, and argue, and that it is how you go about it that makes the difference.

FRIENDSHIP

A controversy has existed over whether members of groups should have outside contact with each other. The early proponents of group therapy had the philosophy that group is meant to help patients learn how to make friends, not provide friends for them. Many female therapists, notably Dr. Melanie Katzman, have spoken out in books and at national conferences disagreeing with the early concept of "no outside involvement" between group members, and instead encourage therapists to promote group members' using each other outside the group for support. Being in a group is obviously a good way of reaching out, contacting others, and developing personal resources. Patients need each other this way. Sometimes just a phone call can prevent a binge, bring someone out of a depressed mood, or offer an alternative to throwing up. If patients agree, names and phone numbers can be exchanged in the beginning, and members can call each other between group sessions. Some members may even form friendships that remain long after the group has ended. It is up to the therapist to recognize and effectively deal with any splitting or undermining effects that outside contact or friendships have on the group.

TYPES OF GROUPS

When forming an eating disorder group, there are decisions to be made about what kind of group it will be. Will you separate patients by disorders, will you allow new patients after the group has been going on for awhile, or will you simply have a drop-in group?

SEGREGATED/HOMOGENEOUS

A homogenous or segregated group includes only people with the same disorder; for example, all anorexics, all bulimics, or all binge eaters. This method of group member selection is used to enhance the similarities among members and avoid the issue of members not relating to one another. Anorexics and binge eaters often complain about being mixed in groups together, as they feel they cannot relate to each other. They suffer from different illnesses. Many experts agree and don't mix them in groups. However, heterogeneous (mixed) groups have certain advantages and can be very therapeutic. For example, in a group of all anorexics, the egocentricity, hypersensitivity, and anxiety can be so high that it can make group interaction impossible. The competition in a group of all anorexics, all wanting to be the best anorexic, comparing notes on who ate less or weighs less, and so on, can overshadow any potential benefits. Depending on the skills of the therapist and available patients and patient selection, mixed groups may be a better alternative.

MIXED/HETEROGENEOUS

The most common heterogeneous group of eating disorder patients consists of anorexics and bulimics. Anorexics and bulimics have so many similarities that they seem to accept fairly readily being mixed in a group setting. Groups with anorexics, bulimics, and binge eaters are also prevalent, especially in many inpatient treatment programs. The working premise is that all of these patients have an unnatural or self-destructive relationship with food and their bodies. Combining groups may provide a more difficult task for the therapist, but potential benefits are exceptional when the group works. Hearing horror stories about the pain and agony of an anorexic often helps bulimics to not want that for themselves and vice versa. Patients can look at each other's strengths and weaknesses and even, strange as it might seem, see themselves in each other and see the many common themes or underlying psychological issues they share that contribute to their dysfunctional relationships with food and weight. Mixed groups provide experiences that break through distortions in thinking in a way that the therapist or another similar patient cannot.

For example, Mary, a binge eater, said to Pam, an anorexic, "How could you sit there and say you are fat? I am fat. If you feel fat, that's one thing, but to say you are fat is wrong."

OPEN OR CLOSED

A group can be short term and closed, allowing no other patients in, or long term, allowing or not allowing others to join throughout the group's existence. These judgments are made depending on factors such as the therapist's philosophy, the patient population, finances, and the group setting. For example, a group in a hospital will generally be ongoing and accept new members whenever there is a new hospital admission. A group run by a therapist in private practice might have eight specific members and last a year or more. Often, groups in private practice are started and then the group itself decides what type of group it wants to be. For example, group participants can make a commitment for six months, agreeing to take a certain number of new members, or they can commit and pay for four weeks at a time and reevaluate after each four-week period. It is important for some pledge to be made to establish a working group where all members have the same commitment and expectations. The group commitment helps separate a therapy group from a support group.

SUPPORT GROUP

A support group is usually a "drop-in" group where new people can come in at any time. An Alcoholics Anonymous or Overeaters Anonymous meeting, where the participants may vary greatly from one group to the next, is an example of a support group. The nature of this kind of group with varying members does not allow for continuity or for the same kind of intimacy and depth as a therapy group. Support groups are usually free and are set up to provide support and education to members, not to provide therapy. Support groups are valuable and have their place, but they are different than a group run by a therapist where the members are committed to coming for a certain period of time.

FORMING THE GROUP

PLACE, TIME, SIZE

The therapist or facilitator, with or without group input, must ultimately determine where the group will meet, for how long it will meet, and how many members to include. A common format is an hour and a half with eight to ten people. Obviously, this does not include the multifamily group or drop-in groups, which are often larger than this and are still effective.

CRITERIA FOR MEMBERSHIP

Having the correct diagnosis should not be the only criterion for allowing patients admittance to the group. Group therapy is not appropriate for many patients. They may not be ready, willing, or capable of sharing with others or hearing what others have to say. Some patients are too self-absorbed, deviant, distraught, or impulsive to be able to benefit from group or be of benefit to anyone else. Some patients simply cannot "be there" for the others, and putting them in a group would be counterproductive for everyone.

The group therapist must ultimately decide who will benefit from group and who will not. An individual interview or screening process is a good idea. Patients for whom the therapist feels group is appropriate but who are resistant should not be coerced, because the likelihood for their success in group is minimal.

CAUTIONS AND CONCERNS

The following are common concerns regarding possible occurrences in group therapy. The therapist must deal with these problems and either make changes or terminate the group.

Patients getting too many negative ideas from each other. If a young girl has never heard of drinking ipecac to induce vomiting and learns this technique in group therapy, who is responsible? Has the group turned into a sharing session of eating disorder techniques? Are the members overly pessimistic about recovery?

Being in the group/having an eating disorder increases patients' self-worth. Although this is tricky, it is important that patients not receive too many secondary gains just for having an eating disorder. Group therapy can sometimes normalize and even glamorize eating disorders. In one instance, a movie director actually went to eating disorder groups looking for actresses for a movie. Patients often feel that having the eating disorder gives them special status and a reason to belong. If they didn't have this disorder, they couldn't be in the group.

Patients get worse or engage in more symptoms to get attention from each other or the therapist. Competition will always exist in groups on some level, but it may also get out of control and become highly unproductive. One member of a group took extra laxatives upon learning that several group members called another participant during the week after she had reported in a previous group taking a similar amount.

Participants feel too much pressure from the other group members and start to withdraw, lie, or not show up. Well-meaning group members often become cotherapists of a group to the point of insisting on change or judging others who don't comply with suggestions. This can be extremely subtle and should be watched for carefully. Group members feeling judged or pressured may not attribute it to other group members and may feel it is their own inadequacy or weakness that is the problem.

MEMBER PREPARATION

It is necessary to prepare participants for the group experience. It is the therapist's job to clarify what group therapy is and the purpose of the group. The therapist must clarify any misconceptions, guide members in what to expect, discuss fears, and provide support. It is important that the therapist set up some definite structures if the group helps out with some of the planning. Especially in an eating disorder group, structure needs to be provided and ground rules set. Handouts on group rules and guidelines are useful.

THERAPIST'S ROLE

Every therapist has his or her own style of running groups. Therapists should also have group rules and guidelines they want followed. Some rules are general and apply to all groups; for example, the rule of confidentiality. Depending on the kind of group, the therapist or the group will decide what to do about tardiness, absences, and so on, but all of this is ultimately the therapist's responsibility. The next section discusses some ground rules that should be given out at an initial group meeting.

GROUND RULES FOR GROUP

The patients will look to the therapist to establish the norms. It is the therapist who establishes the code of behaviors or norms which guide the interaction in the group. The therapist guides the interaction by modeling, encouraging, and teaching when it is appropriate.

An obvious example of this is the need for the therapist to redirect questions and dialogue from him or herself to other members of the group. For example, in the early phase of a group, a therapist was talking to an extremely emaciated, anorexic girl about being cold. She was shivering, yet everyone else was quite comfortable. The therapist told her this was due to the fact that she was too thin and had no insulation or protection from the cold. Another female member of the group asked the therapist, "Does it bother her when you say that?" It is the therapist's responsibility, unless someone else in group does it, to redirect this member to ask the question directly to the person being talked about or to make a statement to the therapist regarding her feelings about the therapist's actions, such as, "It bothers me when you talk to her like that."

Redirecting dialogue is necessary to get the group dealing with each other, and it is one example of the therapist's function in setting desirable standards, such as high level of involvement between group members, nonjudgmental acceptance, high level of self-disclosure, a desire for self-understanding, and a desire for change.

One important standard the therapist sets is the importance of process over content in the group. In running an eating disorder group, members could spend the whole session discussing a topic such as "perfection." Each person could take turns, or there could even be interaction among the members, but all are likely to stick to their own experiences of this topic. This kind of interaction is content oriented. It is important, if the group is to be a true therapy group, to include process interaction, discussing the here and now. "How do you feel about what she just said?" "You look like you don't believe Sherry." "You look nervous and unhappy about that." Members, unless redirected, may continue blindly with content interaction unless the therapist establishes the understanding that process is just as, and probably more, important.

How the group members feel about and relate to each other is of the greatest importance. What group members are thinking and not saying is exactly what they should be saying. The therapist can simply stop periodically and ask a member or members what they are thinking right at that moment, or ask what they have thought about but have not said so far during the session. The therapist must encourage the group members to ask questions of each other. Keeping journals and writing about the group sessions is a good way to bring process interaction into the group. In the journal, members will express much of what they were really feeling during a session. If they are willing, participants can read what they've written at the next group session. This usually brings up important feelings and leads to a good process discussion. Eventually group members start to bring up process comments on their own during the group session.

GROUP TOPICS

Below are some topics or themes useful in eating disorder groups. They can be distributed at the first session to provide guidelines as to with what the group will be concerned and discussing.

GROUP TOPICS

1. Adaptive Functions of Eating Disorder Behaviors

2. Control and Helplessness

3. Family and Personal History Regarding Food and Weight

4. Ability to Nurture and Be Nurtured

5. Perfectionism, Competition, and Loneliness

6. Anger and Assertiveness

7. Body Image and the Need to Develop an Essential, not Ornamental Self

8. Intimacy and Sexuality

9. Spirituality

10. Separation and Individuation

11. The Importance of Sex Roles

12. Women's Conflict around Achievement

13. The Power of Language to Shape Thought Patterns and Subsequent Actions

14. Trust and Mistrust

15. Risk Taking

To end this chapter, here are some excerpts taken from journal entries made by patients in group.

I really felt for Karen today because two weeks ago, she was so excited about her "diet." I knew it wouldn't last for her and sure enough, there we were today, sitting there, listening to her tell us how she blew it. The diet didn't last. Now she's bingeing and throwing up again. I look at her and wonder what goes on in her mind. There's more to it than just being thin. She is so unsure of what she wants and who she should be. Some of the things she says just don't make sense to me, yet I have said them. Seeing her really makes me think about myself.

I had a hard time today looking at Christy. She is so thin, it really made me feel a little sick to see how thin her legs are. She is a walking skeleton. I know we weigh the same, I wonder how they all see me?

Just knowing that everyone else in the group is rooting for me, not judging me but supporting me to get better, has made it so much easier.

I'm surprised at how defensive I get when someone asks a question or wants clarification about something I've said. Tonight the group members told me how hard it is for them to talk to me, especially to ask me anything because I act annoyed and defensive. I guess I always feel suspicious of people's motives and am always thinking I'm being attacked. That's how I felt in my family, exactly like that.

12

ALL IN THE FAMILY

Individuals with eating disorders directly or indirectly affect those with whom they live or who love and care about them. Family patterns of socializing, preparing food, going out to restaurants, and just plain talking to each other are all disrupted. Everything from finances to vacations seems jeopardized and the person with the eating disorder is resented for an illness he or she cannot control.

A family member with an eating disorder is most likely not the only member of the family with problems. It is common to find problems with mood or behavior control in other family members, and the level of functioning and boundary setting among parents and siblings is often poor. In many families there is a history of excessive reliance upon external achievement as an indicator of self-worth, which ultimately or repeatedly fails. Fluctuations between overinvolvement and abandonment may have been occurring for some time, leaving family members feeling lost, isolated, insecure, or rebellious, and without a sense of self.

Parents, who have their own issues both from the past and in the present, are often frustrated, fighting between themselves, and unhappy. Overinvolvement with the eating disordered child is usually a first reaction in trying to gain control of an out-of-control situation. Futile attempts at control are exerted at a time when understanding and supportive direction would be more helpful.

In a marriage where one partner has an eating disorder spouses' concerns are often overshadowed by anger and feelings of helplessness. Spouses often report a decrease of intimacy in their relationships, sometimes describing their loved ones as preferring or choosing the eating disorder over them.

Individuals with eating disorders need help in communicating to their family members and loved ones. Family members and loved ones need help as they experience a variety of emotions, from denial and anger to panic or despair. In the book, *Eating Disorders: Nutrition Therapy in the Recovery Process*, by Dan Reiff and Kim Reiff, six stages that parents, spouses, and siblings go through are delineated.

STAGES OF GROWTH EXPERIENCED BY FAMILY MEMBERS AFTER BECOMING AWARE THAT A PERSON THEY LOVE HAS AN EATING DISORDER

Stage 1: Denial

Stage 2: Fear, ignorance, and panic

    a. Why can't she stop?

    b. What kind of treatment should she have?

    c. The measure of recovery is behavior change, isn't it?

    d. How do I respond to her behaviors?

Stage 3: Increasing realization of the psychological basis for the eating disorder

    a. Family members question their roles in the development of the eating disorder.

    b. There is increased understanding that the process of recovery takes time and that there is no quick fix.

    c. Parents/spouses are increasingly involved in therapy.

    d. Appropriate responses to the food- and weight-related behavior are learned.

Stage 4: Impatience/despair

    a. Progress seems too slow.

    b. The focus shifts from trying to change or control the person with the eating disorder to working on oneself.

---

    c. Parents/spouses need support.

    d. Anger/detachment is felt.

    e. Parents/spouses let go.

Stage 5: Hope

    a. Signs of progress are noticed in the person with the eating disorder and oneself.

    b. It becomes possible to develop a healthier relationship with the person with the eating disorder.

Stage 6: Acceptance/peace

To help family and friends understand, accept, and work through all the problems a loved one with an eating disorder presents, successful treatment of eating disorders often mandates therapeutic involvement with the patient's significant others and/or family, even when the patient is no longer living at home or a dependent.

Family therapy (this term will be used to include therapy with significant others) involves the creation of a powerful therapeutic system consisting of the family members plus the therapist. Family therapy emphasizes responsibility, relationships, conflict resolution, individuation (each person's developing an individual identity) and behavior change among all family members. The therapist assumes an active and highly responsive role within this system, altering the family rules and patterns in a significant way. If the therapist appreciates the vulnerability, pain, and sense of caring within the family, he or she can provide initial support for all family members. Supportive, guided therapy can relieve some of the tension created by tenuous and previously disappointing family relationships.

One goal in family therapy involves helping the family learn to do what the therapist has been trained to do for the patient (for example, empathize, understand, guide without controlling, step in when necessary, foster self-esteem, and facilitate independence). If the therapist can help the family and significant others to provide for the patient what a healing therapeutic relationship provides, lengthy therapy may not be necessary.

In doing family work, the patient's age and developmental status are important in outlining the course of treatment as well as high-lighting the responsibility of family members. The younger the patient is, both chronologically and developmentally, the more responsibility and control the parents will have. On the other hand, patients who are developmentally more advanced require parental involvement which is more collaborative and supportive and less controlling.

SUMMARY OF IMPORTANT TASKS FOR SUCCESSFUL FAMILY THERAPY

The multidimensional task of the therapist in family therapy is exten-sive. The therapist must work on correcting any dysfunction occurring in the various relationships, for this may be where the underlying causal issues have partly developed or at least are sus-tained. Family members, spouses, and significant others need to be educated about eating disorders and, particularly, the patient's unique manifestation of symptoms. All loved ones need help in learning how to respond appropriately to various situations they will encounter. Any serious conflicts between family members, which contribute highly to the development of eating disorder behaviors, must be addressed. For example, one parent may be stricter than the other and have different values, which may develop into serious con-frontations over the raising of the children. Parents may need to learn how to solve conflicts between themselves and nurture each other, which will then enable them to better nurture their child. Faulty organizational structure in the family, such as too much intru-siveness on the part of the parents, too much rigidity, or fused boundary issues, must be pointed out and corrected. Expectations of family members and how they communicate and get their needs met may be underhanded and/or destructive. Individual members of the family may have problems that need to be resolved separately, such as depression or alcoholism, and the family therapist should facilitate this happening. The task of family therapy is so complex and at times overwhelming that therapists often shy away from it, preferring to work solely with individual patients. This can be a grave mistake. Whenever possible, family members and/or significant others should be a part of overall treatment.

The following is an excerpt from a session where an extremely upset father was yelling about the fact that the family had to be in therapy. He felt that there were no family problems except that his daughter, Carla, was sick. This can be a grave mistake. Whenever possible, family members and/or significant others should be a part of overall treatment.

Father: *Why should I listen to this? She is the one with this disgusting sickness. She's the one screwed up in the head. She's the one who is wrong here.*

Therapist: *It is not a matter of right or wrong or blame that I want to address. It is not just a matter of something wrong in Carla's personality. There is also a problem with the combination of personalities. In another family Carla may be seen as a hard worker and very helpful, to you it isn't that way. She thinks you have too many rules and ask too much. There is no way to judge who is right. Who could be the judge? Some families have more rules, some have less. What's important is that you and Carla work out an agreement between the two of you. Each of you will have to give in a little from the positions you now hold.*

The therapist creates an experience of continuity for the treatment and remains its guiding force until the family as a whole trusts both the therapist and the changes that are asked for and slowly taking place in treatment. It is important for the therapist to show patience, continuity, support, and a sense of humor within the context of optimism about the possibilities of all family members for the future. It is best if the family experiences therapy as a welcomed and

159

desired situation which can help foster change and growth. Even though the therapist takes responsibility for the course and pacing of treatment, he or she can share this responsibility with family members by expecting them to identify issues for resolution and to demonstrate greater flexibility and more mutual concern.

ESTABLISHING RAPPORT AND GETTING STARTED

Families with eating disordered individuals often seem guarded, anxious, and highly vulnerable. Therapists must work at establishing rapport to make the family feel comfortable with the therapist and the therapy process. It is important to lessen the anxiety, hostility, and frustration that often permeate the first few sessions. When beginning treatment, the therapist needs to create a strong relationship with each family member and imposes himself or herself as a boundary between individuals as well as between generations. It's important for everyone to express their feelings and viewpoint as thoroughly as possible.

It may be necessary to see each family member alone to establish a good therapeutic relationship with each one. Family members must be recognized in all their roles (i.e., the father as husband, man, father, and son; the mother as wife, woman, mother, and daughter). In order to do this, the therapist obtains background information about each family member early in treatment. Then, he or she provides recognition of each individual's strength, caring, and passion while also identifying and elaborating on individual difficulties, weaknesses, and resentments.

If the individual family members trust the therapist, the family can come together more at ease, less defensive, and much more willing to "work" at therapy. Treatment becomes a collaborative effort where the family and therapist begin to define problems to be solved and to create shared approaches to these problems. The therapist's responsibility is to provide the proper balance between stirring up controversy and crises in order to bring about change, while at the same time making the therapeutic process safe for family members. Family therapists are like directors and need trust and cooperation in order to direct the characters. Family therapy for eating disorders, like individual therapy, is highly directive and involves a lot of "teaching style" therapy.

EDUCATING THE FAMILY

It is important to have information for family members to take home and read or at least suggestions of reading material they can buy. Much confusion and misinformation exists about eating disorders. Confusion ranges from the definitions and differences between the disorders to how serious they are, how long therapy takes, what the medical complications are, etc. These issues will be discussed but it is useful to give family members something to read that the therapist knows will be correct and helpful. With reading material to review, family members can be collecting information and forming questions when they are not in the session. This is important, as therapy is expensive and family therapy will most likely take place no more than once a week. Additional sessions are usually not feasible for most families, especially since individual therapy with the patient is also ongoing. Information provided in the form of inexpensive reading material will save valuable therapy time that would otherwise be spent explaining the same information. The therapy time is better spent on other important issues, such as how the family interacts, as well as questions on and clarification of the material read. It's also comforting for family members to read that other people have been through similar experiences. Through reading about others, family members can see that there is hope for recovery and they can begin to look at what issues in the reading material relate to their own situation.

Literature on eating disorders helps to validate and reinforce information the therapist will be presenting, such as the two to five year length of treatment often quoted. Families may be inclined to be suspicious and wonder if the therapist is simply trying to get two or more years of income. After reading various material on eating disorders, family members are more likely to understand and accept the possibility of lengthy therapy. It is important to note that the therapist should not doom a patient or her/his family into thinking it will absolutely take him/her two years to recover. There are patients who have recovered in much less time, such as six or eight months, but it should be made clear that the longer time period is more likely. Being realistic about the usual lengthy time necessary for treatment is important so that family members don't have unrealistic expectations for recovery.

EXPLORING THE IMPACT OF THE ILLNESS ON THE FAMILY

It is necessary for the family therapist to assess how much the eating disorder has interfered with the feelings and functioning of the family. Is father or mother missing work? Has everything else been put secondary to the eating disorder? Are the other children's needs and problems being neglected? Are the parents depressed or overly anxious or hostile due to the eating disorder, or were they like this before the problem started? This information helps the therapist and family begin to identify whether certain things are the cause or result of the eating disorder. Families need help learning what is appropriate behavior and how to respond (for example, guidelines for how to minimize the eating disorders influence over family life).

The therapist will need to find out if other children in the family are affected. Sometimes other children are suffering silently for fear of being "another bad child" or "disappointing my parents more," or just simply because their concerns were ignored and they were never asked how they were feeling. In exploring this issue, the therapist is making therapeutic interventions from the very beginning by 1) allowing all family members to express their feelings, 2) helping the family examine and change dysfunctional patterns, 3) dealing with individual problems, and 4) simply providing an opportunity for the family to come together, talk together, and work together on solving the problem.

Reassuring family members that the eating disorder is not their fault is crucial. Family members may feel abused and perhaps even victimized by the patient and need someone to understand their feelings and see their sides. However, even though the focus stays off blame, it is important that everyone recognizes and takes responsibility for their own actions that contribute to family problems.

The therapist also addresses the quality of the patient's relationship with each of his/her parents and assists in developing an effective, but different, relationship with both of them. These relationships should be based upon mutual respect, with opportunities for individual assertiveness and clear communication on the part of everyone involved. This depends upon a more respectful and mutually supportive relationship between the parents. As treatment progresses there should be a greater ability on the part of all family members to respect each other's differences and separateness, and enhanced mutual respect within the family.

Sessions should be planned to include appropriate family members according to the issues being worked on at that time. Occasionally, individual sessions for family members, sessions for one family member with the patient, or sessions for both parents, may be necessary.

In situations where chronic illness and treatment failure have led to marked helplessness on the part of all family members, it is often helpful for the therapist to begin with a somewhat detached, inquisitive approach, letting the family know that this treatment will only be effective if it includes all members in an active way. The therapist can define everyone's participation in ways that are different from previous treatments and thus avoid earlier pitfalls. It is common for families who have been faced with chronic symptoms to be impatient and impulsive in their approach to the therapeutic process. In these situations, therapists need to gently probe family relationships and the role of the eating disorder within the family, pointing out any positive adaptive functions that the eating disorder behaviors serve. This often highlights difficulties in family relationships and offers avenues for intervention in highly resistant families. In order to gain the family's participation in the desired fashion, the therapist must resist the family's attempt to get him or her to take full responsibility for the patient's recovery.

DISCOVERING PARENTAL EXPECTATIONS/ASPIRATIONS

What messages do the parents give the children? What pressures are on the children to be or to do certain things? Are the parents asking too much or too little, based on the age and ability of each child or simply on what is appropriate in a healthy family?

Sarah, a sixteen-year-old anorexic, came from a nice family who had the appearance of having things very much "together." The father and mother both had good jobs, the two daughters were attractive, good in school, active, and healthy. However, there was significant conflict and constant tension between the parents regarding the disciplining of and expectations for the children.

As the eldest child got into the teenage years, where there is a normal struggle for independence and autonomy, the conflict between the parents became a war. First of all, the mother and father had different expectations regarding the daughter's behavior and found it impossible to compromise. The father saw nothing wrong with letting the girl wear the color black to school while the mother insisted that the girl was too young to wear black and would not allow it. The mother had certain standards for having a clean house and imposed them on the family even though the father felt that the standards were excessive and complained in front of the children about it. These parents didn't agree on rules regarding curfews or dating either. Obviously this caused a great deal of friction between the parents, and their daughter, sensing a weak link, would push every issue.

Two of the problems regarding expectations addressed in this family were a) the parent's conflicting values and aspirations, which necessitated couple therapy, and b) the mother's excessive expectations for everyone, especially the oldest daughter, to be like herself. The mother would constantly make statements such as, "If I did that when I was in school . . . ," or "I would have never said that to my mother." The mother would also overgeneralize, "all my friends . . . ," "all men . . . ," and "other kids" for validation of rightness. What she was doing was using her past or other people she knew to justify the expectations she had for her own children instead of recognizing her children's own personalities and needs in the present. This mother was wonderful at fulfilling her motherly obligations like buying clothes, furnishing rooms, transporting her daughters to the places they needed to go, but only as long as the clothes, the room furnishings, and the places were those that she would have chosen for herself. Her heart was good, but her expectations for her children to be and think and feel like her or her "friends or sister's kids" were unrealistic and oppressive and one way her daughter rebelled against them was through her eating disorder behavior, "Mom cannot control this."

Unrealistic expectations for achievement or independence also cause problems. Consciously or unconsciously children may get rewarded particularly by their fathers, only for what they "do" as opposed to who they are. These children may learn to depend only on external rather than internal validation.

Children who get rewards for being self-sufficient or independent may feel afraid to ask for help or attention because they have always been praised for not needing it. These children often set their own high expectations. In our society, with the cultural standard of thinness, weight loss often becomes another perfectionistic pursuit, one more thing at which to be successful or "the best." Steven Levenkron's book, *The Best Little Girl in the World*, earned its title for this reason. Unfortunately, once successful at the dieting, it may be very hard to give it up. In our society, all individuals are praised by their peers and reinforced for an ability to diet. Once individuals feel so "in control," they may find they are unable to break the rules they set for themselves. The attention for being thin, even for being too thin, feels good, and too often people just do not want to give it up, at least not until they can replace it with something better.

Individuals with bulimia nervosa are usually trying to be over-controlled with their food half the time, like anorexics, and the other half of the time they lose control and binge. Some individuals may place so many expectations on themselves to be successful and perfect at everything that their bulimic behaviors become the one area where they "go wild," "lose control," "rebel," "get away with something." The loss of control usually leads to shame and more self-imposed rules (for example, purging or starving or other anorexic behaviors, thus starting the cycle over again).

There are several other ways in which I have seen faulty expectations contribute to the development of an eating disorder. The therapist needs to uncover these and work with the patient and the family to set realistic alternatives.

GOAL SETTING

Parents don't know what to expect from treatment or what they should be asking of their sons or daughters who are being treated. Therapists help families set realistic goals. For example, with underweight anorexics, the therapist helps the parents to expect that weight gain will take time and when it begins, no more than a steady, slow weight gain of as little as one pound per week should be expected. In order to meet the weekly weight goal, parents (depending on the patient's age) are usually advised to provide various foods but avoid power struggles by leaving the issue of determining what and how much to eat up to the patient and therapist or dietitian. Setting goals in a family session helps guide parents in assisting their sons or daughters to meet weight goals while limiting the parents' intrusiveness and ineffective attempts to control food intake. An agreement will also need to be made regarding an appropriate, realistic response should lack of weight gain occur. The protocol just described can also be applied for use with binge eaters and/or overweight individuals where weight loss is the agreed-upon goal.

An example of goal setting for bulimia would be symptom reduction, as there may be an expectation on the part of the family that, since the patient is in treatment, she/he should be able to stop bingeing or purging right away. Another example would be setting goals for using alternative means of responding to stress and emotional upset (without resorting to bingeing and purging). Together the therapist and family help the patient discuss goals of eating when physically hungry and managing his or her diet appropriately to reduce episodes of weight gain and periods of anxiety leading to purging behavior.

For bulimics and binge eaters, a first goal may be to eliminate the goal of weight loss. Weight loss considerations should be set aside while trying to reduce binge eating behavior and purgings. It is difficult to focus on both tasks at once. I point this out to patients by asking what they will do if they overeat when weight loss and overcoming bulimia are simultaneous goals. If stopping bulimia is a priority, you will deal with having eaten the food. If weight loss is a priority, chances are you will purge it.

The usual focus on the need to lose weight may be a big factor in sustaining the binge eating, since bingeing often precedes restrictive dieting.

ROLE OF THE PATIENT IN THE FAMILY

A family therapist learns to look for a reason or adaptive function that a certain "destructive" or "inappropriate" behavior serves in the family system. This "functional" behavior may be acted out on an unconscious level. Research on families of alcoholics or drug abusers have identified various roles that the children take on in order to cope. I will list these various roles below, as they can be applied to working with individuals with eating disorders.

Scapegoat. In the case of parental disharmony, the eating disorder may serve as a mechanism to focus the parents' attention onto the child with the eating disorder and away from their own problems. In this way the parents can actually work together on something, their son or daughter's eating disorder. He/she is the scapegoat for the family pain and may often end up feeling hostile and aggressive, having learned to get attention negatively.

Often, as an eating disorder patient begins to get better, the relationship between her parents gets worse. When not sick herself, she ceases to provide her parents with a distraction from their own unhappy lives. This certainly must be pointed out, however carefully, and dealt with in therapy.

The Caretaker or Family Hero. This is the child who takes on too much responsibility and becomes the perfectionist and overachiever. As mentioned under the issue of parental expectations, this child puts the needs of others first. Anorexics are often the child who "never gave us any problems." "She was always so good, we never had to worry or concern ourselves about her."

There is a careful and gentle technique to uncovering and confronting these issues in a family. Yes, the parents need to see if their child has become the caretaker, but they need to know what to do about it and they need to not feel guilty about the past. In this case, they can learn to take more responsibility themselves. They also can learn to communicate better with and focus more attention on the child with the eating disorder, who has been virtually ignored because she was doing so well.

A caretaker often comes from a household that has a chaotic or weak parental system—the child becomes independent and assumes too much control and self-reliance before being mature enough to handle it. He/she is given, or takes out of necessity, too much responsibility. The eating disorder occurs as an extension of the child's self-imposed control system. Anorexia nervosa is the ultimate form of control, bulimia nervosa is a combination of overcontrol combined with a sort of loss of control, rebellion, or at least escape from it. A bulimic controls weight by purging; forcing oneself to purge is exerting control over the binge and the body.

The Lost Child. Sometimes there is no way to overcome a combative parent or abusive family situation. Sometimes there are too many children and the competition for attention and recognition is too tough. Whatever the reason, some kids get lost in a family. The lost child is the child who learns to cope with family pain or problems by avoidance. This child spends a lot of time alone and avoids interaction because she has learned that it is painful. She also wants to be good and not a problem. She cannot discuss her feelings and keeps everything in. Consequently this individual's self-esteem is low. If she discovers that dieting wins approval from her peers (which it almost always does) and gives her something to be good at and talked to about, then she continues because it is reinforcing. "What else do I have?" she might say, or at least think and feel. Also, I have seen the lost child who takes comfort in night binges as a way to ease loneliness and the inability to reach out and make meaningful relationships.

The lost child who develops an eating disorder may also discover a sense of power in having some effect on the family. This power is hard to give up. Even though she may really not want to cause family problems, her new special identity is too hard to surrender. It may be the first real one she has had. Some patients, who are conflicted about desperately wanting their disorder but desperately not wanting to cause the family pain, often tell me or write in their journals that they think it would be better if they were dead.

There are other aspects and examples of the roles played in families, but the important point is that this "role" or function be identified and worked through. Once the patient and other members figure out the roles they have been playing, they can begin to learn more positive alternatives. Awareness of a problem is the first step toward a solution or change. Everyone in the family will have to work at his or her own pace to find healthier, more fulfilling ways of relating to each other and to the world.

ANALYZING AND ADJUSTING THE ORGANIZATIONAL STRUCTURE OF THE FAMILY

Looking at the family structure can help tie all the other components together. This is the family's system for working. Each family has rules its members live or function by that are unspoken. These rules concern such things as "what can and cannot be talked about in this family," "who sides with whom in this family," "conflicts are solved in this way," and so on. Family structure and organization is explored to answer the question, "What makes it necessary for the patient to go to the extreme of having an eating disorder?"

What are the boundaries that exist in the family? For example, when does the mother stop and the child begin? Much of the early focus in family treatment for eating disorders was on the mother and her overintrusiveness and inability to separate herself from her child. In this scenario the mother dotes on the child but also wants to be in on every decision, feeling, or thought the child has. The mother feels that she has been nurturing and giving and expects it all back from the child, wanting the child to be a certain way because of it. There is also the overpleasing mother who is emotionally weak and is afraid of the child's rejection, so she tends to let the child be in charge. The child is in charge too soon to be able to handle it, and inside actually resents that the mother did not help her/him enough.

Marta, a twenty-three-year-old bulimic, came to therapy after her mother, with whom she was still living, called for an appointment. Although the mother wanted to come to the first session, Marta insisted on coming alone. In the first visit, she told me that she had been bingeing and purging for five years and her mother had not said anything to her until a few days before the phone call to me. Marta described how her mother, "came into the bathroom when I was throwing up and asked me if I was making myself sick. I thought, 'Thank God, I will now get some help.'" Marta went on to describe her reluctance to share things with her mother, "Whenever I have a problem she cries, breaks down, and falls apart and then I have to take care of her!" One obvious issue in this family was for the mother to become stronger, allowing the daughter to express her needs and not have to be the parentified child.

One sixteen-year-old bulimic, Donna, and her mother Adrienne alternated between being best friends and sleeping in the same bed together, staying up late to talk about boys, to having fist- and hair-pulling fights when Donna did not do her homework or her chores. The mother in this family gave a lot but demanded too much in return. Adrienne wanted Donna to wear the kind of clothes *she* wanted, date the boys *she* approved of, and even go on a diet *her* way. In wanting to be best friends and expecting her daughter to be a best friend yet still obey her as a parent, Adrienne was sending mixed messages to her daughter.

Mothers who get overly invested in getting their needs met from their daughters get uncontrollably upset when their daughters don't react in the "right" way. This same issue may very well exist in the marriage relationship. With Adrienne, this was one factor in breaking up the marriage. The father was not living at home when Donna came into treatment. The end of the marriage had made the mother even more dependent on Donna for her emotional satisfaction, and the fighting was a result of her daughter not giving it to her. Donna felt abandoned by her father. He had left her there to take care of her mother and to fight with her, and he had not stayed to help her out in this situation.

Donna's bulimia was, in part, her struggle to get back at her mother by having something about which her mother could do nothing. It was a call for help, a plea for someone to pay attention to how unhappy she was. It was a struggle to escape a reality where she could not seem to please herself and her mother at the same time. If she pleased her mother, she wasn't happy, and vice versa. Her bulimic behaviors were a way of trying to get control over herself and make herself fit into what she considered the standards for beauty so that she would be accepted and loved, something she did not feel from either of her parents.

One aspect of Donna's treatment was to show her how her bulimia was not serving any of the purposes she consciously or unconsciously wanted it to serve. We discussed all the above aspects of her relationship to her family and how she needed to make it different, but that her bulimic behavior was just making it all worse. Not only was bulimia not helping solve her underlying issues, it wasn't even helping her to be thin, which is true for almost all bulimics as the bingeing gets further and further out of control.

Other ways of dealing with dieting and the family have to be explored. In Donna's case this involved family participation with both the mother and the father. Progress was made when the mother and father discussed their own problems. Solving them helped lead to the solution of the mother/daughter issues (for example, the mother's expectations and demands). Donna benefited greatly from the knowledge of her parent's role in her feelings and thus her behavior. She began to see herself with more self-worth and to see the futility of her bulimia.

Even though early researchers focused on mothers and mothering, over the last few years there has been more emphasis on the role of fathers in the development of eating disorders. One issue where the effect of the father's role has been discussed is when a father applies his sense of values, achievement, and control to areas where they are misinterpreted or misused. For example, achievement and control should not be values to strive for in the area of weight, body image, and food.

Although children are more biologically dependent on their mother from birth, fathers can provide the traditional role of being "outside representative" while also offering a non-threatening transition from the natural dependency on the mother. The father can help his daughter confirm her own separateness, enhancing her sense of self. As stated by Kathryn Zerbe in *The Body Betrayed*, "When a father is unable to help his daughter move out of the maternal orbit, either because he is physically unavailable or not invested emotionally in her, the daughter may turn to food as a substitute. Anorexia and bulimia nervosa have in common inadequate paternal responses for helping the daughter develop a less symbiotic relationship with her mother. When she must separate on her own, she may take on the pathological coping strategies embedded in eating disorders."

Literature on fathers and eating disorders is scarce. *Father Hunger* by Margo Maine does address this too little discussed but important topic. See Appendix B for more information.

Other issues in the family structure involve how rigid or flexible the family is and the effectiveness of members' overall communication skills. The therapist needs to explore all the various kinds of communication that exist. Effective teaching on how to communicate is very beneficial to all families. Communication skills affect how families resolve their conflicts and who sides with whom on what issues.

ADDRESSING ABUSE ISSUES

Numerous studies have documented a correlation between eating disorders and a history of physical and/or sexual abuse. Although one study by the Rader Institute on sexual abuse and eating disorder inpatients reported a correlation of 80 percent, most research seems to indicate a much lower rate. It is important to understand that the association is not a simple cause-and-effect relationship. Abuse does not cause an eating disorder but can be one of many contributing factors. Both physical and sexual abuse are boundary violations of the body, thus it makes sense that abused individuals manifest both psychological and physical symptoms including problems with eating, weight, and body image.

Both therapist and family therapist should explore family histories asking very specific questions regarding any abuse. Individuals who are abused are reluctant to reveal it or perhaps have no recollection of the abuse. Perpetrators of the abuse are, of course, reluctant to admit it. Therefore, therapists must be well trained and experienced in these matters, paying heed to signs and symptoms of possible abuse that need further exploration.

CHALLENGING CURRENT PATTERNS

Whatever is going on, family members will usually at least agree that what they are presently doing is not working. Coming for help means they haven't been able to solve the problem on their own. If they have not already tried several solutions, they at least agree that something in the family is not working correctly and they can't or don't know how to fix it.

Usually the family is trying to do all the things they are sure will help because they have helped before in other circumstances. Many of the standard approaches used with other problems or with other children are inappropriate and simply don't work with the eating disordered child. Grounding, threatening, taking away privileges, rewarding, and so on will not resolve an eating disorder. Taking the eating disorder patient to the family doctor and having all the medical consequences explained to her or him doesn't work either, nor will planning a diet or guarding the bathroom.

Parents usually have a hard time stopping their own monitoring, punishing, rewarding, and other controlling behaviors in which they are engaging to try to stop the eating disorder even though those methods don't seem to be doing any good. Often many of the methods used to prevent behaviors actually serve to sustain them. Examples of this are: Father yells and screams about the daughter's eating disorder ruining the family, and the daughter's reaction is to go and throw up. The more control a mother exerts over her daughter's life, the more control the daughter exerts with her eating disorder. The more demands for weight gain are made, the thinner the individual gets. If yelling, grounding, threatening, or other punishments worked to control an eating disorder, that would be different—but they don't work and so there is no use in continuing them.

One night early in my career as an eating disorder therapist, I was in a family session when this useful analogy came to me. The father of Candy, a sixteen-year-old anorexic, was attacking her about being anorexic, harassing her, and demanding that she "stop it." The attacks had been going on for weeks prior to their seeking therapy. It was clear that the more attacking the father did, the worse Candy got. The attacking provided distraction for her; thus, she didn't have to face or deal with the real underlying psychological issues which were at the root of her eating disorder. Most of our sessions dealt with the combat that was going on with her father and her mother's ineffectiveness. We were spending most of our time repairing damage that resulted from her parents' attacks concerning what their daughter was or wasn't eating, how much she weighed, why she was doing so and so, and how she was harming the family. Some of these arguments at home ended up in hair-pulling or slapping sessions.

The family was falling apart, and in fact, the more Candy argued with her parents, the more entrenched she became in her disorder. It was clear from watching Candy that the more she had to defend her position, the more she believed in it herself. It was clear that while being attacked by others, she was distracted from the real issues and had no time to really go inside herself and "clean house," or in other words, really look inside and deal with her problems. In the middle of more complaints by Candy's father, I thought of the analogy and I said, "While you are guarding the fort, you don't have time to clean house," and then I explained what I meant. It is important to leave the individual with an eating disorder free from any outside attacks. If the person is too busy guarding themselves against outside intrusion, they will have too much distraction and spend no time going inside themselves and really looking at and working on their own issues. Who has time to work on themselves if they are busy fighting off others? This analogy helped Candy's father see how his behavior was actually making things worse and helped candy be able to look at her own problem. Candy's father learned a valuable lesson and went on to share this with other parents in a multifamily group.

MULTIFAMILY GROUP

A variation on family therapy involves several families/significant others who have a loved one with an eating disorder meeting together in one large group called a multifamily group. It is a valuable experience for loved ones to see how other people deal with various situations and feelings. It is good for parents, and often less threatening, to listen to and communicate with a daughter or son from another family. It is sometimes easier to listen, be sympathetic, and truly understand when hearing someone else's daughter or son describe problems with eating, fear of weight gain, or what helps versus what sabotages recovery. Patients also can often listen better to what other parents or significant others have to say because they feel too angry or threatened and many times shut out those close to them. Furthermore, siblings can talk to siblings, fathers to fathers, spouses to other spouses, improving communication and understanding as well as getting support for themselves. Multifamily group needs a skilled therapist and perhaps even two therapists. It's rare to find this challenging, but very rewarding, type of group in settings other than formal treatment programs. It might prove very useful if more therapists would add this component to their outpatient services.

Family therapists must be careful that no one feels overly blamed. Parents at times feel threatened and annoyed that they are having to change when it is their daughter or son who is "sick and has the problem." Even if family members refuse, are unable, or it is contraindicated for them to attend sessions, family therapy can still occur without them present. Therapists can explore all the various family issues, discover the family roles in the illness, and change family dynamics when working just with the eating disordered patient. However, when the patient still lives at home, it is essential to have the family come to sessions unless the family is so nonsupportive, hostile, or emotionally troubled as to be counterproductive. In this case, individual therapy and possibly group therapy may very well be enough. In some cases, other arrangements can be made for the family members to get therapy elsewhere. It may be better if the patient has his or her own individual therapist and some other therapist does the family work.

175

Treatment for eating disorders, including family therapy, is not a short-term process. There are no magic cures or strategies. Termination of treatment can occur at different times for different family subsystems. When the patient and the entire family are functioning effectively, follow-up sessions are often helpful in assisting family members to experience their own resources in dealing with stresses and transitions. Ultimately, the goal is to create an environment in which the eating disorder behavior is no longer necessary.

It should be noted that although family involvement in the treatment of those with eating disorders, particularly young people, is considered vital, it is not sufficient by itself to produce lasting changes in family members or a lasting cure. Neither will the absence of family involvement doom the eating disordered individual to a lifelong illness. In some instances, family members and loved ones may not be interested in participating in family therapy or their involvement may cause more unnecessary or unresolvable problems than if the were not involved. It is not that uncommon to find family members or loved ones who feel that the problem belongs solely to the person with the eating disorder and that, as soon as he or she is "fixed" and back to normal, things will be fine. In some cases the removal of the eating disordered person from her or his family or loved ones is the indicated treatment, rather than including the significant others in the therapy process. Each therapist will have to assess the patient and the family and determine the best, most effective way to proceed.

13

NUTRITION EDUCATION AND THERAPY

COAUTHORED BY KARIN KRATINA, M.A., R.D.

THE ROLE OF NUTRITION EDUCATION AND NURITION THERAPY

The American Psychiatric Association guidelines recommend nutritional rehabilitation as a first goal in the treatment of anorexia and bulimia. The guidlines do not address binge eating disorders. Since few therapists are formally educated in or choose to study nutrition, a nutrition specialist, commonly referred to as a "nutritionist" (usually a registered dietitian or other individual specializing in nutrition education and treatment) is a useful and often necessary addition to the treatment team of individuals with eating disorders. Eating disordered individuals often know a great deal about nutrition and may believe they do not need to work with a nutritionist. What they don't realize is that much of their information has been distorted by their eating disordered thinking and is not based on reality. For instance, knowing that bananas contain more calories than other fruits becomes, "Bananas are fattening," which becomes, "If I eat a banana, I will get fat," which means, " I cannot eat bananas." These distortions develop gradually and serve to protect those with eating disorders from feeling and dealing with other underlying issues in their lives as well as from having to make decisions regarding whether they will eat certain foods. Statements such as, "If I'm bingeing all I have to think about is what I'm going to eat," or "If I have a rule about food, I don't have to even think about it," are commonly heard from individuals with eating disorders. The nutritionist can help individuals become aware of their faulty thinking or distortions, challenging them to face unrealistic beliefs that cannot be defended rationally.

Unrealistic beliefs and mental distortions about food and eating can be challenged by a therapist in the course of therapy. However, many therapists deal minimally with specific food, exercise, and weight-related behaviors, partly due to the fact that they have many other issues to discuss in their sessions and/or partly due to lack of confidence or knowledge in this area. A certain level of expertise is necessary when dealing with eating disordered individuals, especially those who are "nutritionally sophisticated." Once someone has an eating disorder, knowledge is distorted and entrenched and the faulty beliefs, magical thinking, and distortions will remain until successfully challenged.

Anyone can call themselves a "nutritionist" and there is no way to distinguish by this title alone who has training and competency and who does not. Although there are various kinds of nutritionists who are properly trained and work well with eating disordered clients, a licensed registered dietitian (R.D.) who has a degree from an approved program is the safest choice when looking for a nutritionist, because the R.D. license guarantees that the person has been trained in the biochemistry of the body as well as extensively in the area of food and nutrition.

It is important to understand that not all R.D.s are trained to work with eating disordered clients. (The term *client* is most often used by R.D.s and thus will be used in this chapter.) Most R.D.s are trained with a physical science frame of reference and are taught to explore the quality of a diet with concerns such as, "Is there enough energy, calcium, protein, and variety in the diet for good health?" Even though many R.D.s call their interactions with their clients "nutrition counseling," the format is usually one of nutrition education. Typically clients are educated about nutrition, metabolism, and even about the dangers their disordered eating behaviors could cause. They are also given suggestions and helped to see how changes can be made. Providing information may be sufficient to help some individuals change their eating patterns, but for many, education and support are not enough.

For individuals with eating disorders there are two phases of the nutritional aspect of treatment: 1) the education phase, in which nutrition information is provided in a factual manner with little or no emphasis on the emotional issues, and 2) the experimental phase, where the R.D. has a special interest in long-term relationship-based counseling and works in conjunction with other member, of a treatment team.

In addition to the educational phase, eating disordered individuals will, for the most part, need a second experimental phase, which involves a more intensive intervention from the R.D., which calls for some understanding of the underlying psychological problems involved in eating disorders and a certain amount of expertise in counseling skills.

All registered dietitians have the qualifications for the education phase, but to work effectively with an eating disordered client, R.D.s need to be trained in a "psychotherapeutic" counseling style. R.D.s trained in this type of counseling are often called "nutrition therapists." There is some controversy over the use of the term "nutrition therapist," and the term may be confusing. The reader is advised to check the credentials of anyone doing nutrition education or counseling. For the purpose of this chapter the term *nutrition therapist* refers only to those registered dietitians who have had training in counseling skills, supervision in performing both phases of nutrition treatment for eating disorders, and who have a special interest in doing long- term, relationship-based nutrition counseling. A nutrition therapist works as part of a multidisciplinary treatment team and is usually the team member assigned the task of exploring, challenging, and helping the eating disorder client replace the mental distortions that cause and perpetuate the specific food and weight-related behaviors.

When working with eating disordered individuals, a treatment team is important because the psychological issues involved in the client's eating and exercise patterns are so intertwined. The nutrition therapist needs therapeutic backup and must be in regular contact with the therapist and other members of the team.

Sometimes eating disordered clients, in the effort to avoid psychotherapy altogether, will call a registered dietitian first, instead of a psychotherapist and begin working with the R.D. when not concurrently in psychotherapy. All registered dietitians, including those who are also nutrition therapists should be aware of the eating disorder individuals need for psychotherapy and be able to guide the client to that knowledge, understanding, and commitment. Therefore, anyone working in the area of nutrition should have resources for psychotherapists and physicians skilled in treating eating disorders to whom the client can be referred.

SPECIFIC TOPICS THAT NUTRITION THERAPISTS DISCUSS

Competent nutrition therapists should involve the client in a discussion of the following topics:

- What kind and how much food the client's body needs
- Symptoms of starvation and of re-feeding (the process of beginning to eat normally after a period of starvation)
- Effects of fat and protein deficiency
- Effects of laxative and diuretic abuse
- Metabolic rate and the effect of restricting, bingeing, purging, and yo-yo dieting
- Food facts and fallacies
- How restricting, bingeing, and taking laxatives or diuretics influence hydration (water) shifts in the body and thus body weight on the scale
- The relationship between diet and exercise
- The relationship of diet to osteoporosis and other medical conditions
- The extra nutritional needs during certain conditions such as pregnancy or illness
- The difference between "physical" and "emotional" hunger
- Hunger and fullness signals
- How to maintain weight
- Establishing a goal weight range
- How to feel comfortable eating in social settings
- How to shop and cook for self and/or significant others
- Nutritional supplement requirements

Finding and Choosing a Nutritionist

There are many things to consider when choosing a nutritionist to work with an eating disordered individual. It has already been mentioned that a registered dietitian is the safest bet to ensure adequate education and training in the biomechanics of nutrition. It has also been stated that those registered dietitians who are further trained in counseling skills and are called nutrition therapists are even a better choice. The yellow pages of the phone book, or The American Dietetic Association which has a Consumer Hotline at 1-800-366-1655 may be able to provide readers with the names and numbers of qualified individuals in the caller's area.

The problem is that many individuals do not live in an area where registered dietitians, much less nutrition therapists, are available. Therefore, it is important to consider other ways of finding competent individuals who can provide nutrition treatment. One way is to ask a trusted therapist, doctor, or friend for referrals. These individuals may know of someone who can provide nutrition counseling even though he or she does not fit the registered dietitian or nutrition therapist category. Occasionally other health professionals such as a nurse, medical doctor, or chiropractor are well trained in nutrition and even in eating disorders. In instances where a registered dietitian is not available these individuals may be useful and should not necessarily be excluded from consideration. However, it is not always true that some help is better than no help. Misinformation is worse than no information. Whether or not the person being consulted to provide the nutritional aspect of treatment is a dietitian or a nurse, it is important to ask questions and gather information to gather in order to determine if they are qualified for the position of working as a nutritionist with an eating disordered individual.

Interviewing a Nutritionist

Interviewing a nutritionist over the phone or in person is a good way to obtain information regarding his or her credentials, special expertise, experience, and philosophy. It is important to keep the following considerations in mind:

An effective nutrition therapist should:

- Be comfortable working with a treatment team
- Be in regular contact with the therapist
- Know skilled therapists and be able to refer the client to one if necessary
- Understand that the treatment of eating disorders takes time and patience
- Know how to provide effective interventions without a meal plan
- Know how to address hunger and satiety issues
- Be able to address body image concerns

An effective nutrition therapist should not:

- Simply provide a meal plan
- Give and expect a client to follow a rigid meal plan
- Indicate the client will not need therapy
- Tell a client they will lose weight as they normalize eating behaviors
- Shame the client on any level
- Encourage a client to lose weight
- Suggest that certain foods are fattening, forbidden, addictive and should be avoided
- Support a diet of less than 1,200 calories

Karin Kratina, R.D., is a nutrition therapist specializing in eating disorders. She believes that dietitians who work with eating disorders should be nutrition therapists but also recognizes that this is not always possible. She has provided questions to ask a professional for nutritional counseling. Karen has also provided the response she would give to each question to help the reader better understand what kind of knowledge, philosophy, and response to look for.

QUESTIONS TO ASK AND ANSWERS TO LOOK FOR WHEN INTERVIEWING A NUTRITIONIST

1. Question: *Could you describe your basic philosophy in treating eating disorders?*

Response: *I believe that food is not the problem but a symptom of the problem. I work with long term goals in mind and don't expect immediate changes in my clients. Over the course of time I will discover and challenge any distorted beliefs and unhealthy eating and exercise practices you have and it will be up to you to change them. I prefer to work in conjunction with a treatment team and stay in close communication with its members. The team usually includes a therapist and may include a psychiatrist, a medical doctor, and a dentist. If you (or proposed client) are not currently in therapy, I will provide feedback on the need for therapy, and if needed, refer you to someone who specializes in the treatment of eating disorders.*

2. Question: *How long could I expect to work with you?*

Response: *The length of time I work with any individual client varies significantly. What I usually do is discuss this with other members of the treatment team, as well as with the client to determine what the needs are. However, recovery from an eating disorder can take a significant amount of time. I have worked with clients briefly, especially if they have a therapist who is able to address food issues. I have also worked with clients for over two years. I could give you a better indication of the amount of time I would need to work with you after an initial assessment and a few sessions.*

3. Question: *Will you tell me exactly what to eat?*

Response: *Sometimes I develop meal plans for clients. In other cases, after the initial assessment, I find certain clients would be much better off without a specific meal plan. In those cases, I usually suggest other forms of structure to help clients move through their eating disorder. (Those who most desire a structured meal plan, for example, compulsive eaters, will benefit the least from them, while those who tend to prefer not to have a structured meal plan, such as anorexics, often benefit from them.)*

4. Question. *I want to lose weight, will you put me on a diet?*

Response: *This is a somewhat tricky question, because the appropriate response of, "No, I will not put you on a diet, I do not recommend that you try to lose weight now because it is counter productive to recovery from an eating disorder," will often result in a client choosing not to come back.*

(A favorable response should include information to the client that most often weight loss and recovery do not go hand in hand.) What I have found in my work with people with eating disorders is that diets often create problems and interfere with recovery. Dieting actually contributes to the development of eating disorders. I have found that "non hunger eating" is what usually causes people to gain weight, or makes it more difficult for them to reach their set point weight range.

5. Question: *On what kind of meal plan will you put me (my child, friend, and so on)?*

Response: *I try to work with a flexible meal plan that does not get caught up in calories or weighing and measuring food. Sometimes clients do better without meal plans. However, we can get specific if we need to do so. What is important is that there are no forbidden foods. This does not mean you have to eat all foods but we will explore and work on your relationship with different foods and the meaning they have for you.*

6. Question: *Do you work with hunger and fullness?*

Response: *Dealing with hunger and fullness are part of my job. Usually clients who have eating disorders or have a long history of dieting tend to ignore their signals of hunger, and feelings or fullness are highly subjective. What I do is explore with you various signals that come from different areas of your body to determine exactly what hunger, fullness, satiety, and satisfaction mean to you. We can do things like use a graph on which you rate your hunger and your fullness so that we can "fine-tune" your knowledge of and ability to respond to your body's signals.*

7. Question: *Do you work in conjunction with a therapist or doctor? How often do you speak with them?*

Response: *Nutrition is only part of your treatment plan, psychotherapy and medical monitoring is another. If you do not have a professional in those other areas I can refer you to those with whom I work. If you already have your own I will work with them. I believe that communication is important with all of the members of your treatment team. I usually speak with the other treating professionals once a week for a period of time and then, if appropriate, reduce it to once a month. However, if your exercise or eating pattern changes significantly at any given time, I would contact the rest of the treatment team to inform the members and discuss with them what difficulties might be happening in other areas of your life.*

8. Question: *Do you now or have you ever received professional supervision from an eating disorder professional?*

Response: *Yes, I have received both training and supervision. I also continue to get supervision or consultation periodically.*

OTHER INFORMATION TO OBTAIN

1. Fees: If you are unable to afford the nutritionist's standard fee, can adjustments be made or a payment schedule be arranged?

2. Hours: Is the nutritionist able to schedule you at a convenient time? What is the policy regarding missed appointments?

3. Insurance: Does the nutritionist accept insurance? Will he or she help submit claims to an insurance company?

WHAT TO AVOID

Individuals with eating disorders often go into the field of nutrition as a result of their own obsession with food, calories, and weight. Any nutritionist should be assessed for signs of eating disordered thinking or behavior including "fat phobia." Many individuals with eating disorders are fat phobic. If the nutritionist is also fat phobic, nutrition therapy will be negatively affected.

Fat phobia can refer to dietary fat or body fat. Many people are afraid of eating fat and of being fat and this fear creates a negative attitude toward food with a fat content of any kind and fat people. The existence of fat makes these fat phobic individuals fear the prospect of losing control and becoming fat. The prevailing cultural attitude is that fat is bad and fat people should change. Unfortunately, many nutritionists have perpetuated fat phobia. When discussing body size and weight, individuals should look for a nutritionist who does not use a chart to determine a client's proper weight. The nutritionist should discuss the fact that people come in all shapes and sizes and there is no one weight that is a perfect body weight. Clients should be discouraged by the nutritionist from trying to make their bodies conform to a certain selected weight but rather encouraged to accept that if they give up bingeing, purging, and starving, and learn how to properly nourish themselves, their body will reach its natural weight. However, avoid a nutritionist who thinks natural eating alone will always restore a person to a normal, healthy weight. For example, in the case of anorexia nervosa, an excessive amount of calories, beyond what is considered normal eating, is necessary for the anorexic to gain weight. It may take as many as 4,500 calories or more per day to begin weight gain in severely emaciated individuals. Anorexics must be helped to see that in order to get well they need to gain weight, which will require an excessive amount of calories and they will need specific help in how to get those calories into their diet. After weight restoration a return to more normal eating will sustain weight but a higher calorie level than individuals without a history of anorexia is usually required. Binge eaters who become obese from bingeing and who desire to return to their more normal weight, may have to eat a diet that is lower in calories than the amount originally needed to sustain their pre-bingeing weight. It is important to reiterate that these circumstances as well as all areas involved in the nutritional treatment of eating disorders require special expertise taking into account a variety of circumstances.

How Often Do Clients Need to See a Nutritionist?

How often a client will need to see the nutrition therapist is based upon a number of factors and is best determined with input from the therapist, the client, and other significant members of the treatment team. In some cases only intermittent contact is maintained throughout recovery as the psychotherapist and client deem necessary. In other cases continuous contact is maintained and the nutritionist and psychotherapist work together throughout the recovery process.

Usually clients will meet with a nutrition therapist once a week for a thirty minute to sixty minute session, but this is highly variable. In certain instances a client may want to meet with a nutritionist two or three times a week for fifteen minutes each time, or, especially as recovery progresses, sessions can be spread out to every other week, once a month, or even once every six months as a checkup, and then on an as-needed basis.

Models of Nutrition Treatment

Listed below are various treatment models that can be used with eating disordered clients depending upon the severity of the clients illness and on the training and expertise of both the nutritionist and the psychotherapist.

Food Plan Only Model
This involves a one, or two-session consultation where an assessment is made, specific questions are answered, and an individual food plan is designed.

Education Only Model
The nutritionist meets with the client six to ten times discussing various issues in order to meet the following five objectives:

1) Collect a detailed history with relevant information in order to:

- Determine the variety of and quantity of weight loss and disordered eating behaviors

187

- Determine nutrient amount and intake patterns
- Identify effect of behaviors on client's lifestyle
- Develop treatment plans and goals

2) Establish a collaborative, empathic relationship.

3) Define and discuss principles of food, nutrition, and weight regulation, for example:

- Symptoms and bodily responses to starvation
- Metabolic shifts and responses
- Hydration (water balance in the body)
- Normal and abnormal hunger
- Minimum food intake to stabilize weight and metabolic rate
- How food and weight-related behaviors change during recovery
- Optimal food intake
- Set point

4) Present hunger and intake patterns (calories included) of recovered persons.

5) Educate the family on meal planning, nutrient needs, and effects of starvation and other eating disorder behaviors. Strategies for dealing with food and weight-related behaviors should be done in conjunction with the psychotherapist.

THE EDUCATION/BEHAVIOR CHANGE MODEL

This model necessitates that the nutritionist has special training and experience in treating eating disorders.

Education Phase: This comes first and early in treatment (see education model above).

Behavior Change or Experimental Phase: The second, or experimental, phase of this model begins only when the client is ready to work on changing food and weight-related behaviors. Sessions with the nutritionist are intended to be the forum for planning strategies for behavior change, thus freeing psychotherapy sessions for exploration of psychological issues. The primary objectives are:

1) Separate food and weight-related behaviors from feelings and psychological issues.

2) Change food-related behaviors *slowly* until intake patterns are normalized. Behavior change is most effective when coupled with education. Treatment must be individualized and not over-simplified. Clients will need constant explanation, clarification, reiteration, repetition, reassurance and encouragement. Topics that will need to be covered include:

- being purge free or eating better for months does not mean recovery
- setbacks are normal and are learning opportunities
- self-monitoring techniques should be chosen and used carefully
- target specific medical or cosmetic concerns first (results are easier to see)
- make changes little by little

3) Slowly increase or decrease weight. Proceeding too quickly may cause the client to become defensive and withdraw.

4) Learn to maintain a healthy weight without abnormal or destructive behaviors.

5) Learn to be comfortable in social eating situations (usually in later stages of recovery). Changes in social eating habits can be directly related to eating and weight issues but can also be due to relationship difficulties in general. (Refusing to eat may be a way of controlling the family or avoiding abuse or embarrassment.)

NUTRITIONAL SUPPLEMENTATION AND EATING DISORDERS

It is common sense to assume that individuals who restrict or purge their food may have specific nutrient deficiencies. There has even been some question and research as to whether certain deficiencies existed before the development of the eating disorder. If it were determined that certain deficiencies predisposed, or in some way contributed, to the development of eating disorders this would be valuable information for treatment and prevention. Regardless of which came first, nutritional deficiencies should not be overlooked or undertreated and correcting them must be considered a part of an overall treatment plan.

The area of nutrient supplementation is a controversial one even in the general population and even more so for eating disordered individuals. First of all, it is difficult to determine specific nutrient deficiencies in individuals. Second, it is important not to impart to clients that they can get better by the supplementation of vitamins and minerals instead of the necessary food and calories. It is common for clients to take vitamins, trying to make up for their inadequate intake of food. Vitamin and mineral supplements should be recommended only in addition to the recommendation of an adequate amount of food.

However, if supplements will be consumed by clients, especially when adequate food is not, the least that can be said is that clinicians may be able to prevent certain medical complications by prudently suggesting their use. A multi-vitamin supplement, calcium, essential fatty acids, and trace minerals may be useful for eating disordered individuals. Protein drinks which also contain vitamins and minerals (not to mention calories) can be used as supplements when inadequate amounts of food and nutrients are not being consumed. A professional should be consulted regarding these matters. For an example of how future research in the area of specific nutrients may be important in the understanding and treatment of eating disorders, the following section on the relationship of zinc deficiency to appetite disturbance and eating disorders has been included.

ZINC AND EATING DISORDERS

A deficiency of the mineral zinc in eating disorder patients has been reported by several researchers. It is a little-known fact that a deficiency in the mineral zinc actually causes loss of taste acuity (sensitivity) and appetite. In other words, zinc deficiency may contribute directly to reducing the desire to eat, enhancing or perpetuating a state of anorexia. What may start out as a diet motivated from a desire, whether reasonable or not, to lose weight accompanied with a natural desire to eat, may turn into a physio-logical desire not to eat, or some variation on this theme.

Several investigators, including Alex Schauss, Ph.D., and Carolyn Costin, M.A., M.F.C.C., who coauthored a book, *Zinc and Eating Disorders* have discovered that through a simple taste test reported years ago in the English medical journal, the *Lancet*, most anorexics, and many bulimics, seem to be zinc deficient. Furthermore, when these same individuals were supplemented with a certain specific solution containing liquid zinc, many experienced positive results and, in some cases, even remission of eating disorder symptoms. More research needs to be done in this area, but until then it seems fair to say that zinc supplementation looks promising and, if done wisely and under the supervision of a physician may provide a sub-stantial benefit with no harm. For more information on this topic, consult the Schauss and Costin book, which is to be re-released in fall 1996 in a new edition by Keats Publishing. This material explores nutritional supplementation for eating disorders and specif-ically how zinc is known to affect eating behavior, how to determine if one is zinc deficient, and various reported results of zinc supple-mentation in cases of anorexia nervosa and bulimia nervosa.

14

THE PSYCHIATRIST'S ROLE AND MEDICATION

THE PSYCHIATRIST

A psychiatrist, knowledgeable about eating disorders, is an integral part of the treatment team. Psychiatrists are medical doctors trained in the use of mind-altering medications who can perform psychotherapy and prescribe drugs. Depending on their preference, psychiatrists perform psychotherapy, prescribe medication, or both.

A psychiatrist can be brought in as part of a treatment team at any time, but is usually consulted in the beginning as part of assessment, diagnosis, and treatment. A dietitian or therapist working with a client may decide that additional help is needed and a referral for medication that affects mental functioning is warranted. As with all professionals, it is important that the psychiatrist have experience in treating eating disorders and is understanding of the complexity and special needs of this population. Aside from this, there are other things to look for when choosing a psychiatrist.

A psychiatrist:

1. Should be willing to work collaboratively as part of a treatment team.

2. Should not be too quick to suggest, or rely upon, medication particularly when other methods have not been tried and nutritional rehabilitation has not been started.

3. Should communicate regularly with other members of the treatment team.

4. Should clearly explain the expected benefits of any medication prescribed and its side effects.

5. Should be empathic and understanding toward the patient.

6. Should be board certified or board eligible.

7. Should be able to discuss the current research and trends in eating disorder treatment.

8. Should communicate regularly with family members when appropriate.

9. Should clearly spell out all policies regarding fees, emergencies, paging procedures, cancellation policies, what to do in case of problematic medication reactions, and other issues.

The psychiatrist is a valuable treatment team member, if not the leader of the team. Whether or not medication is being prescribed, the psychiatrist can add another dimension and perspective to evaluation and treatment, ideally one that is integrative in nature. Psychiatrists should have an understanding of the biological aspects of eating disorders and other medical or psychological disorders that go along with them. Psychiatrists treating eating disorder patients should keep updated in the field of assessment and treatment with mind-altering medications for eating and related disorders.

THE PSYCHIATRIST AS PART OF A TREATMENT TEAM

It is vital that therapists, psychiatrists, and other physicians or treatment team members working with an eating disorder patient have a good working relationship with each other. Clinicians need to work as a team, giving patients and significant others the same or similar input. Release forms should be obtained from the patient so that all parties may contact each other to discuss the case on an ongoing basis.

The therapist and physician (hereafter used to refer to both the psychiatrist and the medical doctor) must work together and with input from the team on the treatment approach, including what they expect from the patient, the kind of diet and exercise advice to be given, the need for supplements, recommendations to the parents, and criteria for hospitalization. If the therapist and physician are not working together, with the same goals, the patient hears different messages and uses this as an excuse not to listen to anyone because, "No one really knows what is best." Patients may think, "They can't even agree on what to do so why should I listen to them?" In order not to undermine what one another says or does, clinicians must remain in constant contact with each other regarding the patient.

Communicating frequently is important even if it takes extra work, because someone, especially if he/she hasn't had experience with eating disorder patients, may unknowingly make statements that are counterproductive or contrary to the others' treatment. An example of this counterproductiveness happened when the physician of a seventeen-year-old anorexic patient told her parents that they needed to "lay down the law" and should not allow her to have any kind of diet foods like nonfat milk, diet soda, or low-fat dinners, and that she must gain 2 pounds per week. This was in contradiction to what the therapist was telling the family and the patient.

It is difficult for a therapist or family member to tell a physician that he or she has done something wrong or is negating other treatment taking place. Even when this is discussed, the physician may disagree. In the example above, the proof may come when the patient will not do what the physician has suggested anyway and it is realized that there is much more to treatment than simply "laying down the law." In other conflicts, the physician may appropriately prescribe a necessary hospitalization to a reluctant therapist or naive parents. In any case, the physician, therapist, and all members of a treatment team should communicate and work closely together to avoid adding unnecessary confusion, difficulties, delays, or doubts to the already complex problems patients have.

MEDICATION

Dr. Arnold Anderson, a leading researcher in the field of eating disorders, said at a lecture on medication and eating disorders, "To every complex problem there is a simple answer . . . . and it's wrong." People would like to find a simple answer to the complex problem of eating disorders and, in looking, have gone down the "Isn't there medication for this?" path. The use of psychotropic (mind-altering) medication, otherwise known as "pharmacotherapy" or "psychopharmacology," may indeed play a significant role in the treatment of some cases of eating disorders, but it has not proven by any means to be a cure. Pharmacotherapeutic solutions are sought for a variety of clinical challenges presented by individuals with eating disorders; these are summarized below.

POSSIBLE USES OF PHARMACOTHERAPY IN EATING DISORDER TREATMENT

1. Other coexisting psychiatric conditions (along with the eating disorder)

2. Weight restoration or loss

3. Normalize thinking processes

4. Induce/reduce hunger, increase/decrease satiety

5. Reduce sensitivity to stress

6. Relapse prevention

A high degree of other psychiatric disorders and conditions (called psychiatric comorbidity) exists in eating disordered individuals. Anorexics and bulimics are commonly diagnosed with anxiety disorders, including social phobia, panic disorder, obsessive-compulsive disorder (OCD), or post-traumatic stress disorder (PTSD). Other common diagnoses include depression, substance abuse, and borderline personality disorder. These coexisting diagnoses would seem to suggest pharmacotherapy as a feasible treatment response. The crucial question, however, is, "Which came first, the eating disorder or the comorbid (coexisting) psychiatric condition?" In some cases, nutritional rehabilitation and weight restoration alone have been enough to eliminate obsessive-compulsive behavior and depression, whereas in others, they are not. Ideally, the use of medication should be tried only after nutritional rehabilitation has been initiated.

However, this presents the proverbial "Catch 22" when nutritional rehabilitation cannot be accomplished, such as in a recalcitrant anorexic, and the treating professionals often search for medication to help accomplish that goal. Under these circumstances, trial and error and more trial seem to be the order of the day.

Frustrated researchers became excited when studies on bulimia nervosa indicated that it may be closely related to mood disorders, particularly depression. Some researchers reported that as many as 80 percent of the bulimic patients studied had major mood disorders at some point during their lives. There was also a high incidence in their family histories. This led to the argument that heredity and genetics play a major role in depression and bulimia nervosa and that both could be the result of the same type of biological disorder that runs in families. Further convincing evidence showed up in the treatment response, since a high percentage of bulimics responded positively to antidepressant medication even when not depressed.

The use of pharmacological agents in the treatment of eating disorders is undergoing increasing exploration and research and will most likely be a continuing factor in the treatment of a variety of eating disorder components. However, when reviewing studies on the effectiveness of certain medications, it is important to keep in mind that not just effectiveness but comparative effectiveness with other drugs or techniques, as well as side effects, must be considered. For example, studies using fluoxetine (Prozac) with bulimia nervosa have shown a high degree of effectiveness; however, cognitive behavioral therapy shows a greater degree of effectiveness with fewer side effects and longer lasting results! Most experts and treatment programs tend to use a combination of the two. Additionally, medications which can cause weight gain, such as clomipramine (Anafranil), used for obsessive-compulsive disorder, or lithium, used for manic depression, may backfire when the individual becomes even more restrictive with eating, loses trust, and becomes noncompliant with the medication. Other medications, such as naltrexone (Trexan), an opiate antagonist that eliminates the euphoric effects of opioids used with addicts and alcoholics to curb cravings and reduce the beneficial "high" they get from their drugs, have shown promise in the treatment of eating disorders, especially anorexia nervosa. Controlled studies are now underway. Medications used to influence hunger and satiety have been ineffective overall in treating anorexia nervosa and bulimia nervosa, partly due to side effects. However, a combination of medications (phentermine and fenfluramine) used to decrease hunger and food cravings facilitates weight loss in obese individuals and binge eaters and has recently shown promising results. These medications also have side effects but, more importantly, when the medication is stopped, the weight lost is often regained.

As far as treating cognitive behavioral disturbances, there are certain drugs that can help improve thought processes and clear thinking. These include a wide variety ranging from antianxiety agents, such as alprazolam (Xanax), to medicine for attention deficit hyperactivity disorder, such as methylphenidate (Ritalin), to antipsychotic (also known as neuroleptic) medications for hallucinations or delusional thinking such as risperdone (Risperdal) or haloperidol (Haldol).

Various medications such as neuroleptics or antianxiety agents are used to reduce sensitivity to stress and resultant anxiety, such as alprazolam (Xanax), klonazepam (Klonopin), and lorazepam (Ativan). These can work well in the short term for general anxiety, provide immediate relief, and may have some usefulness as premeal agents to alleviate distress associated with eating. However, these agents do not successfully treat the core issues of an eating disorder and are usually best used in conjunction with antidepressants, which also reduce anxiety and sensitivity to stress.

The role of medication in preventing relapse has become increasingly more interesting and promising with information from the newest studies, particularly those involving anorexia nervosa, which will be discussed below. The following material will summarize the current information on the use of medication in treating various eating disorders.

THE MEANING OF MEDICINE

Aside from the possible direct beneficial and adverse effects of medication of any kind, there is the important issue of what taking medication means or symbolizes to any given individual. The act of taking mind-altering medication symbolizes different things to different people, but commonly it means that "I'm sick" or "defective" or "imperfect" or "bad" or "crazy" or "out of control." Since issues of control and self-worth are already predominant in people with eating disorders, often this becomes an obstacle to effective treatment, particularly in cases with significant coexisting problems, and even in cases in which medications have clearly proved effective. When patients with eating disorders begin to feel better, they frequently want to stop the medicine(s) when it may be an important reason why they are better. This only ends up contributing to the already high relapse rate in eating and related disorders. Patients need help in understanding that medication is best thought of as a powerful tool that a person with an eating disorder can choose to use in the struggle for full recovery.

ANEXORIA NERVOSA AND MEDICATION

Despite what many think, anorexia nervosa has so far been shown to be relatively resistant to treatment with drugs. Many medicines have been tried for various reasons, with a report here and there about the effectiveness of a certain medicine in certain cases, but overall none have been shown in controlled studies to have any particular effectiveness with the core issues of anorexia nervosa. Even tetrahydrocannabinol (marijuana) was clinically tried in hopes of stimulating appetite (causing the "munchies") but it produced only unhappy moods instead.

Recently, however, a breakthrough has occurred that was reported by Dr. Walter Kaye at the International Association of Eating Disorder Professionals conference in August 1995 (from the University of Pittsburgh, Western Psychiatric Clinic and Institute). The breakthrough was discovered in a controlled medication trial of fluoxetine (Prozac) with anorexics. Prozac, and less so Zoloft and Paxil, are the most commonly known of the group of antidepressants referred to as selective serotonin reuptake inhibitors (SSRIs). Until recently even these medications, the drugs of choice for the treatment of bulimia nervosa, were falling short with anorexia nervosa. However, according to Walter Kaye, the newest research shows that fluoxetine (Prozac) did show significant results in anorexia, but with a crucial difference in how it was used. When administered after nutritional rehabilitation and weight restoration, fluoxetine showed significant advantages over a placebo in preventing the all-too-common relapse. This appears to work by the drug's causing a significant reduction in obsessions and compulsions related to food and body image. More research needs to be done, but for now it seems that initially behavioral and nutritional therapy should be the foundation of treatment for anorexia nervosa, with the use of fluoxetine and perhaps even other SSRIs as an adjunct to prevent relapse.

BULIMIA NERVOSA AND MEDICATION

As with anorexia nervosa, many of the same medications have been tried with bulimia nervosa with little or limited success. The exception has been antidepressant agents, which have shown promise since the 1980s. Antidepressant medication doesn't work for everyone, some patients (about 20 to 33 percent) have complete remission of symptoms, and others have significant reductions in cravings to binge, purge, and engage in other bulimic behaviors.

The class of antidepressants known as the SSRIs, discussed above, such as Prozac, Zoloft, and so on, are the newer versions of antidepressants since the original tricyclics and MAOIs (monoamise oxidase inhibitors). Tricyclics such as desiprimine, imiprimine, and nortriptyline showed effectiveness but had many side effects, such as weight gain, which were not well tolerated by eating disorder patients. Additionally, tricyclic overdose is the third leading cause of death in emergency rooms, and as such is extremely dangerous in depressed patients, the very ones it most effectively treats. The lethality of tricyclic overdose is only enhanced by the medical effects of eating disorders, especially lowered potassium in the body.

The MAOIs include tranylcypromine (Parnate) and phenelzine (Nardil) and show efficacy in reducing bulimic symptoms. However, individuals taking MAOIs must be on a very restrictive low tyrosine (an amino acid) diet which, if broken, can cause a hypertensive crisis (very high blood pressure, possibly resulting in serious side effects such as stroke or death). More than any other type of medication, the SSRIs have been shown to decrease the core bulimic symptoms of depression, poor regulation of hunger and satiety, sensitivity to stress, and obsessive thinking and behavior, without undue side effects. For more information on SSRIs and their side effects, refer to the section below describing the psychotropic medications most commonly used in eating disorders.

BINGE EATING DISORDER (BED) AND MEDICATION

As has been previously stated, the research on BED is minimal, but growing. However, several clinicians believe that binge eating is less a matter of willpower than brain chemistry. In some cases, clinicians and researchers are using SSRIs with binge eating disorder for the same reasons they use it for bulimia. Serotonin helps us feel full, so it is theorized that people with binge eating disorder may want to eat all the time because they have too little of the neurotransmitter serotonin and thus never feel satisfied (satiated).

A newer and increasingly popular combination of fenfluramine and phentermine is currently being prescribed to overweight individuals as an antibinge, appetite suppressant, and weight loss medication. Fenfluramine increases serotonin activity and has been shown to be helpful in increasing satiety, but also may cause people to feel sleepy and slowed down. Phentermine affects norepinephrine and dopamine, other neurotransmitters, and acts as a stimulant and appetite suppressant, countering sleepiness. One study conducted by Dr. Michael Weintraub and researchers at the University of Rochester Medical School reported that dieters who took fenfluramine with phentermine lost an average of nearly 16 percent of their body weight in thirty-four weeks. This was more than three times as much as the control group not taking the drugs. This study and others indicate promising short-term results but nothing about the long-term effects. In fact, current data suggests that these medications need to be continued for the weight loss to remain, and yet no one knows the results of long-term use. Many patients have diarrhea, headaches, nausea, and dry mouth and do not tolerate these medications well, while others either don't have these side effects, learn to tolerate them, or experience them only temporarily in the beginning. On the other hand, side effects such as hypertension may be a serious and even fatal problem with phentermine. A physical exam and periodic blood work should be required of anyone wishing to take this medication. In summary, although the results are encouraging, long-term results and side effects of the combination of fenfluramine and phentermine are unknown, and may or may not outweigh the very real medical risks of obesity.

GUIDELINES FOR WHEN TO USE ANTIDEPRESSANT MEDICATIONS

1. After nutritional rehabilitation has begun

2. After full patient history and medical evaluation is complete

3. After full family history and evaluation

4. After review of valid, reliable, published data-based trials

5. After/with psychotherapy

6. When antidepressant-responsive coexisting conditions are clearly identified, particularly when they predate the onset of the eating disorder

PSYCHOTROPIC MEDICATIONS COMMONLY USED IN EATING DISORDERS

ANTIDEPRESSANTS

Selective Serotonin Reuptake Inhibitors: Easily tolerated, readily absorbed after oral intake. May cause gastric irritation. Price range $1.50–$2.00 per pill. Low risk of suicidal overdose with these medications. Used for obsessive-compulsive behaviors, depression, and anxiety, and may have the effect of decreasing binge behavior in higher doses when used in bulimics or binge eaters. May cause further weight loss and appetite loss in anorexics. Risks versus benefits will have to be carefully assessed, given that SSRIs may diminish obsessive, rigid thinking and ritualistic behavior traits. Not to be used in pregnancy, particularly first trimester, unless absolutely necessary. This class of medications is not addicting but there may be side effects with abrupt withdrawal of Paxil and Zoloft. Gradual tapering is recommended. Drug interactions do occur. Monoamine oxidase inhibitors cannot be used within two weeks of SSRIs. Generally this extends five to eight weeks after discontinuation of Prozac.

Most common side effects: anxiety, nervousness, insomnia, agitation, fatigue, drowsiness, sweating, tremor, anorexia (loss of appetite), diarrhea, dizziness, lightheadedness, sexual dysfunction, and decreased libido.

Examples of general dosing:

Prozac (fluoxetine)   10–80 mg a day

Zoloft (sertraline)   25–200 mg a day

Paxil (paroxetine)   10–50 mg a day

Luvox (fluvoxamine)   (approved for OCD) 50–300 mg a day

Serzone (nefazodone) 100–600 mg a day

Tricyclics: Reduces depression and may diminish bingeing behaviors. Generally cause increased appetite and weight gain. Have more side effects than SSRIs. Much lower threshold for use in suicide attempt, as they significantly affect heart function in higher doses.

Commonly used in overdose attempts. Generally cause more seda- tion than SSRIs. Much cheaper than SSRIs. Rapidly absorbed from the stomach. Certain medications may increase blood levels without actual increase in dose. This may place the person at increased risk for side effects or inadvertent overdose. Can cause side effects with abrupt discontinuation. Tapering is recommended; just as with SSRIs, don't use with MAO inhibitors. Therapeutic blood levels can be ben- eficial. Cost: approximately $30.00 per one hundred 100 mg tabs.

Common side effects: constipation, blurry vision, urinary hesi- tancy, can affect cardiac function, weight gain, increased appetite, and may decrease libido.

Examples of general dosing:

Desipramine   100–300 mg

Nortriptyline   (similar to Desipramine) 50–150 mg a day

Combination Serotonin-Norepinephrine Reuptake Inhibitor: A new antidepressant, venlafaxine (Effexor) has not yet been shown to be of value in eating disorders, but theoretically it should. Weight gain or loss may occur, with corresponding alteration in appetite. There is no clear advantage over SSRIs in regard to side effects. In fact, it may have a more stimulating effect. This drug does tend overall to have fewer side effects than the tricyclics. Lower suicide potential for overdose than tricyclics but may be higher than SSRIs.

Common side effects:
nausea and rises in blood pressure.

Examples of general dosing:
37.5 mg two times a day to 300 mg a day total (in two divided doses)

MOOD STABILIZERS
Used primarily for mood stabilization in bipolar (manic depressive) disorder or mood swings. May help stabilize mood instability in per- sons with borderline personality organization and various disorders of brain function. Can sometimes be used as augmentors in individ- uals who are not responding to antidepressants.

Depakote/valproic acid derivatives: Primary use is as anticonvulsant. May cause liver failure as more severe side effect. Can be fatal. General dosage range 500–2,000 mg. Causes less weight gain than lithium, but more than Tegretol. Blood serum levels must be checked. Gastrointestinal side effects may occur. Toxic levels can be fatal.

Tegretol: Anticonvulsant. Worse side effect aplastic anemia. Can be fatal, but rare (1 in 50,000). Gastrointestinal side effects do occur. Blood levels must be checked. Causes less weight gain than lithium and Depakote. Toxic levels can be fatal. Dose range 200–2,000 mg.

Lithium salt: May cause weight gain, acne, retention of water, hypothyroidism, excessive secretion of urine, excessive thirst. Replacement of water loss is essential or toxicity will occur. Toxic levels will kill and are more likely with decreased potassium. Patients generally will not use if aware of risk of weight gain. Dose range 600–3,000 mg in eating disordered clients. Probably should be avoided in eating disorders due to lithium toxicity associated with low potassium and dehydration.

ANTIANXIETY MEDICATIONS

Generally benign in regard to side effects, but have significant effects in overdose. Most important concern is addiction potential. Short-term use is acceptable and long-term use sometimes necessary in severe anxiety disorders not responsive to SSRIs. In order of most to least addicting: Xanax, Ativan, Klonopin (most commonly used).

Examples of general dosing:

Xanax	.25–1 mg (lower dose two to four times per day)
Ativan	.5–2.0 mg two to four times per day as needed
Klonopin	.25–1.0 mg two to four times per day

NEW RESEARCH IN THE AREA OF BIOLOGICAL TREATMENT

PHOTOTHERAPY

Eating disorder symptoms have been reported to fluctuate across the seasons. Most strikingly, individuals with bulimia nervosa have features in common with people with seasonal affective disorder (SAD), or winter depression. Recent preliminary data indicate that light therapy (phototherapy) may help to decrease bulimic as well as depressive symptoms. Light is thought to act like a drug by enhancing normal serotonin function. This approach may be an important adjunct to treatment in certain patients. *Winter Blues*, by Norman Rosenthal, is a resource for more information.

ASSESSING AND PRESCRIBING MEDICATION USING QUANTITATIVE ELECTROENCEPHALOGRAPHY

This chapter cannot conclude without discussing a new, innovative, and controversial approach to the diagnosis and treatment of the underlying biochemical individuality that may play a part in the origins of eating disorders.

As has been stated elsewhere, some researchers propose that disordered eating behaviors, specifically anorexia and bulimia, are a type of obsessive-compulsive disorder, mood disorder, anxiety disorder, or addictive disorder. In general, antidepressants are most frequently recommended with the hope that mood, anxiety, appetite, impulse control, and attitudes about eating will improve or normalize. Antidepressants most often recommended include certain tricyclic antidepressants, selective serotonin reuptake inhibitors, and monoamine oxidase inhibitors.

It is clear that the present behavior-based system of medical prescribing is inconsistently or only partially effective. The controversy surrounding what role medicine should have in disordered eating behaviors, and the inconsistent treatment outcomes in various studies, is due to the lack of a physiologic marker in clinical practice by which to make objective medical treatment decisions.

In no other branch of medicine is the physician expected to perform accurate diagnosis and treatment without objective biophysical measurement of organ function. Cardiologists have EKG and cardiac function tests; family practice physicians, pediatricians, and internists have pulmonary, gastric, kidney, and liver function tests. (Of course, normal functioning of these organs is necessary for normal brain function and therefore may be of interest to the psychiatrist.)

Current psychiatric practice relies on patient history and interview, general medical laboratory tests, and rating scales or psychological performance tests to sort patients into different behavioral and syndromal classifications. Medication is based on this sorting system, despite the fact that there is an inconsistent correlation between psychiatric behavioral diagnoses and responses to medications prescribed. Lacking an objective test of brain function, psychiatrists currently prescribe on the basis of existing scientific studies of large groups of subjects. If there is no data available, a trial-and-error basis is used for patients with disordered eating behaviors with the eventual expectation of achieving positive results; for example, symptom reduction and relief.

Following an initial psychiatric consultation, one or two medicine trials usually require from four to twelve weeks to determine compatibility and responsivity. Some medicine trials take months to a year or two, and others are endless in nonresponsive patients. The endurance of problems and side effects in sequential medicine trials requires considerable patience on the part of both doctor and patient. A demand for more accurate medical treatments and better outcomes has stimulated the search for physiologic markers that guide treatment. Research in progress in the field of biological psychiatry suggests that a physiologic marker may be able to be detected through brain-wave measurement techniques that would indicate what, if any, medication is indicated for an individual.

NEUROMETRIC ANALYSIS AS A MARKER FOR PRESCRIBING MEDICINE

In 1986 physicians at the NeuroPharmacologic Institute began to explore quantitative electroencephalography (QEEG) as a tool to understand brain function in psychiatry. They were interested in identifying brain-wave features that would correlate with responsivity to different types of psychiatric medicines. It was believed by these physicians that among the objective physiologic technologies available, the neurometric method of quantitative electroencephalography (QEEG) appeared as the most practical functional test because it was safe (noninvasive), included a large, well-replicated normal database, had a potential for broad distribution, and was easily adapted to a variety of clinical settings.

The physicians at the NeuroPharmacologic Institute set up a rigorously controlled EEG/QEEG laboratory and initially tested treatment-resistant and nonresponsive patients. By keeping precise computerized records, they correlated patients' clinical histories, diagnoses, ineffective and effective medicines taken, and QEEG brain-wave features.

In a retrospective study of patients with attentional disorders and mood disorders, these physicians found that responsivity to medicine type correlated more closely with QEEG brain-wave features than with clinical diagnoses. From this data, they were able to identify several QEEG brain-wave features that responded to different types of medicine. Different brain-wave frequencies are labeled alpha, delta, theta, and so on. For example, patients with excess frontal alpha frequency (eight to twelve cycles per second activity) responded to antidepressants, patients with excess frontal theta frequency (four to eight cycles per second activity) responded to stimulants, and patients with excess frequency coherence (synchrony) responded to anticonvulsants or lithium carbonate. These results were reported in the neurological literature, in the *Journal of Clinical Electroencephalography*, April 1995. The NeuroPharmacologic Institute currently is evaluating these medicine correlations in double-blind studies with the UCLA Department of Psychiatry and with other research institutions.

Additionally, trials which already indicate positive results are underway in conjunction with the Eating Disorder Center of California and the Monte Nido Residential Treatment Center for Eating Disorders, both located in Malibu, California.

As with any new technology, more research is required, and as the research develops, we will continue to see improvement in our ability to diagnose and treat the underlying biochemical and neurological predispositions in all individuals, including those with eating disorders.

This chapter has been devoted mainly to the use of psychotropic medication. Eating disordered individuals have coexisting medical conditions and symptoms which also benefit from medication.

The use of other types of medication in the treatment of eating disorders is certainly indicated for various medical complications which arise, but proper precautions must be taken. For example, prescribing hormone replacement therapy for an anorexic who has stopped menstruating may be a viable choice, with the precaution that there is no proof that the medication will prevent osteoporosis and taking it might even foster a false sense of security by masking the return of normal menstrual function. Another example would be prescribing laxatives for a bulimic complaining of constipation. On one hand this might be contraindicated, but with another individual it may be necessary, particularly if the person has become laxative dependent, in which case slowly weaning the individual off is a more likely scenario. The following chapter discusses these and other topics in the medical management of eating disorders, particularly anorexia and bulimia.

15

MEDICAL MANAGEMENT OF ANOREXIA NERVOSA AND BULIMIA NERVOSA

BY PHILIP S. MEHLER, M.D.

Note: This chapter is primarily geared toward professionals and discusses some of the extreme medical consequences and interventions used in the treatment of anorexia nervosa and bulimia nervosa. For interested parents and significant others, medical terms have been defined.

Of the entire gamut of psychological disorders treated by clinicians, anorexia nervosa and bulimia nervosa are the ones most frequently punctuated by accompanying medical complications. Although many of these are more annoying than serious, a distinct number of them are indeed potentially life threatening. The mortality rate for these disorders exceeds that found in any other psychiatric illness and approaches 20 percent in the advanced stages of anorexia nervosa. Thus, a clinician cannot simply assume that the physical symptoms associated with these eating disorders are just functional in origin. Physical complaints must be judiciously investigated and organic disease systematically excluded by appropriate tests. Conversely, it is important, from a treatment vantage point, to avoid subjecting the patient to expensive, unnecessary, and potentially invasive tests.

Competent and comprehensive care of eating disorders must involve understanding the medical aspects of these illnesses, not just for physicians but for any clinician treating them, regardless of discipline or orientation. A therapist must know what to look for, what certain symptoms might mean, and when to send a patient for an initial medical evaluation as well as for follow-up. A dietitian may be the team member who performs the nutrition evaluation instead of the physician, and he or she must have adequate knowledge of all medical/nutritional aspects of eating disorders. A psychiatrist may prescribe medication for an underlying mood or thought disorder and must coordinate this with the rest of the treatment.

In this chapter, the major medical complications inherent to these disorders will be described. Although there is clearly a continuum in the spectrum of physical illnesses encountered for anorexia and bulimia, with much clinical overlap, for the purpose of this chapter the discussions of anorexia and bulimia and their unique medical complications will be separated.

ANOREXIA NERVOSA

Most medical complications are a direct result of weight loss. There are a number of easily observable skin abnormalities which are seen including brittle nails, thinning hair, yellow-tinged skin, and a fine downy growth of hair on the face, back, and arms, which is referred to as lanugo hair. All of these changes revert to normal with weight restoration. There are other, more serious complications involving a variety of systems in the body.

GASTROINTESTINAL SYSTEM
The gastrointestinal tract is affected by the weight loss inherent to anorexia nervosa. There are two main issues in this regard.

Complaints of early satiety and abdominal pain. It has been shown by well-performed studies that transit time out of the stomach and through the digestive tract is significantly slowed in individuals with anorexia nervosa. This, in turn, can produce complaints of early satiety (fullness) and abdominal pain. Although it is clearly logical to surmise that such a complaint in this population may be part of the illness and represent an attempt to avoid the psychological pain of beginning to once again eat normally, there may clearly be an organic basis to this concern. A quality thorough physical examination and evaluation will be able to define the correct source of these complaints. If the complaints are truly organic and no metabolic cause is found to explain them, treatment with an agent that speeds emptying of the stomach should afford the patient relief; reducing the caloric load and rate of refeeding (beginning to eat normally after self-induced starvation) will also be therapeutic. These problems resolve with weight gain.

Complaints of constipation. Many anorexics are troubled by constipation, particularly early on in the refeeding process. This is in part attributable to the slowed gastrointestinal transit time described above. In addition, there is a reflex poor functioning of the colon secondary to a history of inadequate food intake. It is important to keep in mind that complaints of constipation are frequently due to a patient's false perception of what causes constipation. It is important to forewarn these patients from the outset that it normally may take three to six days for food to pass through the digestive system. Thus, it may be impractical to expect a bowel movement the first day after beginning to increase daily caloric intake. In addition to forewarning, it is important to educate patients about intake of adequate liquids and fiber as well as a judicious amount of walking, because the bowel becomes sluggish when an individual is sedentary. An extensive medical workup for constipation is generally unnecessary unless a series of abdominal examinations confirm obstruction and progressive distention (bloating).

CARDIOVASCULAR SYSTEM

Just as the other body systems are affected by weight loss, the cardiovascular system is also not spared. Severe weight loss causes thinning of the heart muscle fibers and a resultant diminished cardiac volume. As a result of this process, there is a reduction in maximal work capacity and aerobic capacity. A slowed heart rate (forty to sixty beats/minute) and low blood pressure (systolics of 70 to 90 mm Hg) are commonly found in these patients. These changes are not dangerous unless there is coexisting evidence of heart failure or an arrhythmia (irregular heartbeat). There is also an increased prevalence of a heart valve abnormality known as mitral valve prolapse. While generally benign and reversible with weight gain, it can produce palpitations, chest pain, and even arrhythmias.

One other cardiac concern is known as the refeeding syndrome. All malnourished patients are at risk for the refeeding syndrome when nutritional repletion is initiated. This syndrome was first described in survivors of concentration camps after World War II. There are multiple causes for this syndrome. The potential for starvation-induced low blood levels of phosphorus following intake of foods high in calories or glucose is one of the main causes of this sobering syndrome. Phosphorous depletion produces widespread abnormalities in the cardiorespiratory system, which can be fatal. In addition to phosphorous, the refeeding syndrome also evolves due to changes in potassium and magnesium levels. Further, abrupt blood volume expansion and inappropriately aggressive nutritional intake may place excessive strain on the shrunken heart and cause the inability of the heart to maintain adequate circulation.

The crucial issue when refeeding anorexic patients is to identify beforehand which patients may be at risk. Generally speaking, it is the severely emaciated, malnourished patient with prolonged starvation who is at risk for refeeding syndrome. However, in some cases, patients who have been deprived of nutrition for seven to ten days is potentially in this category. There are general guidelines to follow to avoid these problems. The overall general rule in adding calories is, "Start low, go slow." It is of extreme importance to monitor electrolytes during the refeeding period and to ensure that they are normal prior to the beginning of refeeding. In severe cases, particularly patients requiring hospitalization or tube feeding, checking electrolytes every two to three days for the first two weeks and then, if stable, decreasing the frequency seems wise. A supplement may be indicated to help avoid phosphorous depletion. From a clinical standpoint, following the pulse and respiratory rates for unexpected increases from the baseline as well as checking for fluid retention are a crucial part of the treatment plan in avoiding refeeding syndrome.

EKG abnormalities are also common in anorexia, such as sinus brachycardia (slow heart rate), which is usually not dangerous. However, some cardiac irregularities can be dangerous, for example, prolonged QT intervals (measurement of electrical impulses) and ventricular dysrhythmia (abnormal heart rhythms). Some have opined that a baseline EKG is therefore indicated to screen for these findings.

ENDOCRINE SYSTEM

Although not quite as dramatic, anorexia can have profound negative effects on the endocrine system. Two major areas are the cessation of menstrual periods and osteoporosis, both of which are physiologically interrelated. While the exact cause of the amenorrhea (lack of menstruation) is not known, low levels of the hormones involved in menstruation and ovulation are present in the setting of an inadequate body fat content. Clearly there is also an important contribution from the tenuous emotional state of these patients.

Reversion to the age-appropriate secretion of these hormones requires both weight gain and remission of the disorder. In the interim, if the amenorrhea persists for longer than six months, hormone replacement therapy is used empirically if there is no contraindications to its usage. This recommendation, along with an adequate intake of dietary calcium, is predicated on the increased risk of osteoporosis seen in patients with amenorrhea. Some studies suggest that the lost bone density may be irreversible. In case of prolonged amenorrhea, a referral should be made for medical follow-up and treatment planning.

HEMATOLOGICAL SYSTEM

Not infrequently, the hematological (blood) system is also affected by anorexia. Approximately one-third of individuals with anorexia nervosa have anemia and leukopenia (low white blood cell count). The relevance of this low white blood cell count for the functioning of the immune system of the patient with anorexia nervosa is controversial. Some studies have indeed found an increased risk of infection due to impaired cellular immune function.

In addition to the low white cell count, anorexic patients typically have low body temperature. Thus, the two traditional markers of infection, namely fever and a high white cell count, are often lacking in these patients. Therefore, there has to be heightened vigilance toward the possibility of an infectious process when these patients report some unusual symptom.

The hematological system is thus similar to other body systems that can be ravaged by anorexia nervosa. However, nutritional rehabilitation, if done in a timely and well-planned fashion, in concert with competent medical supervision, promotes a return to normal in all these systems.

Most anorexics can be treated as outpatients. Inpatient hospitalization is recommended for patients whose weight loss is rapidly progressive or whose weight loss is greater than 30 percent of ideal body weight, as well as for those with cardiac arrhythmias or symptoms of inadequate blood flow to the brain.

BULIMIA NERVOSA

Unlike anorexia nervosa, most of the medical complications of bulimia nervosa directly result from the different modes of purging utilized by these patients. It is functionally more understandable if the complications inherent to a particular mode of purging are reviewed separately.

SELF-INDUCED VOMITING

An early complication resulting from self-induced vomiting is parotid gland enlargement. This condition, referred to as sialadenosis, causes a round swelling near the area between the jawbone and the neck and in severe cases gives rise to the chipmunk-type faces seen in chronic vomiters. The reason for parotid swelling in bulimia has not been definitively ascertained. Clinically, in bulimic patients, it develops three to six days after a binge-purge episode has stopped. Generally, abstinence from vomiting is associated with the ultimate reversal of the parotid swelling. Other standard treatment modalities include heat applications to the swollen glands, salivary substitutes, and the use of agents that promote salivation, most commonly tart candies. In the majority of cases, these are effective interventions. For stubborn cases, an agent such as pilocarpine, may promote shrinking of the size of the glands. Rarely, parotidectomies (removal of the glands) have to be performed to alleviate this problem.

216

Another oral complication of self-induced vomiting is termed perimyolysis. This refers to erosion of the enamel on the surface of the teeth near the tongue which is presumably due to the presence of the acid in vomit which passes through the mouth. Patients who induce vomiting at a minimum frequency of three times per week for a year will show erosion of tooth enamel. Vomiting may also cause an increased incidence of dental cavities, inflammation of the gums, and other periodontal diseases. At the same time, a frequently voiced complaint of extreme sensitivity to cold or hot food is a result of exposed teeth dentin.

The proper dental hygiene for these patients is somewhat unclear. However, it is obvious that they need to be cautioned against immediately brushing their teeth after vomiting because it will hasten the erosion of the weakened enamel. Rather, rinsing with a neutralizing agent, such as baking soda, has been recommended. Patients should also be encouraged to seek regular dental treatment.

A potentially more serious complication of self-induced vomiting is the damage it causes to the esophagus. These patients complain of heartburn due to the stomach acid's irritant effect on the esophageal lining, which causes a condition known as esophagitis. Similarly, repeated exposure of the esophageal lining to the acidic stomach contents can result in the development of a precancerous lesion referred to as Barrett's esophagus. Another esophageal complication of vomiting presents as a history of vomiting bright red blood. This condition is known as a Mallory-Weiss tear, which is due to a tear in the mucosal lining.

Aside from encouraging the cessation of vomiting, the approach to complaints which involve dyspepsia (heartburn/sour taste in the mouth) or dysplagia (difficulty swallowing) is comparable to that utilized in the general population with these complaints. Initially, together with the recommendation to cease vomiting, the simple suggestion of antacids is offered. The second level of intervention involves drugs known as histamine antagonists, such as cimetidine, plus an agent that induces gastric contractions such as cisapride, to strengthen the gate between the stomach and the esophagus, which in turn prevents acidic contents from refluxing back and irritating the esophagus. Proton-pump-inhibitors that inhibit acid secretion in the stomach such as omeprazole, are the third line and most potent therapy for resistant cases. Generally, this will suffice for most patients and resolve their symptoms. The important point to be aware of is the potential harmful implications of severe and stubborn dyspepsia. Since resistant cases may be harbingers of a more serious process, referral to a gastroenterologist should be recommended so that an endoscopy can be performed and definitive diagnosis made.

One other important condition with regard to the esophagus is Boerhaave's syndrome, which refers to a traumatic rupture of the esophagus due to forceful vomiting. It is a true medical emergency. Patients with this condition complain of the acute onset of severe chest pain which is worsened by yawning, breathing, and swallowing. If this condition is suspected, prompt referral to an emergency room is indicated.

Lastly, vomiting causes two main electrolyte disorders, hypokalemia (low potassium) and alkalosis (high blood alkaline level). Either of these, if severe enough, can result in serious cardiac arrhythmia, seizures, and muscle spasms. It does not suffice to place these patients on supplemental potassium, because the body cannot absorb the potassium. The beneficial effects of supplemental potassium are nullified unless there is restoration of the volume status either with intravenous saline or oral rehydration solutions such as Pedialite or Gatorade. One final point about self-induced vomiting: some bulimics use ipecac to induce vomiting. This is dangerous because it is toxic to the heart. Because of ipecac's long elimination time, repeated ingestion can result in potentially fatal cumulative doses. Heart failure and arrhythmia can result.

LAXATIVE ABUSE

If the mode of purging is through laxative abuse, there are also potential problems with potassium and acid-base aberrations. It is worth telling patients that laxatives are a very ineffective method to induce weight loss because caloric absorption occurs in the small bowel and laxatives affect the large bowel by promoting the loss of large volumes of watery diarrhea and electrolyte depletion.

The main body system which is affected by laxatives is the colorectal area. This information refers strictly to stimulant laxatives that contain senna, cascara, or phenolphthalein and directly stimulate colonic activity. These types of laxatives, if used in excess, damage the colonic neurons which normally control gut motility and contractions. The result is an inert, noncontractile tube which is referred to as the "cathartic colon syndrome." This causes significant problems with fecal retention, constipation, and abdominal discomfort. Loss of colonic function can become so severe that a colectomy (surgery) is needed to treat intractable constipation.

It is crucial to identify laxative abusers early in the course of treatment, before permanent colonic damage has occurred, so that they can be encouraged to seek the assistance of a physician who is adept at withdrawing patients from stimulant laxatives. Laxative withdrawal can be an extremely difficult situation, which is made worse by fluid retention, bloating, and swelling. The mainstays of treatment involve educating patients that it may take weeks to accomplish restoration of normal bowel habits. Patients need to be advised about the importance of ample fluid intake, a high-fiber diet, and judicious amounts of exercise. If constipation persists, a glycerin suppository or a nonstimulating osmotic laxative (works by shifting fluids), such as lactulose, may be useful. Most patients are successfully detoxed with this type of program, but patience is necessary to endure the transient bloating which will resolve in one to two weeks with salt restriction and leg elevation. Progressive abdominal pain, constipation, or distention warrants an abdominal X ray and further evaluation.

DIURETICS

Another mode of purging which can produce medical problems is the abuse of diuretics. This mode is infrequently utilized except by medical personnel who may have access to these medications, although they are also available in over-the-counter preparations containing pamabrom, caffeine, or ammonium chloride. The main complication associated with diuretic abuse is fluid and electrolyte imbalance. In fact, the electrolyte pattern is basically the same as that seen with self-induced vomiting, which is potentially dangerous due to heart problems caused by low potassium levels.

There is also a reflexive development of lower leg edema (swelling) with abrupt cessation of diuretic abuse. Generally the edema can be controlled and treated with salt restriction and leg elevation. It is worthwhile to give a brief educational talk to patients with edema explaining that the condition is self-limited and caused by a reaction from the body which diuretics promote, albeit transiently.

DIET PILLS/APPETITE SUPPRESSANTS

Another method used to avoid weight gain and/or promote weight loss is the use of diet pills. Diet pills are not actually considered a form of purging but are used as a compensatory reaction to binge eating in the category of bulimia nervosa known as "non-purging type." Most diet pills stimulate the sympathetic nervous system and are amphetamine-type derivatives. The adverse effects of diet pills include hypertension (high blood pressure), palpitations, seizures, and anxiety attacks. There is no long-term dependence syndrome associated with the usage of diet pills and abrupt cessation is medically safe.

Individuals suffering from anorexia nervosa or bulimia nervosa may be troubled with a myriad of medical complications. However, with proper identification and an effective and safe treatment plan, most of these are reversible. Medical management may thus be the building block for a successful psychiatric treatment program.

A NOTE ON BINGE EATING DISORDER

Managing binge eating disorder patients most likely involves the same medical considerations to be taken into account when treating obese individuals, such as heart or gallbladder disease, diabetes, high blood pressure, and so on. Most symptoms associated with binge eating will be a result of the accompanying weight gain associated with this disorder. Occasionally people have binged to the point of becoming breathless when their distended stomachs press up on their diaphragms. In very rare cases a medical emergency may occur if the stomach wall becomes so stretched that it is damaged or even tears.

MEDICATION

One last aspect of medical management involves the use of medication to treat the coexisting psychological conditions that cause or contribute to eating disorders. Prescribing and managing this type of medication is sometimes undertaken by the family physician or internist, but is more often relegated to a psychiatrist who has special training in psychopharmacology. The information regarding mind-altering medication for use with eating disorders is extensive and is covered in chapter 14.

16

WHEN OUTPATIENT TREATMENT IS NOT ENOUGH

E ating disorder treatment is a long-term process involving a potentially life-threatening situation. Treatment is extremely expensive
with therapy most likely extending for over two years. Outpatient
therapy refers to individual, family, or group therapy sessions taking
place in a therapist's or other professional's office and usually conducted one to three times per week. Individual sessions generally run
forty-five minutes to an hour and family or group sessions are usually
sixty to ninety minutes. Sessions can be arranged for more or less
time if needed and as deemed appropriate by the treating professional. The cost of outpatient treatment, including therapy, nutritional
counseling, and medical monitoring, can extend to $100,000 or more.
Most eating disorder treatment takes place on an outpatient basis.

There may come a time when outpatient treatment is insufficient
or contraindicated due to the severity of the eating disorder. Treatment in a more intense structured setting, such as a hospital or
residential facility, may be required when symptoms are out of control and/or the medical risks are significant. If treatment necessitates
a round-the-clock or more acute program such as an inpatient hospital stay, this alone can be $30,000 or more per month with some
patients needing several months or repeated hospitalizations.

Most people consider a round-the-clock treatment program as a
last resort, however, if specifically designed for eating disorders, this
kind of program can be an excellent option even in the beginning of
treatment. There are a variety of settings which provide more
intense levels of care than outpatient therapy. When looking for a
treatment program it is important to understand the difference
between the intensity and structure of different levels of care. The
various options include inpatient, partial hospitalization or day

treatment programs, residential treatment facilities, and halfway or recovery houses. These options will be described below.

ROUND-THE-CLOCK TREATMENT OPTIONS

INPATIENT

Inpatient treatment means twenty-four-hour care in a hospital setting which can be a medical or psychiatric facility, or both. The cost is usually quite high, around $1,200 to $1,400 per day. Inpatient treatment at a strictly medical hospital is usually a short-term stay to treat medical conditions or complications that have arisen as a result of the eating disorder. In some cases, a patient may stay longer simply because his or her medical condition is severe. In other cases, patients stay longer in a medical hospital than is medically necessary because there is no other facility close by to treat the patient. This is particularly true if the hospital has provisions or a treatment protocol for eating disorders. The rest of the inpatient treatment of eating disorders takes place in psychiatric hospitals that utilize nearby or associated medical facilities when necessary. It is very important that these psychiatric hospitals have trained eating disorder professionals and a treatment program or special protocol for treating these patients.

PARTIAL HOSPITALIZATION OR DAY TREATMENT

Often individuals need a more structured program than outpatient treatment but do not need twenty-four-hour care. Additionally patients who have been in an inpatient program can often step down to a lower level of care but are not ready to return home and begin outpatient treatment. In these cases partial programs or day treatment programs may be indicated. Partial programs come in a variety of forms. Some hospitals offer programs a few days per week, or in the evening, or a few hours each day. Day treatment generally means the person is in the hospital program during the day and returns home in the evening. These programs are becoming more prevalent, in part due to the cost of full inpatient programs, and also due to the fact that patients can receive great benefits from these programs without the additional burden or stress of having to leave home entirely. Due to the amount of variation in these programs it is not possible to give a fee range.

RESIDENTIAL

The majority of eating disordered individuals are not medically or psychologically unstable and do not require hospitalization. However, a substantial benefit may be received if these individuals can have supervision and treatment on a twenty-four-hour-per-day basis. Bingeing, self-induced vomiting, laxative abuse, compulsive exercise, and restricted eating do not necessarily lead to medical instability and thus do not qualify by themselves as criteria for hospitalization. If this is the case, many insurance companies will not pay for hospitalization since coverage requires the individual to be medically compromised. However, eating disorder behaviors can become so habitual or addictive that trying to reduce or extinguish them on an outpatient basis can seem almost impossible. Residential treatment facilities offer an excellent alternative, providing round-the-clock care in a more relaxed, affordable, nonhospital setting.

Residential facilities vary greatly in the level of care provided, so it is important to investigate each program thoroughly. Some programs offer sophisticated, intensive, and structured treatment very similar to a hospital inpatient program but in a more relaxed environment and in some cases even a renovated house or estate. These facilities often utilize physicians and nurses but not on a 24-hour-per-day basis and the residents are referred to as clients, not patients, as they are medically stable, not requiring acute medical care. Other residential facilities are less structured and provide far less treatment, often centered around group therapy. This type of residential program falls somewhere above recovery or halfway houses (see below) but with less structure than the type of residential program described here.

Some individuals go directly to residential treatment programs, while others spend time in an inpatient facility and then transfer to a residential program. Residential treatment is becoming very popular as a choice for treating eating disorders. One reason for this is the cost. Some residential programs charge as little as one-third of the fees of most inpatient facilities. Cost varies but is usually between $400 to $900 per day. Furthermore, residential programs can offer a crucial and important treatment feature not feasible in an inpatient setting. In residential settings patients have the opportunity to be increasingly involved in meal planning, shopping, cooking, exercise, and other daily living activities in which they will need to participate upon returning home. These are problem areas for eating disordered individuals that cannot be practiced and resolved in a hospital setting. Residential facilities offer treatment and supervision of behaviors and daily living activities, providing clients with increasing responsibility for their own recovery.

RECOVERY OR HALFWAY HOUSE

A recovery or halfway house can easily be confused with residential treatment and in some cases there is a fine line of distinction between them. Recovery houses have far less structure than most residential programs and are usually not equipped for individuals who are still engaging in symptomatic eating disorder behaviors, or other behaviors needing a good deal of supervision. Recovery houses are more like transitional living situations where residents can live with others in recovery, attending group therapy and recovery meetings, and participating in individual therapy either as part of the house program or with an outside therapist. The idea was originally developed for drug and alcohol addicts so they could have a place to live with other recovering addicts attending group therapy and/or recovery meetings under the supervision of a "house parent." This was designed to help individuals practice sober living skills, before going back to live with their families or on their own. These recovery homes are far less expensive than hospitals and even less than residential facilities. Fees can range from as little as $600 up to $2,500 per month, depending on the services provided. However, it must be kept in mind that most halfway or recovery houses provide far less treatment and supervision than is necessary for many eating disordered individuals.

WHEN TO HOSPITALIZE

It is always the best circumstance when an individual chooses to enter into a treatment program by choice and/or before it becomes a necessity. A person may decide to seek treatment in a hospital or residential setting in order to get away from the normal daily tasks and distractions and focus exclusively and intensely on recovery. However, it is often as a result of medical evaluation or a crisis situation that the decision to go to, or put a loved one in, a treatment program is made. To avoid panic and confusion, it is important to establish criteria for and goals of any hospitalization in case such a situation arises. It is essential that the therapist, physician, and any other treatment team members agree on hospitalization criteria and work together so that the patient sees a competent, complimentary, and consistent treatment team. The criteria and goals should be discussed with the patient and significant others and, when possible, agreed upon at the beginning of treatment or at least prior to admission. Involuntary hospitalization should be considered only when the patient's life is in danger.

In relation to the specific eating disorder behaviors, the primary goal of hospitalization for the severely underweight anorexic is to institute re-feeding and weight gain. For the binge eater or bulimic, the primary goal is to establish control over excessive bingeing and/or purging. Hospitalization may be needed to treat coexisting conditions such as depression or severe anxiety that are impairing the individual's ability to function. Furthermore, many eating disordered individuals experience suicidal thoughts and behaviors and need to be hospitalized for protection. A patient may be hospitalized strictly for a medical condition or complication such as dehydration, electrolyte imbalance, fluid retention, or chest pain, in which case a medical hospital may be sufficient. The decision regarding where to hospitalize must be decided on a case-by-case basis. When hospitalization is intended to address any of the eating disorder issues, it is important to look for a treatment program or hospital unit specializing in the care of eating disordered patients. Below are some reasons why a decision to hospitalize might be made.

SUMMARY OF REASONS FOR HOSPITALIZATION

1. Postural hypotension (low blood pressure).

2. Cardiac dysfunctions such as irregular heartbeat, prolonged QT interval, ventricular ectopy.

3. Pulse less than 45 beats/minute (BPM) or greater than 100 BPM (with emaciation).

4. Dehydration/electrolyte abnormalities such as a serum potassium level less than 2 milligrams equivalents per liter, fasting blood glucose level less than 50 milligrams per 100 milliliters, creating a level greater than 2 milligrams per 100 milliliters.

5. Weight loss of more than 30 percent of ideal body weight or rapid, progressive weight loss (1 to 2 pounds per week) in spite of competent psychotherapy.

6. Outpatient treatment failure: a) patient is unable to complete an outpatient trial, for example, can't physically drive to or remember sessions, or b) treatment has lasted six months with no substantial improvement.

7. Observation for diagnosis and/or medication trial.

8. Tendency toward suicide.

9. Chaotic or abusive family situation.

10. Inability to perform activities of daily living.

Hospitalization should not be regarded as an easy or final solution to an eating disorder. Minimally, hospitalization should provide a structured environment to control behavior, supervise feeding, observe patient after meals to reduce purging, provide close medical monitoring and, if necessary, provide invasive medical treatment. However, some treatment programs for eating disorders offer an established protocol and a trained staff and milieu that provide empathy, understanding, education, and support, facilitating cessation or dramatic reduction of eating disorder thoughts and behaviors. For this reason, hospitalization does not have to be a last resort. In fact, professionals should avoid the connotation that indicates, "If you get too bad, or if you don't improve, I'm going to have to hospitalize you and I know you don't want that." Hospitalization should not be feared nor should it be seen as a punishment. It is better for individuals to understand that if they are unable to battle their eating disorders with outpatient therapy alone, then more help for them will be sought in a treatment program where they will be provided the care, nurturing, and added strength they need to overcome their oppression by their eating disorders. When framed to the patients as "an opportunity to take the necessary time out from other responsibilities to focus on recovery in a setting where your thoughts and behaviors are understood," hospitalization or some other round-the-clock treatment option can be viewed as a welcomed, albeit scary, choice individuals make from the healthy part of them that wants to get better.

Letting eating disorder individuals be included in all of their treatment decisions, including when to go to a treatment program, is valuable. Control issues are a consistent theme seen in individuals with eating disorders. It is important not to let a "me against them" relationship develop between the therapist or treatment team and the person with the eating disorder. The more control individuals have in their treatment, the less they will need to act out other means of control (for example, lying to the therapist, sneaking food, or purging when not being observed). Furthermore, if an individual has been included in the decision making process regarding hospitalization or residential treatment, there is less trouble getting compliance when admission is necessary. Consider the following example.

Alana, a seventeen-year-old high school senior, first came in for therapy when she weighed 102 pounds. Alana's mother brought her to see me because of her concern for Alana's recent weight loss and her fear that Alana was overly restricting her food intake, having taken her diet too far for her 5′ 5″ frame and her propensity for exercise. Alana was reluctant and angry that her mother had dragged her to a therapist's office; "It's my mother who has a problem, not me. She won't get off my back."

I sent Alana's mother out of the room and asked Alana if perhaps there was anything I could possibly help her with since she and I both had at least another thirty minutes to kill. When Alana couldn't really think of anything, I suggested that one thing I might do is help her get her mother off her back. This, of course, perked her up a little and she immediately agreed. After talking to her for a while and explaining how I work on getting parents to stay out of their kid's eating, I invited Alana's mother in and explained to both of them that as long as Alana was going to be seeing me there would be no reason for her mother to discuss her eating habits or her weight. Her mother was unhappy about this and offered several protests, but I held firm that this was no longer her territory and in fact made matters worse, which she conceded. However, Alana's mother needed reassurance that Alana would not be allowed to starve herself to death, which was an almost obsessive fear for this parent due to the recent unexpected death of her husband. Therefore, I told them that I would not allow Alana's condition to worsen without more intense intervention and that I was sure Alana had no intention of that either. Here is where I let Alana in on a major treatment decision:

Carolyn: *Alana, at what weight do you think you would need to be hospitalized?*

Alana: *I don't know, but I'm not going to let that happen. I'm not going to lose any more weight. I've already told everybody that.*

Carolyn: *Okay, so you've agreed to not lose more weight, but you're a smart girl. To reassure your mom, let her know that you do have some idea of what would be unreasonable or unhealthy to the point where you would need to go to a treatment program for more help.*

Alana: *(Fidgeting a bit and looking uncomfortable, not willing to say anything, most likely for fear of being trapped and held to it.)*

Carolyn: *Well, do you think 80 pounds would be taking it too far? Would you need to go then?*

Alana: *Of course, I'm not stupid. (Most, but not all, anorex-
           ics think they can control the weight loss and don't
           imagine they will ever be at the extreme weight often
           seen in other anorexics.)*

Carolyn: *I know, I already said I thought you were smart. So
           do you think 85 pounds would be too low?*

Alana: *Yes.*

Carolyn: *What about 95?*

Alana: *Well, no not really. I don't think I'd need a hospital
           or anything but it's not going to happen anyway.*

Carolyn: *(At this point I know I have her in a position to set-
           tle on a weight criterion for going into a treatment
           program.) Okay, so I think we can agree that you
           think that 85 is too low but 95 is not, but that in
           any case, you are willing to stay at your current
           weight of 102. Is that right?*

Alana: *Yes.*

Carolyn: *So then for your mom's sake and since you have
           said you will not lose any more weight, let's make an
           agreement. If you do lose weight to the point where
           you get down to, say, 90 pounds, you will in essence
           be telling us that you cannot stop and therefore need
           to go to a treatment program?*

Alana: *Sure, yeah, I can agree to that.*

Throughout this discussion Alana played a major role in decision making for her treatment. She got to have her mom "off her back" and she picked the weight criterion for hospitalization. I did have to spend some time with Alana's mother reassuring her that this was the best approach and that letting Alana pick the weight criterion would help us out in the event that hospitalization was necessary. I also needed to see if Alana could maintain her weight and improve her diet through outpatient therapy. However, in Alana's case the writing was on the wall. All of Alana's behaviors described to me earlier in the session by her mother pointed to the fact that she probably would indeed continue to lose weight because, as with most anorexics, her extreme fear of gaining would keep her restricting to the point where she would most likely continue to lose. Alana did get down to 90 pounds and reluctantly, though compliantly, went into a treatment program. The process of having Alana establish the weight criterion made a huge difference in her willingness to go when it became necessary. Additionally, there was no panic or crisis when the time came and the therapeutic relationship bond was not disrupted by me "doing something to her" or fostering the "me against them" attitude I discussed earlier.

In Alana's case there was no medical condition or emergency situation necessitating hospitalization. Rather, hospitalization was followed through with when outpatient therapy was not working and an eating disorder treatment program was a means for her to get the help she really needed to get better. A good eating disorder program provides not only structure and monitoring but a number of curative factors that facilitate recovery.

Curative Factors of Inpatient or Residential Treatment

(The term patient or inpatient will be used to refer to an individual in a round-the-clock treatment program and the terms hospital, and hospitalization will refer to any round-the-clock program.)

A. Separates Patient from Home Life, Family, and Friends

1. Family members may have had a significant role in the development or sustaining of the disorder. Secondary gains with the family or with friends may be exposed and may even diminish when patients are removed from those people.

2. The therapist can take a more active role as both authoritarian and nurturer and facilitate the necessary trust and relationship needed for recovery.

3. When the patient is absent from the family, the therapist can see the functional significance that the patient had in the family. The "role" the patient plays in the family may be an important aspect of treatment. Furthermore, how the family functions without the patient will be helpful in determining causes and treatment goals.

4. Being away from normal routines such as work, taking care of children, and daily living responsibilities, which often serve as distractions from dealing with the issues and behaviors, can help patients to focus attention where it is needed.

B. Provides a Controlled Environment

1. Putting a patient in a controlled environment exposes otherwise hidden issues such as food rituals, laxative abuse, rigidity in eating behaviors, mood around meal times, reactions to weighing, and so on. Exposing the patient's true patterns and behaviors is necessary in order to deal with these issues, discovering the meaning they have for the patient, and finding alternative, more suitable behaviors.

2. A controlled, structured environment assists the patient in breaking addictive patterns. Popcorn and frozen yogurt diets will not be able to be continued. Vomiting directly after meals will be difficult in programs providing direct supervision after meals. Weight is usually monitored and yet kept from the patients in order to protect them from their own reactions to the information and to break them from being addicted to weighing and to the number on the scale. Furthermore, having a certain schedule to follow, including planned meals, helps reintroduce structure into what is often a chaotic pattern. A healthy, realistic schedule may be learned and then utilized upon returning home.

3. Another useful aspect of the controlled environment is medication monitoring. If medication is warranted, such as an antidepressant, it can be more carefully monitored as to compliance, side effects, and how well it is working. Observation of the reaction

to medication, blood tests, and dosage adjustments are more easily carried out in a hospital setting.

C. OFFERS SUPPORT FROM PEERS AND A HEALING ENVIRONMENT

1. Patients in a treatment program are there with other individuals with similar issues, problems, and feelings. The camaraderie, support, and understanding of others is a well-documented healing factor.

2. A good treatment team in a hospital also provides a healing environment. It's members can be positive role models for self-care and can be an example of a healthy "family" system. The treatment team can provide a good experience of the balance between rules, responsibility, and freedom.

The duration of time spent in a treatment program will depend upon the severity of the eating disorder, any complications, and the treatment goals. Inpatient treatment dealing with the eating disorder should include family and/or significant others throughout its course unless the treatment team determines there is good reason not to do so. Prior to discharge, family members can work with the treatment program staff to establish treatment goals and realistic expectations for the entire family.

Hospitalization can help break any addictive patterns or cycles and start a new behavioral process for the patient, but it is not the cure. Long-term follow-up is necessary. Success rates for hospitalization are hard to come by, but there are many aspects to choosing the right program, which will not be the same for everybody.

The cost of inpatient treatment is anywhere from $15,000 to $45,000 per month or more and, sadly enough, many insurance companies have exclusions in their policies for eating disorder treatment, which some have referred to as a "self-inflicted" problem. Careful assessment of cost and reimbursement possibilities should be done prior to admission unless there is an emergency situation. This is an outrage to people familiar with those suffering and/or those treating these individuals. There are some recovery homes or halfway houses that charge far less, even as little as $600 to $2,500 per month. However, these programs are not as intense or highly structured and are inadequate for individuals needing higher levels of care. When considering admission to a treatment program it is important to review the philosophy, staff, and schedule of various program options. To help patients and their families in the selection of an appropriate treatment program, the following "ingredients" were developed by Michael Levine, Ph.D., and presented at the Thirteenth National NEDO Conference in Columbus, Ohio.

INGREDIENTS OF A GOOD EATING DISORDERS TREATMENT PROGRAM

1. Nutritional counseling designed to restore and maintain a body weight normal for that person. This is a body weight the person can maintain easily without dieting and without being obsessed with eating.

2. Behavioral lessons designed to teach eating patterns that restore control to the person's body, not to some diet or some cultural ideal of slenderness. In other words, cognitive-behavioral lessons in how to live with food, not without it.

3. Some form of psychotherapy aimed at overcoming the eating disordered person's characteristic overvaluation of weight and shape as central determinants of self-worth. In general, this psychotherapy will address pathological attitudes about the body, the self, and relationships. The focus here is on development of a person, not refinement of a "package."

4. Some form of individual and/or group psychotherapy and/or behavioral therapy which helps the person not only renounce illness, but embrace health. In this regard, the person will probably need to learn (a) how to feel and to trust, and (b) specific skills for assertion, communication, problem solving, decision-making, time management, etc. At many colleges support groups are a very useful adjunct to individual therapy.

235

5. Where it has been deemed appropriate after a careful psychiatric evaluation, judicious use of antidepressant medication, for example, fluoxitene (Prozac) or anti-anxiety medication.

6. Some form of education, support, and/or therapy which helps family and friends assist in the process of recovery and future development.

7. In addition, many clients can get positive results from short-term intensive treatment. The key is that continuation and intervention be the same treatment team, and care involves and addresses relapse.

The list of ingredients supplied above by Michael Levine is a good guide but choosing a treatment program will still be a difficult decision to make with many factors to consider. The following questions will provide additional information which is useful in making the right decision.

QUESTIONS TO ASK WHEN CHOOSING A TREATMENT PROGRAM

1. What is the overall philosophy of treatment, including the program's position on psychological, behavioral, and addictive approaches?

2. How are meals handled? Is vegetarianism allowed? What happens if the meal plan isn't followed?

3. Is there an exercise component other than walks or recreational activities?

4. How many patients have been treated and/or are some available to speak with you?

5. What kind of background and qualifications do staff members have? Are any or many recovered?

6. What is the patient schedule (for example, how many and what kind of groups are held daily? how much leisure time is there? how much supervision versus treatment takes place?)?

7. What are the arrangements for individual therapy? Who performs it and how often?

8. What are the outpatient or aftercare treatment and follow-up services?

9. What is considered noncompliance and what are the consequences?

10. What is considered to be the average length of stay and why?

11. What are the fees? Are there any extra fees besides those quoted that may occur? How are fees and payments arranged?

12. What books or literature are given or recommended?

13. Is it possible to meet with a staff member, visit a group, or talk to current patients?

Since different patients will be looking for different things in a treatment program, providing "the right" answers to the above questions is not possible. Individuals considering a treatment program for themselves or a loved one should ask the questions and get as much information as they can from various programs in order to compare options and select which program is most suitable. A list and brief summary of various treatment programs specializing in eating disorders is supplied in Appendix A.

The following information on Monte Nido, my residential program in Malibu, California, provides an idea of the philosophy, treatment goals, and schedule of a 24-hour care facility specializing exclusively in eating disorders.

MONTE NIDO TREATMENT CENTER

LEVEL SYSTEM

Our level system allows for increased freedom and responsibility as clients progress in the program. Each client has a written contract which they help create. The contract shows the current level they are on and spells out the goals for that level. Each client's program is individualized even though there are certain activities, reading assignments, and other requirements for every level. A copy of the contract is given to each client and one is kept in their chart.

Special Privileges: If deemed appropriate, clients may have special privileges in their contract which allow for things not usually spelled out on the level they are on.

Level Changes: When clients feel they are ready, they can request to move to the next level. Level changes and decisions are discussed in individual sessions and the contract group. Clients must request at the beginning of the group for time to discuss their level change request. Clients will receive feedback from the staff and peers in the group. The matter is taken by the group leader to the treatment team for a final decision. The client will then be told that same day or the next day whether or not the level change was approved.

Down Leveling: Occasionally clients are moved up to a level and find that it is too difficult to accomplish the tasks on that level. A client may be down leveled to an appropriate level with more structure until they are ready to try again.

Weight: Unless otherwise contracted, weight is taken and recorded once weekly with bulimics and twice weekly with anorexics, with the client's back to the scale. Only the therapist, the clinical director, or director may tell the client her weight or any changes in weight.

Meal Times and Place: Clients will be asked not to go to the kitchen or begin any meal preparation until scheduled meal or snack time and not without staff present until they are on Level IV or Level III by contract. Clients are to eat meals in the dining room or other area supervised by staff until Level IV.

Snacks: Snacks will be served two or three times each day according to client needs. Protocol for snacks is the same as meals; according to the clients level and contract.

ENTRY LEVEL

The first phase in our level system is the Entry Level. Entry Level begins with the client's admission into the facility and when the first contract is made. During this time clients are getting acquainted with our program and will be given an Entry Level contract which lists certain tasks to be accomplished. Assessments will begin right away, and the treatment team will be getting to know the client. During Entry Level, clients are on a "grace" period with no formal requirements for eating unless otherwise contracted or ordered. This gives us time to know the client and what his or her needs will be. In some cases an initial calorie assignment may be made. During Entry Level, clients will attend meals with other clients and a staff member, but no formal eating requirement is made.

PROGRAM OVERVIEW

Eating disorders are progressive and debilitating illnesses requiring medical, nutritional and psychological intervention. Individuals suffering from eating disorders often need a structured environment to achieve recovery. However, all too often a person does well in a highly structured, regimented environment only to fall into relapse upon returning to a less structured situation. Our residential program is designed to meet the individual needs of clients and their families in a way that gives them a higher level of responsibility and "teaches" them how to recover. The atmosphere at Monte Nido is professional and structured, but it is also warm, friendly, and family like. Our dedicated staff, many of whom are recovered themselves, serve as role models, and our environment inspires people to commit to overcoming obstacles that are interfering with the quality of their life.

The program at Monte Nido is designed to provide behavior and mood stabilization, creating a climate where destructive behaviors can be interrupted. Clients can then work on the crucial underlying issues which caused and/or perpetuate their disordered eating and other dysfunctional behaviors. We provide a structured schedule with education, psychodynamic and cognitive behavioral therapy, corrective eating patterns, healthy exercise, life skills training and spiritual enhancement, all in our beautiful, serene country setting.

Our treatment philosophy includes restoring biochemical functioning and nutritional balance, implementing healthy eating and exercise habits, changing destructive behaviors, and gaining insight and coping skills for underlying emotional psychological issues. We believe that eating disorders are illnesses which, when treated correctly, can result in full recovery where the individual can resume a normal, healthy relationship to food.

Nutrition and exercise are not simply a part of our program. We recognize these as crucial areas of recovery. Therefore, we require assessments on nutritional status, metabolism, and biochemistry, and we teach patients what this information means in terms of their recovery. Our exercise physiologist and fitness trainer perform thorough assessments and develop a fitness plan suitable for each clients needs. Our detailed attention to the nutrition and exercise component of treatment reveals our dedication to these areas as part of a plan for a healthy, lasting recovery.

Every aspect of our program is designed to provide clients with a lifestyle they can continue upon discharge. Along with traditional therapy and treatment modalities, we deal directly and specifically with eating and exercise activities that can't be adequately addressed in other settings but, nevertheless, are crucial for full recovery.

Planning, shopping, and cooking meals are all part of each client's program. Dealing with these activities is necessary since they will have to be faced upon returning home.

Clients participate in exercise according to individual needs and goals. Exercise compulsion and resistance are addressed with the focus on developing healthy, non-compulsive, life-long exercise habits. We are uniquely set up to meet the needs of athletes who require specialized attention in this area.

240

Activities include: weight training, regular and water aerobics classes, stretch and tone classes, hiking, dance, and rehabilitation for sports injuries.

Individual and group therapy establish and solidify the other treatment components. Through intensive individual sessions and group work, clients gain support, insight into their problems, and the ability to transform them. Increasing confidence is gained in appropriately selecting meals and exercise activities, while using other methods to deal with underlying issues. Outings and passes are provided to assess each client's growth in handling real life situations. Upon returning from an outing or pass, clients process their experience in both individual and group sessions in order to learn from it and plan for the future.

Group Topics include:

- Cognitive Behavioral Therapy
- Communication Skills
- Self-Esteem
- Stress/Anger Management
- Body Image, Women's Issues
- Art Therapy
- Assertiveness
- Family Therapy
- Sexuality & Abuse
- Life Skills
- Career Planning

We are innovative and unique. Our director, Carolyn Costin, M.A., M.Ed., M.F.C.C., recovered herself for more than twenty years, has sixteen years of experience as a specialist in the field of eating disorders. Her extensive expertise, including a directorship of five previous inpatient eating disorder programs, combined with her unique, hands-on empathetic approach, has achieved high success rates with full recovery. Carolyn and our staff can empathize, offer hope, and serve as role models while providing skills for recovery.

PHASES OF TREATMENT

1. Initial interview, clinical assessment

2. Comprehensive history and physical by our or your medical doctor

3. Admission and orientation to the program

4. Comprehensive psychological assessments, including a psychiatric evaluation

5. Nutrition/Exercise assessments and initial meal and exercise plan established

6. Treatment team establishes a treatment plan

7. Active involvement begins in therapy, education, activities, and family sessions

8. Client works through the phases of the program, gaining understanding, control, and confidence, and establishes a life-long plan for recovery and wellness

9. Staff helps client transition through a level system providing increasing responsibility for self care

10. Treatment team, with client, re-evaluates discharge criteria and discharge date

11. Discharge with plan for aftercare

TREATMENT COMPONENTS

- Individual, Group and Family Therapy (Cognitive Behavioral & Psychodynamic Therapies)
- Psychiatric Evaluation and Treatment
- Medical Monitoring
- Communication and Life Skills Training
- Meal Planning, Shopping, and Cooking
- Nutrition Education and Counseling
- Exercise, Fitness, and Rehabilitation Program
- Art Therapy and Other Experiential Therapies

- Occupational, Career Planning
- Biochemical, Nutritional Stabilization
- Body Image Treatment
- Sexuality, Relationships, Co-Dependency
- Recreation and Relaxation
- Education Groups—Topics include: stress, psychological development, self-esteem, compulsive behaviors, sexual abuse, spirituality, anger, assertiveness, relapse, shame, women's issues

TREATMENT OBJECTIVES

Our objective is to help each client achieve a clear understanding of her eating disorder, its effect on her life and what is necessary for her personal recovery. Our goal is to develop and initiate a plan for recovery that will be able to be maintained upon discharge. We assist clients to:

1. Eliminate starving, bingeing, purging and compulsive eating

2. Establish nutritious, healthy eating patterns

3. Get into balance nutritionally, biochemically, and metabolically

4. Gain insight into disordered thinking

5. Gain insight into the underlying causes of the disordered eating behaviors

6. Learn appropriate expression of anxiety regarding food and weight issues

7. Work towards achieving an "ideal body weight" within an accepted range

8. Gain insight into destructive attitudes and behaviors

9. Develop a balanced weight maintenance plan involving food and exercise.

10. Improve body image

11. Use journal writing and self-monitoring

12. Discover and utilize alternative coping skills other than the eating disorder or any other self-destructive acts

243

13. Work with their significant others in the development of improved understanding and improved communication in order to break patterns that enable the eating disorder to continue

14. Alleviate depression and anxiety and improve self esteem

15. Identify and constructively express emotions and receive support in developing coping strategies for living free of destructive behaviors

16. Use independent experiences and therapeutic passes in order to create a life-style that can be continued upon discharge

17. Develop relapse prevention techniques

Figure 16-1 WEEKLY SCHEDULE FOR THE MONTE NIDO FACILITY RESIDENTIAL EATING DISORDER TREATMENT

MONDAY	TUESDAY	WEDNESDAY	THURSDAY	FRIDAY	SATURDAY	SUNDAY
6:30-7:30 Wake-up/Dress/Vitals/Meds	6:30-7:30 Wake-up/Dress/Vitals/Meds	6:30-7:30 Wake-up/Dress/Vitals/Meds	6:30-7:30 Wake-up/Dress/Vitals/Meds	6:30-7:30 Wake-up/Dress/Vitals/Meds	6:30-7:30 Wake-up/Dress/Vitals/Meds	6:30-7:30 Wake-up/Dress/Vitals/Meds
7:30-8:00 **Breakfast**	7:30-8:00 **Breakfast**	7:30-8:00 **Breakfast**	7:30-8:00 **Breakfast**	7:30-8:00 **Breakfast**	7:30-8:00 **Breakfast**	7:30-8:00 Sleep In!
8:00-9:00 Physical conditioning	8:00-9:00 Doctor Appts.	8:00-9:00 Physical conditioning	8:00-9:00 Physical conditioning	8:00-9:00 Physical conditioning	8:00-9:00 Physical conditioning	8:00-8:30 Breakfast
9:00-10:00 (9:45 Snack) Personal Time	9:00-10:00 (9:45 Snack) **NUTRITION**	9:00-10:00 (9:45 Snack) Personal Time	9:00-10:00 (9:45 Snack) Personal Time	9:00-10:00 (9:45 Snack) Personal Time	9:00-10:00 (9:45 Snack) Personal Time	8:30-9:30 Stretch & Tone
10:00-10:30 Goals	10:00-11:30 **Contract Group with Staff**	10:00-11:00 Body Image Group	10:00-11:30 Cogn Behavioral	10:00-11:00 Cogn Behavioral	10:00-11:00 *Visiting/Free Time*	9:30-10:30 Snack Spirituality
10:30-12:00 *Primary Group*	11:30-1:15 Staffing & Treatment Planning	11:00-12:00 Primary Group	11:30-12:00 Cogn Behavioral Assignment	11:00-12:00 **NUTRITION GROUP**	11:00-12:00 Discharge/Relapse Planning	10:30-12:00 Visiting/Free Time
12:00-1:00 Lunch	11:30-1:30 Lunch Outing	12:00-1:00 Lunch	12:00-1:00 Lunch	12:00-1:00 Lunch/ Staffing	12:00-1:00 Lunch	12:00-1:00 Lunch
1:00 Food/Feelings Grp 1:30-2:30 Cognitive Behavioral	1:30-2:00 Food/Feelings Grp	1:00 Food/Feelings Grp 1:30-2:30 Nutrition & Exercise	1:00-2:00 *Primary Anger/Assertiveness*	1:00– Food/Feelings Grp 1:15-2:30 *Primary Group*	1:00-2:00 Body Image Grp	OUTING
2:45-3:00 Snack	2:00-3:00 Exercise Physiology	2:45-3:00 Snack	2:45-3:00 Snack	2:45-3:30 Snack/Free Time	2:45-3:00 Snack	
3:00-4:30 Ind. Therapy * Ind. Assignments/Activities	3:00-3:30 Snack 3:30-5:00 Ind. Therapy * *Ind. Assignments/Activities	3:00-4:30 Ind. Therapy * *Ind. Assignments/Activities	3:00-4:30 Ind. Therapy * *Ind. Assignments/Activities	3:30-5:00 Exercise Physiology	3:00-4:00 Multi Family/Relationship Grp	
5:00-5:30 *Comm Meeting*	5:00-5:30 *Comm Meeting*	5:00-5:30 *Comm Meeting*	5:00-5:30 *Comm Meeting*	5:00-5:30 *Comm Meeting*	4:00-5:30 Individual Assignts/Passes	
5:30-6:30 **Dinner/Food & Feelings**	5:30-6:30 **Dinner/Food & Feelings**	5:30-6:30 **Dinner/Food & Feelings**	5:30-6:30 **Dinner/Food & Feelings**	5:30-6:30 **Dinner/Food & Feelings**	5:30-6:30 **Dinner/Food & Feelings**	5:30-6:30 **Dinner/Food & Feelings**
6:30-7:30 **Education/Special Topics	6:30-7:30 **COMMUNITY INVOLV**	6:30-7:30 Creativity Group	6:30-7:30 Spirituality	6:30-7:30 Recreation/Exercise	6:30-7:30 Recreation/Exercise	6:30-7:30 Recreation/Exercise
7:30-9:00 (8:15 PM Snack) Visting/Indiv. Time Ind.Therapy /Recov Mtng	7:30-9:30 (8:15 PM Snack) **COMMUNITY INVOLV**	7:15-9:00 (8:15 PM Snack) Visting/Indiv. Time Ind.Therapy	7:15-9:00 (8:15 PM Snack) Visting/Indiv. Time Ind.Therapy	7:15-9:00 (8:15 PM Snack) Visting/Indiv. Time Ind.Therapy	8:00-9:00 (8:15 PM Snack) Visting/Indiv. Time 8:00-9:00 *Visiting/Free*	7:30 8:00 Community Mtg & Contracts (8:15 PM Snack)
9:30-10:00 Stress Management	9:30-10:00 House Meeting	9:30-10:00 Stress Management	9:30-10:00 Stress Management	9:30-10:00 Stress Management	9:30-10:00 Stress Management	9:30-10:00 Stress Management

**Education/Special Topics = Medical Issues, Sexuality, Relationships, Addictions, Women's Issues

*Ind. Assignments/Activities = Individualized treatment protocols; journaling, reading assignments, exercise physiology, and rehabilitation . . . .

17

INCREASING AWARENESS AND PREVENTION

E ating disorders are rampant in our society, yet adequate prevention programs do not exist. Extensive programs aimed at preventing alcoholism and drug abuse have proven their value and been accepted into school curricula. On the other hand, very few schools or colleges have programs on education and prevention of eating disorders.

The increase in eating disorders, the high cost of treatment, the longevity of these illnesses, and the high mortality rate make it imperative that programs be implemented to prevent them. Since 86 percent of victims report the onset of their illness by age twenty, education programs should focus on early ages in order to maximize preventive efforts. With the increasing number of elementary school children ending up in eating disorder hospital programs, the need for early education and prevention efforts is crucial.

Prevention programs must include males. It is a mistake to think of eating disorders as a "women's issue." First of all, the number of males reporting eating disorders is on the rise, and second, males are affected by and have an effect on the phenomenon of eating disorders. Males need to know not only how to deal with a loved one who has an eating disorder but how they can help prevent eating disorders in our society. Male athletes, fathers, brothers, boyfriends, and so on need to be involved.

There are several organizations which include the prevention of eating disorders as one of their goals and purposes. These organizations are listed in Appendix B, "Resources," and they include Eating Disorders Awareness and Prevention, Inc. (EDAP), an organization that officially began in 1987 in response to the enormous number of individuals suffering from eating disorders and the lack of any organization dedicated exclusively to prevention and education. A task force of mental health professionals from all over the United States, with headquarters in Seattle, work together in this national organization dedicated to the primary and secondary prevention of eating disorders. EDAP sponsors and organizes Eating Disorders Awareness Week (EDAW) which takes place every year during the second week of February. Each state has a coordinator and steering committee which help to organize community events and activities throughout EDAW and the year. Scheduled events include workshops, hotlines, radio shows, and media events such as scale bashing or "Fearless Friday," a day for everyone to refuse to diet. EDAP's targeted audiences have expanded from the college aged, to high school and junior high students and, more recently, to the families of newborns and toddlers.

EDAP and other professionals have created educational materials for use in the schools. Books, tapes, and workbooks are now available, many of which can be purchased through Gurze Books, located in Carlsbad, California (see the resource section for more information). The following list of recommendations is for those interested in the prevention of eating disorders. Not all items will apply to everyone.

GENERAL PREVENTION IDEAS FOR A VARIETY OF CIRCUMSTANCES

A. FOR PARENTS, THERAPISTS, DOCTORS, OR JUST SOMEONE WHO CARES:

1. *Discuss society's thinness mania and myth.* It's important to talk about the cultural pressure to be thin and beautiful. Discuss the dieting hype and advertising propaganda promoting the myth of thinness. Talk to young children, peers, and others about these issues and how the propaganda can lead to eating problems and eating disorders. Teach others to appreciate and respect persons of all sizes. Speak out against the objectification of people on

TV, movies, videos, beauty pageants, bodybuilding competitions, and so on. Avoid other obvious sources of objectification, such as pornography and sexist films.

2. *Educate people about healthy dieting.* Help steer people away from fad or quack diets, diet pills, and so on. Help them learn to listen to hunger and satiety cues and respond to the body's needs rather than the pressure from other people or the media. Dieting and weight loss myths need to be exposed. The phrase "diets don't work" has become a cliché. Provide the necessary information to make the cliché be understood as a reality.

3. *Teach and practice good nutrition and exercise habits.* Make it a point to read up on these topics and put your knowledge to use. Share the knowledge with others. Many people really don't know much about proper quality nutrition and exercise. Even doctors have very little knowledge on these subjects. When exercising, focus on coordination, balance, breathing, enjoyment, and improved health and body acceptance rather than on calories burned or resulting changes in appearance.

4. *Avoid criticizing your own body.* If you criticize your body, you will perpetuate the message that a body is more important than the person who owns it. Too much emphasis on looks leads to distorted ideas about happiness and what is truly important in life. Don't objectify yourself by frequently weighing, scrutinizing yourself in mirrors, comparing yourself to others, or talking about the need to lose weight. If you can't do these things, get help for yourself.

5. *Discuss cultural influences.* Using various cultures and time periods, discuss cultural influences and pressures placed on people, especially females, but increasingly males, to look a certain way. Discuss ways to combat these pressures.

6. *Develop self-esteem.* Read books on raising self-esteem. Learn and practice positive self-talk to boost self-esteem and reject negative messages from media, society, and other people, including yourself. Help others have a healthy, strong self-esteem. Love people

and make them feel loved for who they are on the inside. Encourage others to be themselves and foster love of self. Model healthy ways to nurture yourself, meet emotional needs, and cope with stress that are not focused on food, weight, appearance, or other self-destructive behaviors.

7. *Do not push to excel.* Very often people get the feeling that they are loved for their accomplishments or what they do rather than who they are. Children who experience this may grow up feeling that if they aren't excelling or being the best, they aren't lovable or loved. It's okay to encourage kids or others to try hard, but they must feel loved and praised for things other than performance. Too much anxiety and stress on performance and perfection can drive a person to seek relief from this by using unhealthy means.

8. *Balance rules/limits and freedom/responsibility.* It is hard to know when to push a child to eat his/her dinner or stop eating candy. A good rule of thumb is to follow the notion that it is your responsibility to provide good, wholesome, healthy food and it is your child's responsibility to eat it. Don't be too rigid. Children should also have treats provided. Being too strict may cause certain foods to attain an elevated status, thus making them more desirable. (The book, *How to Get Your Kid to Eat, But Not Too Much* by Ellen Satter is a good resource on this subject.)

9. *Avoid pushing anyone to lose weight.* Some people do need to lose weight for health reasons. However, be careful not to promote the idea that if you aren't thin, you aren't acceptable. Young people often rebel at any kind of pushing to diet and may begin eating in secret. On the other hand, the person may feel desperate and resort to fad diets, diet pills, laxatives, and so on, all of which are unhealthy and could lead to rebound bingeing.

10. *Avoid or confront sarcastic comments or jokes about weight.* Calling someone "fatty" does not serve any purpose other than to make that person feel terrible and lose more self-esteem, which only perpetuates the problem. Let people know that making fun of fat

people is cruel and offensive. Show your dislike for tasteless items such as bumper stickers that say things like "no fat chicks." When people objectify others by judging their appearance, explain why it bothers you and ask that they stop.

11. *Focus on health, not weight.* Even if people are trying to lose weight, talk to them about being healthier, not thinner. Talk about healthy foods, foods with life force, not just fattening versus nonfattening foods. Promote the message that there are no fattening foods, only fattening eating habits. Someone's health is more important than his or her weight. Even in a weight loss program, the focus should be on losing fat, not just indiscriminate weight, and this is not determined by the scale.

12. *Love, regardless of looks.* Looks and attractiveness play a part in most relationships, but the degree or extent is important to discuss. Appearance should not mean more than other inner qualities. Make sure not to complain about your own looks or the appearance of others.

13. *Communicate effectively.* Good communication is important for healthy, happy relationships. This can't be emphasized enough. Be open and honest and allow others to be the same. Learn assertive communication skills for expressing feelings rather than "stuffing" or denying them. Read books, take courses, get counseling early if there are any problems in this area.

14. *Help others to help themselves.* Help people cope with their problems by reaching out to them and letting them know you are there in a nonjudgmental way to listen and to offer guidance whenever you can. Be supportive and encouraging. Help them to seek further help for themselves if they need to do so. Help locate a therapist, group, counselor, dietitian, and so on.

15. *Provide literature* for your children, students, patients, and so on regarding healthy eating, exercise, self-esteem, dieting, and eating disorders. (Carefully scrutinize any material on eating disorders as most books and articles give people ideas and have the opposite effect from prevention.)

B. PREVENTION IN THE SCHOOLS

1. *Survey.* Determine how many students have body image problems or are engaging in dieting, other eating disorder behaviors, and/or compulsive exercise.

2. *Library books.* Provide books in the school library on eating disorders, healthy nutrition, dieting, and exercise practices. Let the student body know these are there.

3. *Health class.* Health classes need to give more attention to these areas:

   • Nutrition
   • Dieting
   • Exercise
   • Eating disorders

4. *Guest speakers.* Bring in guest speakers on eating disorders, body image, and healthy eating for classroom or assembly presentations.

5. *Contact and Communicate.* If you suspect someone in your school has an eating disorder, make contact with him or her and talk about your concern for the person. Focus on feelings, not on weight. See if you can get the person to seek help. Also, if the problem is serious, contact parents. Eating disorders can be fatal and parents should be notified.

6. *Support groups.* Set up a support group on campus for dealing with the following issues:

   • Nutrition/Exercise
   • Self-esteem
   • Dieting
   • Body image

7. *Literature/exposure.* Have pamphlets, magazines, articles, and posters around, fostering good habits and alerting students to the dangers of eating disorders.

8. *Referral.* Know referral sources in case you are in a position to offer these to someone. Have referral resources available for the students to casually pick up in the nursing office, library, or counselor's office. Students often don't want to admit to having a problem but will pick up literature to read anonymously. This may encourage them to seek help.

9. *Medical checkups.* If you suspect someone has a problem you might suggest to him/her or to his/her parents that he/she at least have a medical exam, but be sure to warn them that lab values are almost always normal except in extreme cases and do not indicate a clean bill of health.

10. *Speakers for staff and parents.* Sponsor guest speakers on eating disorders to educate the staff and parents about the subject of body image and dieting.

TREATMENT PROGRAMS

If outpatient therapy is not enough what are the other treatment options and how does one find them? There are countless hospitals, residential programs, and other facilities that treat eating disordered individuals along with other types of patients but do not have a special program for them. This appendix is not meant to be a comprehensive list but as a summary of the types of progams available. The list includes only those facilities that are widely known for their specific treatment programs for eating disorders. The following list of facilities was compiled by interviewing key members of the eating disorder organizations listed in Appendix B, by attending national conferences where treatment centers are represented, and by requesting literature from programs who nationally advertise their treatment of eating disorders. The list is current as of September 1996, but is in no way meant to be an exhaustive one. Please keep in mind that the information supplied may change and therefore the best thing to do when researching program options is to call and get the most updated information. If you have trouble finding a program, you can also contact any of the organizations listed in Appendix B, or you can call The Eating Disorder Center as my office maintains an up-to-date list and helps place individuals in treatment programs.

The description of each of the following programs was taken directly from written materials provided by the facility and from interviews with the contact person, director, or other individual acting as a spokesperson. The facilities are divided into categories according to the level of care they offer. However, the facilities which offer a variety of options are placed in the category of the highest level of care provided.

INPATIENT HOSPITALS

BETHESDA PSYCHIATRIC HEALTH CENTER

Level of Care: Inpatient, full and partial day treatment
Address: 4400 East Cliff Avenue, Denver, Colorado 80222
Phone number: (303) 759-6195
Summary description: This program is on a psychiatric unit with only three to four eating disorder patients at a time. The program is not Twelve Step or addiction based; however, there is one Overeaters Anonymous group per week. The length of stay averages three to four weeks. The program focuses on many issues including spirituality, childhood, cognitive behavioral, empowerment of individual, developing relationships with others, and so on.

The program has three phases: I. Stabilization—designed to break the eating disorder cycle, establish medical stability, and allow for a psychological focus beyond symptoms and food. Once medically stable, patients go to cottages to sleep without round-the-clock supervision. II. Transition—continuation of support, allowing integration of "new" self and others, transition to outpatient/aftercare status. III. Maintenance—individuals have completed phases I and II and developed an individualized plan for continuing care. The patients participate in the after-school/work program. They participate actively in group, including the family program. They demonstrate awareness of behaviors/attitudes. They develop a relapse survival plan and have active participation in Phase III nutrition and activity. The phases are arranged with a gradual decrease in treatment intensity. The length of time spent in phases will be decided by the treatment team with each patient. All aspects of treatment are based on individual needs, not a preset schedule.

LINDEN OAKS HOSPITAL

Level of Care: Private psychiatric hospital
Address: 852 West Street, Naperville, Illinois 60540-6400
Phone: 1-800-955-OAKS or (630) 305-5500
Summary description: Linden Oaks Hospital is a full-service psychiatric hospital meeting the behavioral, emotional, and dietary needs of

preadolescents, adolescents, and adults struggling with anorexia and bulimia. The program utilizes a multidisciplinary treatment team approach in conjunction with services specially designed to meet the unique needs of the eating disordered client. Inpatient, partial hospitalization, intensive outpatient, and outpatient treatment are available.

THE LAUREATE
Level of Care: Psychiatric clinic and hospital with inpatient, partial, and residential programs
Address: 6655 S. Yale, Tulsa, Oklahoma 74136
Phone: 1-800-322-5173, (918) 491-8106, (918) 298-7804
Summary description: The Laureate program incorporates a combination of the Twelve Step philosophy along with other treatment modalities. Team members believe in the motto, "Replace the eating disorder with relationships." The groups offered include family of origin, nutrition, health, living skills, body image, spirituality, inner-child, codependency, assertiveness, exercise, and trauma.

THE MEADOWS
Level of Care: Inpatient
Address: 1655 North Tegner Street, Wickenburg, Arizona 85390
Phone: 1-800-MEADOWS, (520) 684-3926, Fax (520) 684-3935
Summary description: Eating disordered patients are on a unit with patients who have other diagnoses, but the facility specializes in eating disorders. The program is primarily group based, not one-on-one treatment. The program offers a significant Twelve Step orientation. The average length of stay is five to six weeks. The eating disorder program includes specific education and treatment of eating disorders, combined with codependency, relapse prevention, art and movement therapy groups, sexuality, grief, nutrition/food plan, psychotherapy for mental/thought distortions, body image, self-defeating eating patterns, and behavioral changes needed for resolution of eating disorder.

THE MENNINGER CLINIC

Level of Care: Psychiatric facility with inpatient, residential, and partial programs

Address: Box 829, Topeka, Kansas 66601-0829

Phone: (913) 273-7500, ext. 5311, 1-800-351-9058

Summary description: An active, structured, four-week basic program designed to help the patient gain the symptom control necessary to facilitate psychological recovery. Depending on individual needs, some patients may stay beyond the four-week period. Individual and group therapy modalities are a keystone of the Menninger Clinic's program.

THE RADER INSTITUTE

Level of Care: Most Rader programs offer inpatient and partial treatment

Address: Rader has several locations around the country but the central corporate office is located in California at 1663 Sawtelle Boulevard, Los Angeles, California 90025

Phone: 1-800-255-1818 (corporate office in Los Angeles)

Summary description: The Rader Institute programs are based on the disease/addiction model and incorporate cognitive behavioral and psychodynamic treatment into the Twelve Step approach. The primary goals of treatment are to arrest coexisting depression, to interrupt the dysfunctional eating behavior, and to assist in the development of coping skills to address emotional issues. The program also assists the patient in connecting inappropriate behavior patterns to unresolved emotional issues, and provides the tools necessary to help patients resolve these issues. By providing appropriate education to the patient, family members, and significant others regarding the dynamics of the disorder, the program helps to facilitate these goals and, therefore, the recovery process. Administered by a staff of caring, experienced professionals, many of whom are recovering from an eating disorder themselves, the Radar Institute eating disorder treatment program helps patients understand what caused their self-destructive behavior in the first place. All aspects of the patient's life are analyzed and addressed in a supportive environment. The unit offers a highly structured, controlled milieu and a primary therapy group is held daily. Other components of the program include working on self-esteem, relationships, anger, body image, sexuality, stress, and relapse prevention. In-house and community Twelve Step recovery meetings are essential components of the treatment protocol. The average length of stay is three to six weeks.

RIDGEVIEW INSTITUTE, GEORGIA
Level of Care: Inpatient psychiatric and substance abuse hospital
Address: 3995 South Cobb Drive, Smyrna, Georgia 30080
Phone: 1-800-329 9775, ext. 4114
Summary description: Ridgeview center takes five to ten eating disordered patients at a time on a women's unit with patients who have other problems or addictions. Ridgeview is not a Twelve Step program, but Twelve Step meetings are offered, such as Alcoholics Anonymous and Overeaters Anonymous. Ridgeview cited these aspects of their program: body image, women's issues, nutrition, group therapy, relationships, music therapy, journaling, focus groups after every meal, and an ANAD (National Association of Anorexia Nervosa and Associated Disorders) group once a week.

RIVER OAKS NEW ORLEANS
Level of Care: Inpatient, partial, and residential
Address: 1525 River Oaks Road West, New Orleans, Louisiana 70123
Phone: 1-800-366-1740, (504) 734-1740, Fax (504) 733-7020
Summary description: Treatment for eating disorders is provided in the trauma, dissociative disorders, and sexual compulsivity programs at River Oaks Hospital for individuals with a history of problem eating patterns as well as trauma, abuse, or neglect. A specialized team, consisting of a clinical psychologist, movement/expressive therapist, and nutritionist, evaluates each client and develops an individualized treatment plan which addresses restrictive eating, compulsive overeating, purging, and distorted body image in the context of the client's past trauma. Individuals are helped to understand their problem eating patterns as an adaptation to traumatic circumstances.

259

Specialized expressive and experiential techniques are aimed at integrating the sense of fragmentation inherent in eating disorders while cognitive behavioral techniques focus on changing distorted thinking and compulsive behavior. This highly individualized program uniquely recognizes the client's need for control and safety expressed through problem eating patterns while facilitating growth and trauma integration and resolution.

THE WILLOUGH AT NAPLES, FLORIDA
Level of Care: Inpatient psychiatric/chemical dependency hospital/day and partial programs available
Address: 9001 Tamiami Trail East, Naples, Florida 33962
Phone: 1-800-722-0100, (813) 775-4500
Summary description: The Willough at Naples is a ninety-two-bed unit and specializes in eating disorders and chemical dependency. The treatment objective is a blending of the psychodynamic, medical, and behavioral approach with the traditional Twelve Step and family system models. Its professionals believe eating disorders are addictive, progressive, and potentially fatal diseases that require a comprehensive treatment approach.

PROGRAMS ASSOCIATED WITH A UNIVERSITY

MEDICAL UNIVERSITY OF SOUTH CAROLINA, INSTITUTE OF PSYCHIATRY
Level of Care: Inpatient, partial, and outpatient programs
Address: 171 Ashley Avenue, Charleston, South Carolina 29425-0742
Phone: 803-792-0092
Summary description: The eating disorder program of the Institute of Psychiatry provides comprehensive treatment based on a biopsychosocial model. The interdisciplinary team provides a variety of treatment modalities including nutritional rehabilitation, cognitive behavioral therapy, family therapy, and psychopharmacology (drug treatment).

UNIVERSITY OF CALIFORNIA AT LOS ANGELES, NEURO PSYCHIATRIC
INSTITUTE
Level of Care: Inpatient and partial program
Address: UCLA, A South, 405 Hilgard Avenue, Los Angeles,
California 90095
Phone: (310) 794-2093
Summary description: UCLA offers complete inpatient/day hospi-
tal/outpatient treatment for anorexia and bulimia involving intensive
individual, group, and family therapies combined with nutrition
counseling and medical support. Medical consultation is provided as
needed through UCLA Medical Center. Principles of treatment rest
on an integration of dynamic, expressive, and cognitive behavioral
therapies with minimal use of behavior modification. Intensive outpatient module for patients eighteen years and older provides
individual and group-based treatment.

UNIVERSITY OF KANSAS SCHOOL OF MEDICINE, WICHITA
Level of Care: Inpatient and outpatient
Address: 8901 East Orme, Wichita, Kansas 67207
Phone: 1-800-322-8901, (316) 686-5000
Summary description: A comprehensive program specializing in the
care of anorexia nervosa, bulimia nervosa, and other related disorders.
The program offers individual, group, and family psychotherapy.
Educational, directive, cognitive behavioral, and insight-oriented
approaches are offered.

UNIVERSITY OF MINNESOTA HOSPITAL EATING DISORDER PROGRAM,
MINNEAPOLIS
Level of Care: Inpatient, partial program, and outpatient
Address: Box 393 Mayo, University of Minnesota Hospital,
Minneapolis, Minnesota 55455
Phone: (612) 626-6871
Summary description: University of Minnesota offers complete inpa-
tient/day hospital/outpatient treatment for adolescents and adults
for anorexia and bulimia involving intensive individual, group, and

family therapies combined with nutrition counseling and medical support. Medical consultation is provided as needed through University of Minnesota Hospital. Principles of treatment rest on an integration of educational, cognitive behavioral, and interpersonal therapies.

UNIVERSITY OF IOWA HOSPITALS AND CLINICS
Level of Care: Inpatient and partial hospitalization programs
Address: UIHC, 200 Hawkins Drive, 2887 JPP, Iowa City, Iowa 52242
Phone: (319) 356-1354, (319) 353-6149
Summary description: The multidisciplinary team approach at the University of Iowa Hospitals and Clinics, Department of Psychiatry, is comprised of staff physicians, resident physicians, nurses, social workers, dietitians, occupational therapists, recreational therapists, and psychologists. The inpatient eating disorders program centers around a therapeutic milieu where the interactional issues that arise are used to help patients understand their ways of dealing with relationships and stressors. Initially, patients are closely supervised while they establish healthy eating behaviors. As the patient progresses and a healthy goal weight is attained, supervision is decreased and independent eating in realistic settings is encouraged. Typical lengths of stay vary considerably according to individual need. A general range would be five to ten weeks for anorexia nervosa and two to six weeks for bulimia nervosa. All treatment includes individualization of care. A partial hospitalization program has been opened this year.

WESTERN PSYCHIATRIC INSTITUTE AND CLINIC, UNIVERSITY OF PITTSBURGH MEDICAL CENTER
CENTER FOR OVERCOMING PROBLEM EATING (COPE)
Level of Care: Inpatient psychiatric hospital, research facility, partial and outpatient options
Address: Western Psychiatric Institute and Clinic, University of Pittsburgh Medical Center, 3811 O'Hara Street, Pittsburgh, Pennsylvania 15213
Phone: (412) 624-3507, (412) 624-0227

Summary description: COPE offers assessment, diagnosis, and treatment for individuals with eating disorders including anorexia nervosa, bulimia nervosa, and binge eating disorder. The COPE program consists of comprehensive assessments including psychiatric, medical, psychosocial, and nutritional evaluations. Treatment is designed to address the specific needs of individuals who may require different levels of care.

RESIDENTIAL TREATMENT CENTERS

MONTECATINI
Level of Care: Residential
Address: 2516 La Costa Avenue, Rancho La Costa, California 92009
Phone: (619) 436-8930
Summary description: Montecatini is a female-only treatment center for eating disorders and chemical dependency. The center consists of two houses, each of which accommodates six patients. One house serves as the main treatment center while the other is a step-down version of care where patients transition after spending time in the main house. The program lasts a minimum of three months. The program has a Twelve Step orientation and is group therapy based. Individual therapy is only done for the first couple of weeks and thereafter if there is an urgent problem. Clients also see the dietitian weekly on a group basis except for the first time. Clients have graduated freedoms for meals, observation after meals, passes, and so on. Clients are on a buddy system and, for the first two months, they are not allowed to be left alone at any time. Family therapy is offered after clients have been in the program for one month. The family comes to the facility for two to three days for intense family therapy, with lodging away from the facility.

MONTE NIDO RESIDENTIAL TREATMENT FACILITY
Level of Care: Residential
Address: 27162 Sea Vista Drive, Malibu, California 90265
Phone: (818) 222-9534
Summary description: Monte Nido (Mountain Nest) is a private six bed facility designed and created by recovered professionals to heal women suffering from anorexia and bulimia nervosa and/or exercise addiction. Located in the hills of Malibu, California, Monte Nido is a secluded, gated estate surrounded by a state park, and hiking trails leading to the beach. In this home setting providing both comfort and real life challenges, a highly structured program takes place. Psychodynamic, cognitive behavioral, spiritual, and experiential approaches are utilized. Individualized treatment is a priority, including individual therapy at least three times per week. Clients progress through a level system, gaining increasing freedom and responsibility. Every aspect of the program is designed to provide the ability for clients to practice a lifestyle they can continue upon discharge. For example, shopping, meal planning, cooking and fitness training are a part of each client's personalized program. Monte Nido also offers a unique program for athletes. Clinical staff includes therapists, psychiatrists, and counselors, along with a registered dietitian, nurse, physician, exercise physiologist, and fitness trainer. A majority of the staff members are recovered themselves, and Monte Nido promotes the philosophy that eating disordered individuals can become fully recovered, where issues of food, exercise, and body image are no longer necessary as a means of self-expression and are not used in self-destructive ways. Average length of stay is two months, but shorter or longer stays can be arranged on a case-by-case basis.

REMUDA RANCH ARIZONA
Level of Care: Residential treatment center also offering extended care houses
Address: Box 2481 Jack Burden Road, Wickenburg, Arizona 85358
Phone: 1-800-445-1900, (602) 684-3913

Summary description: Remuda Ranch offers a comprehensive, individualized program which provides a careful balance of medical, nutritional, psychological, and spiritual components. The program allows each patient to gain the confidence necessary to live richer, happier, and healthier lives. The treatment program is exclusively for women and is a Christian-oriented facility with an emphasis on the Twelve Step approach. The program promotes the idea that the patient needs to get to the root of emotions and be able to separate them from his/her issue with foods. There is a mandatory family week that is used to confront unfinished business.

RENFREW CENTER
Level of Care: Residential, day treatment, partial programs
Address 1: 475 Spring Lane, Philadelphia, Pennsylvania 19128
Phone: 1-800-736-3739
Address 2: 7700 Renfrew Lane, Coconut Creek, Florida 33073
Phone: 1-800-332-8415
Summary description: Originally Renfrew was exclusively dedicated to eating disorders; however, both programs, in Florida and Philadelphia, are now comprehensive women's mental health centers offering services across the continuum of care for a range of psychiatric diagnoses. The residential program is a highly structured program with thirty to forty groups per week and individual therapy. Family participation is encouraged once a week in family sessions, and phone contact is made if distance is a problem. Renfrew's philosophy is described as a "feminist philosophy" with the goal of empowerment. There are no locked doors. Renfrew is not a Twelve Step program but support is available if needed/required for attendance at AA or OA meetings. The focus of treatment is psychological and group subjects include self-esteem, assertiveness, nutrition, substance abuse, body image, family issues, eating patterns, interpersonal relations, women's issues, life skills, sexuality, risk taking, transitions, art, movement, anger, and psychodrama.

HOSPITAL

THE INSTITUTE OF LIVING
Level of Care: Outpatient, inpatient, day hospital, and residential
Address: 400 Washington Street
Hartford, Connecticut 06106
Phone: (860) 545-7200, (860)545-7203, 1-800-673-2411
Summary description: The Institute of Living offers a specialized program for the treatment of eating disorders in children, adolescents, and adults and provides a continuum of care that includes outpatient, day hospital, and inpatient services. Residential and consultation services are also available. The initial assessment is provided by an eating disorder specialist. Treatment recommendations are geared toward the individual needs of the patient to provide comprehensive treatment in the least restrictive environment possible. A dedicated interdisciplinary team includes eating disorder specialists in the fields of psychiatry, psychology, nutritional science, dance therapy, nursing, and social work. Patients may refer themselves, or they may be referred by health care professionals, schools, friends, or family members.

HALFWAY/RECOVERY HOUSES

ALTERNATIVE SOLUTIONS, E.D.
Level of Care: Recovery house
Address: 2207 Anniversary Lane, Newport Beach, California 92660
Phone: (714) 722-0505
Summary description: Alternative Solutions literature describes the program as an extended care facility (halfway house) and a supportive living environment. Alternative Solutions prefers stays as long as six to nine months for best results. The residents work with a multidisciplinary team to reinforce the dynamics of recovery from compulsive behavior patterns. Residents should be able to fully participate in all groups, activities, and meetings, but the ability to live in recovery without engaging in symptomatic behavior is expected.

Appendix B

Resources

Eating Disorder Organizations

AABA, American Anorexia & Bulimia Society
293 Central Park West, #1R
New York, NY 10024
Phone: (212) 501-8351, referrals over the phone

Academy for Eating Disorders
Business Office—c/o Division of Adolescent Medicine
Montefiore Medical Center
111 East 210th Street
Bronx, NY 10467
Phone: (718) 920-6781
Fax (718) 920-5289

ANAD, National Association of Anorexia Nervosa and
Associated Disorders
P.O. Box 7
Highland Park, IL 60035
Phone: (847) 831-3438

ANRED, Anorexia Nervosa and Related Eating Disorders, Inc.
P.O. Box 5102
Eugene, OR 97405
Phone: (503) 344-1144

EDAP, EATING DISORDER AWARENESS AND PREVENTION
603 Stewart Street, Suite 803
Seattle, WA 98101
Phone: (206) 382-3587

IAEDP, INTERNATIONAL ASSOCIATION OF EATING DISORDER
PROFESSIONALS
123 N.W. 13th Street, #206
Boca Raton, FL 33432
Phone: (407) 338-6494

OA, OVEREATERS ANONYMOUS (look for a local listing in your tele-
phone directory)
World Services Offices
P.O. Box 44020
Rio Rancho, NM 87124

NEDO, NATIONAL EATING DISORDERS ORGANIZATION
6655 S. Yale Avenue
Tulsa, OK 74136
Phone: (614) 436-1112

SUGGESTIONS FOR FURTHER READING

There are countless books on eating disorders too numerous to mention. However, several books stand out as important works in the field
and/or that have been influential in my own understanding of eating
disorders and my development as a therapist in treating them. In
addition, there are certain books that my patients and their families
have found particularly useful and have consistently commented on
over the years. Therefore, the following list includes those books as
suggested for further reading but should not be considered comprehensive by any means. Following each book listed there is a code
indicating what audience the book is being suggested for:

"S" Indicates the book is for significant others and family members

"I" Indicates the book is useful for the individual suffering from an eating disorder

"P" Indicates the book is appropriate for professionals

BOOKS

The Body Betrayed, Zerbe, Katherine. Washington, D.C., London: American Psychiatric Press, 1993. **S I P**

Body Self and Psychological Self, Krueger, David. New York: Brunner Mazel, 1989. **P**

The Beauty Myth, Wolf, Naomi. New York: William Morrow, 1991. **S I P**

Beyond the Food Game: A Spiritual and Psychological Approach to Healing Emotional Eating. Latimer, Jane. Denver, Colo.: LivingQuest, 1993. **S I P**

Eating Disorders: Nutrition Therapy in the Recovery Process. Reiff, D. W., K. Reiff. K. Aspen, Md.: 1992. **S I P**

Father Hunger, Maine, Margo. Carlsbad, Calif.: Gurze Books, 1991. **S I P**

Feminist Perspectives on Eating Disorders, Fallon, Patricia, M. Katzman, S. Wooley, et al. New York: Guilford Press, 1994. **S I P**

The Golden Cage, Bruch, Hide. Cambridge, Mass.: Harvard University Press, 1978. **S P**

Handbook of Psychotherapy for Anorexia Nervosa and Bulimia. Garfinkel, P. E., and D. M. Garner (Eds.). New York: Guilford Press, 1985. **P**

How to Get Your Kid To Eat . . . But Not Too Much, Satter, Ellyn. Palo Alto, Calif.: Bull Publishing Co., 1987. **S P**

Living Binge Free, Latimer, Jane. Denver, Colo.: LivingQuest, 1988. **I P**

Making Peace with Food, Kano, Susan. New York: Harper & Row Publishers, 1989. **I P**

Mothering Ourselves, Bassoff, Evelyn. New York: Plume, 1992.
S I P

Medical Issues and the Eating Disorders, Garfinkel, Paul. New York: Brunner Mazel Publishers, 1993. **P**

The Obsession; Reflections on the Tyranny of Slenderness, Chernin, Kim. New York: Harper and Row, 1981. **S I P**

Overcoming Binge Eating, Fairburn, Christopher. New York: The Guilford Press, 1995.

Reviving Ophelia, Pipher, Mary. New York: Ballantine Books, 1994. **S I P**

Sexual Abuse and Eating Disorders, Schwartz, M., and L. Cohen, New York: Brunner Mazel, 1996. **P**

Special Problems in Managing Eating Disorders, Yager, Joel (Ed.). Washington, D.C.: American Psychiatric Press, 1992. **P**

Surviving an Eating Disorder: Strategies for Family and Friends, Siegel, Michele, Judith Brisman, and Margot Weinshel. New York: Harper and Row, 1988. **S P**

Treating and Overcoming Anorexia Nervosa, Levenkron, Steven. New York: Scribner, 1982. **S I P**

When Food Is Love: Exploring The Relationships Between Intimacy and Eating, Roth, Geneen. New York: Dutton, 1991.
S I P

Your Dieting Daughter, Costin, Carolyn. New York: Brunner Mazel, 1996. **S P**

BIBLIOGRAPHY

Agras, W. S., et al. "Pharmacologic and Cognitive Behavioral Treatment for Bulimia Nervosa: A Controlled Comparison." *American Journal of Psychiatry* 149:82–87, 1992.

———, et al. "One-Year Follow-Up of Psychosocial and Pharmacologic Treatment for Bulimia Nervosa." *Journal of Clinical Psychiatry* 55 no. 5:179–183, 1993.

Alcoholics Anonymous. New York: Alcohol Anonymous World Services, 1995.

Andreason, N. C., et al. "The Family History Approach to Diagnosis" *Archives of General Psychiatry* 43:421–429, 1986.

Bemis, K. "'Abstinence' and 'Non Abstinence' Models for the Treatment of Bulimia." *International Journal of Eating Disorders* 4:389–406, 1985.

Bernstein, Jerrold G. *Drug Therapy in Psychiatry*, 3d edit. St. Louis, Mo.: Mosby-Year Book, Inc., 1995.

Biederman, J., et al. "High Frequency of HLA-Bw16 in Patients with Anorexia Nervosa." *American Journal of Psychiatry* 141:1109–1110, 1984.

———, et al. "Depressive Disorders in Relatives of Anorexia Nervosa Patients with and without a Current Episode of Nonbipolar Major Depression." *American Journal of Psychiatry* 142:1495–1497, 1985.

Brewerton, T.D. "Toward a Unified Theory of Serotonin Dysregulation in Eating and Related Disorders." *Psychoneuroendocrinology* 20:561–590, 1995.

Brisman, J., and M. Siegal. "Bulimia and Alcoholism: Two Sides of the Same Coin?" *Journal of Substance Abuse Treatment* 1:113–118, 1984.

Brody, C. *Women's Therapy Groups.* New York: Springer Books, 1987.

Bruch, H. *The Golden Cage: The Enigma of Anorexia Nervosa.* New York: Vintage Books, 1979.

Butler, S., and C. Wintram. *Feminist Groupwork.* London: Sage Publications.

Chernin, Kim. *The Hungry Self.* New York: Harper and Row, 1986.

Darby, P. L., et al. "Anorexia Nervosa and Turner Syndrome: Cause or Coincidence?" *Psychological Medicine* 11:141–145, 1981.

Davidson, and S., and M. Davidson (eds.). *Behavioral Medicine: Changing Health Lifestyles.* New York: Brunner Mazel, 1980.

Diagnostic and Statistical Manual of Mental Disorders, 3rd ed. revised. Washington, D.C.: American Psychiatric Association Press, 1987.

Dolan, B. "Cross-Cultural Aspects of Anorexia Nervosa and Bulimia: A Review." *International Journal of Eating Disorders* 10 no. 1:67–78, 1991.

Eaves, I.J., et al. "Testing Genetic Models for Multiple Symptoms." *Behavioral Genetics* 17:331–341, 1987.

Eaves, L.J. "Including the Environment in Models for Genetic Segregation." *Journal of Psychiatric Research* 21:639–647, 1987.

Eichenbaum, Luise, and Susie Orbach. *Between Women: Love, Envy, and Competition in Women's Friendships.* New York: Viking Penguin, 1988.

Elsron, R.C., and K.C. Yelverron. "General Models for Segregation Analysis." *American Journal of Human Genetics* 27:31–45, 1975.

Fallon, Patricia, et al. *Feminist Perspectives on Eating Disorders.* New York: Guilford Press, 1994.

Fichter, M. "Symptomatology, Psychosexual Development, and Gender Identity in 42 Anorexic Males." *Psychological Medicine* 17:409–418, 1987.

Fichter, M.M., and R. Noegel. "Concordance for Bulimia in Twins." *International Journal of Eating Disorders* 9:255–263, 1990.

Fluoxetine Bulimia Nervosa Collaborative Study Group. "Fluoxetine in the Treatment of Bulimia Nervosa: A Multicenter, Placebo-Controlled, Double Blind Trial." *Archives of General Psychiatry* 49:139–147, 1992.

Gainsley, Bruce. "Treatment of Anorexia with Prozac." *Journal of Clinical Psychiatry* 51 (September 1990):378–382.

Garfinkel, P., and D. Garfinkel (eds.). *Anorexia Nervosa: A Multidimensional Perspective.* New York: Brunner Mazel, 1982.

———. *Handbook of Psychotherapy for Anorexia Nervosa and Bulimia.* New York: Guilford Press, 1985.

———, et al. "The Heterogeneity of Anorexia Nervosa." *Archives of General Psychiatry* 37:1036–1040.

Garner, D. M., et al. "Validity of the Distinction Between Bulimia With and Without Anorexia Nervosa." *American Journal of Psychiatry* 142:581–587, 1985.

———, et al. "The Eating Attitudes Test: Psychometric Features and Clinical Correlates." *Psychological Medicine* 12 no. 4:871–878, 1982.

Gelenberg, Alan J. *The Practitioner's Guide to Psychoactive Drugs, Third Edition.* New York and London: Plenum Medical Book Company, 1991.

Grabowski, A. "Recovered? What's That?" *ANAD: Working Together* (September 1990):1–3.

Hall, Lindsey, and Leigh Cohn. *Bulimia: A Guide to Recovery.* Carlsbad, Calif.: Gurze Books, 1992.

Hall, R.C.W., et al. 'Sexual Abuse in Patients with Anorexia Nervosa and Bulimia." *Psychosomatics* 30:79–88, 1992.

Handbook of Daily Readings. Overeaters Anonymous: Los Angeles, 1980.

Harper-Giuffre, H., and K.R. MacKenzie. *Group Psychotherapy for Eating Disorders.* Washington, D.C.: American Psychiatric Association Press, 1992.

Hatsukami, D., et al, J. "Similarities and Difference on the MMPI Between Women with Bulimia and Women with Alcohol or Drug Abuse Problems." *Addictive Behaviors* 7:435–439, 1982.

Hoffman L., and K. Halmi. "Psychopharmacology in the Treatment of Anorexia Nervosa and Bulimia Nervosa." *Psychiatric Clinics of North America* 16 no. 4:767–778.

Just for Today. Overeaters Anonymous: Los Angeles, 1979.

Kaminer, Wendy. *I'm Dysfunctional, You're Dysfunctional.* New York: Vintage Press, 1992.

Kearney-Cooke, A. "Group Treatment of Sexual Abuse Among Women with Eating Disorders." *Women and Therapy* 7:5–22, 1988.

Kendall, P.C., and S.D. Hollon (eds.). *Cognitive Behavioral Interventions: Theory, Research and Procedures.* New York: Academic Press, 1979.

Kennedy, S.H., and D.S. Goldbloom. "Current Perspectives on Drug Therapies for Anorexia Nervosa and Bulimia Nervosa." *Drugs* 41 no. 3:367–377, 1991.

Kinoy, Barbara, et al. *When Will We Laugh Again? Living and Dealing with Anorexia Nervosa and Bulimia.* New York: Columbia University Press, 1984.

Lerner, Harriet Goldhor. *The Dance of Anger: A Women's Guide to Changing the Patterns of Intimate Relationships.* New York: Harper and Row, 1985.

Malenbaum, R., et al. "Overeaters Anonymous: Impact on Bulimia. *International Journal of Eating Disorders* 7:139–143, 1988.

Marlatt, G.A. *Alcohol Use and Problem Drinking: A Cognitive Behavioral Analysis.* New York: Academic Press, 1979.

——, and J.R. Gordon. "Determinants of Relapse: Implications for The Maintenance of Behavior Change." *Behavioral Medicine: Changing Health Lifestyles.* (P.O. Davidson and S.M. Davidson, eds.) New York: Brunner Mazel, 1980.

Marrazzi, M.A., et al, (eds.). "Naltrexone Use in the Treatment of Anorexia Nervosa and Bulimia Nervosa." *International Clinical Psychopharmacology* 10:163–172, 1995

McFarland, Barbara, and Tyeis Baker-Baumann. *Feeding the Empty Heart: Adult Children and Compulsive Eating.* San Francisco: Harper and Row, 1988.

Mehren, E. "A Sobering Alternative." *Los Angeles Times* (April 13, 1992).

Minuchin, Rosman. *Psychosomatic Families: Anorexia Nervosa in Context.* Cambridge, Mass.: Harvard University Press, 1978.

Murray, Mary. "The New Diet Pills." *Allure* (February 1995).

O'Connor, P. *Friendship Between Women, A Critical Review.* New York: Guilford Press, 1992.

Oppenheimer, et al. "Adverse Sexual Experiences in Childhood and Clinical Eating Disorders: A Preliminary Description." *Journal of Psychiatric Research* 19:157–161, 1985.

Pfeiffer, Carl C. *Nutrition and Mental Illness.* Rochester, Vt.: Healing Arts Press, 1987

Pope, H.G., and K.I. Hudson. "Is Childhood Sexual Abuse a Risk Factor for Bulimia Nervosa?" *American Journal of Psychiatry* 149:455–463, 1992.

Questions & Answers About Compulsive Overeating and the OA Program of Recovery. Overeaters Anonymous: Los Angeles, 1979.

Reiff, D. W., and K.K. Reiff. *Eating Disorders: Nutrition Therapy in the Recovery Process.* Aspen, 1992.

Robbins, Tony. Personal Power Seminar. San Diego, Calif., 1990.

Root, M.P., and P. Fallon. "The Incidences of Victimization Experiences in a Bulimic Sample." *Journal of Interpersonal Violence* 3 no. 2:161–173, 1988.

Rosenthal, N.E. *Winter Blues: Seasonal Affective Disorder—What It Is and How to Overcome It.* New York: Guilford Press, 1993.

Roth, Geneen. *Breaking Free from Compulsive Eating.* New York: Signet, 1986.

———. *When Food Is Love: Exploring the Relationships Between Intimacy and Eating.* New York: Dutton, 1991.

Satter, Ellen. *How to Get Your Kid to Eat . . . But Not Too Much.* Palo Alto, Calif.: Bull Publishing Company, 1987.

Schauss, Alexander, and Carolyn Costin. *Zinc and Eating Disorders.* Keats Publishing, 1981.

Schwartz, Barrett . "Family Therapy for Bulimia," *Handbook of Psychotherapy for Anorexia Nervosa and Bulimia.* (Garner and Garfinkel, eds.) New York: Guilford Press, 1985.

Schwartz, M., and L. Cohen. *Sexual Abuse and Eating Disorders.* New York: Brunner Mazel, 1996.

Sears, Barry. *Enter The Zone.* New York: HarperCollins, 1995.

Sheppard, Kay. *Food Addiction, The Body Knows.* Health Communications, Inc., 1989

Siegel, Michele, et al. *Surviving an Eating Disorder: Strategies for Family and Friends.* New York: Harper and Row, 1988.

Stunkard, Albert. March "A Description of ED in 1932." *American Journal of Psychiatry* 147 no. 3:263–268, 1990.

Suffin, Stephen C., and Emory W. Hamlin. "Neurometric Subgroups in Attentional and Affective Disorders and Their Association with Pharmacotherapeutic Outcome. *Clinical Electroencephalography* 26 no. 2:76–83, 1995.

Tannen, D. *Gender and Discourse.* New York: Oxford University Press, 1994.

Tessina, T. "Recovery Beyond Recovery: The Real Thirteenth Step." *The California Therapist* (November/December 1991):47–48.

To the Newcomer. Overeaters Anonymous: Los Angeles, 1979.

The Tools of Recovery. Overeaters Anonymous: Los Angeles, 1981.

Vandereycken, W. "The Addiction Model in Eating Disorders: Some Critical Remarks and a Selected Bibliography." *International Journal of Eating Disorders* 9:95–101, 1990.

Visser, Margaret. *The Rituals of Dinner*. New York: Grove Weidenfield, 1991.

Waltos, D.L. "Historical Perspectives and Diagnostic Considerations." *Occupational Therapy in Mental Health* 6 no. 1:1–13, 1986.

Wellborne, Jill, and Joan Reingold. *The Eating Sickness*. Brighton Sussex, England: Harvester Press, 1984.

Wooley, Susan. "Sexual Abuse and Eating Disorders, the Concealed Debate." Chapter 9 in *Feminist Perspectives on Eating Disorders*. New York: Guilford Press, 1994.

Yager, J., (ed.). "The Twelve-Step Approach and Psychotherapy: An Integrated Model." *Eating Disorders Review* 4 (March/April 1993):1–3.

Zerbe, Kathryn J. *The Body Betrayed*. Washington, D.C.: American Psychiatric Association Press, 1993

INDEX

A

activity disorder, 27, 29-39
  approaching individual with, 35-36
  cognitive distortion in, 32-33
  exercise avoidance and, 34-35
  in females, 29
  in males, 27
  physical symptoms of, 34
  risk factors, 36-38
  signs and symptoms of, 30-32
  treatment for, 38-39
adaptive functions of eating disorders,
  53-64
  addictive cycle and, 56-57
  development of, 56-57
  listed, 57
adaptive self. *See* eating disorder self
addiction
  adaptive functions and, 56-57
  eating disorders treated as, 100-107
addiction-based therapy, 95, 100-107
affection, showing, 92
affective disorders, and eating disorders,
  62
American Dietetic Association Consumer
  Hotline, 181
Anafranil (clomipramine), 197
Anderson, Arnold, 26, 195
anorexia
  versus anorexia nervosa, 72
  "holy," 49-51
  meaning of, 5-6
anorexia athletica, 30
anorexia nervosa, 3-8
  body image disturbance in, 47
  cardiovascular concerns, 213-215
  as common, 1, 47
  cultural influences on, 47, 49, 50
  diagnostic criteria, 3-4
  DSM IV on, 3-4
  gastrointestinal complaints, 212-213
  hematological system in, 215-216
  hormonal effects, 215
  in males, 23-24, 27-28
  medical complications of, 212-216
  medical management of, 212-216
  medications and, 198, 199-200
  mind-set of persons with, 6-7

mortality rate and prognosis, 20
  nutritional rehabilitation of, 186
  outside Western world, 47
  starvation related to power in, 49-50,
    54
  starvation related to purity in, 49-50
  symptoms associated with, 4-7, 79-80
antianxiety medications, 205
antidepressants, 72, 197, 200-201, 202
  dosages and side effects, 203-204
appearance, not commenting on, 92
appetite suppressants, use of, 220
assessment
  behavioral, 65-67, 68, 79
  medical, 65, 79-84
  professional, 68-78
  psychological, 65
  by significant others, 65-67
  standardized tests for, 75-78
attention, need for, 121-122
awareness of eating disorders, increasing,
  247-248

B

Beck, Aaron, 98
Beck Depression Inventory, 78
BED. *See* binge eating disorder
behavioral assessment, 65
  by professionals, 68-78
  by significant others, 66-67
belief, 107
  in possibility of recovery, 114
Bell, Richard, 49-51
binge, meaning of, 15
binge abstinence, *versus* substance
  abstinence, 105
binge eating, and bulimia nervosa, 9, 10
binge eating disorder, 4, 12-17
  addictive or dissociative, 13
  as backlash to dieting, 1
  deprivation-sensitive, 13
  DSM IV on, 13-15
  versus eating or overeating, 105
  exercise resistance and, 39-44
  goal setting in, 166-167
  in males, 24
  medical management of, 220-221

279

medications and, 201-202
obesity and, 13, 16, 186, 220-221
populations affected by, 16
statistics on, 21
subjective views of, 16-17
biological predisposition, 61-64
activity disorder and, 37-38
obesity and, 16
blaming, avoiding, 91
body image disturbance
in anorexics, 9
in bulimics, 9
DSM IV on, 46-47
and exercise resistance, 42
PBIS test for assessing, 77-78
body shape, cultural influences on,
45-48
bribing, avoiding, 92
Brown, Dennis, 23-24, 26
Bruch, Hilda, 1, 77, 96
bulimia, meaning of, 9
bulimia nervosa, 8-13
binge eating and, 9, 10
body image disturbance in, 47
cognitive behavioral therapy for, 100
as common, 1, 47
DSM IV on, 8, 19
families of patients with, 10, 165
goal setting in, 166
in males, 23-24
medical complications of, 79-80
medical management of, 216-219
medications and, 72, 197, 200-201
mood disorders and, 197
mortality rate and prognosis, 20-21
from patient's perspective, 11-12
percentage of anorexics developing, 7
phototherapy for, 206
test for assessing, 77
therapy session excerpts, 125-142
Twelve Step programs and, 103
BULIT-R measure, 77

C
calorie counting, 7
caregivers, lack of responsiveness from,
55-56
caretaker role, 167-168
Carpenter, Karen, 1-2
Chernin, Kim, 53
child rearing practices, and activity
disorder, 37

cognitive behavioral therapy, 95,
98-100, 197
cognitive distortion
about food, challenging, 178
in activity disorder, 32-33
challenging in therapy, 117-118
and eating disorders, 32-33
cognitive distortions, 98-100
Cohen, Lee, 59
colon, damage to, 219
communication skills, 251
complaints, 71, 83
compulsive eating disorder. See binge
eating disorder
confrontation, 144-145
constipation, 213
contracts, behavioral, 116-117
control, 5
fear of loss of, 6, 7-8
need for, 122, 168, 229
OA on, 106-107
rigid, 5, 6-8, 49
in therapy, 115-116
controlled environment, 233-234
Costin, Carolyn, 191, 241-242
Cousins, Norman, 107

D
dental treatment, 217
depression, 62, 71-72
assessing, 78
bulimia nervosa and, 197
Diagnostic and Statistical Manual of
Mental Disorders IV
on anorexia nervosa, 3-4
on binge eating disorder, 14-15
on body image disturbance, 47
on bulimia nervosa, 8, 19
on EDNOS, 17-18
dialogue technique, 111-112
dichotomous thinking, 121
dietary assessment, 73-74
diet history, 73-74
dieticians, registered, 124, 178, 179-180,
211-212. See also nutrition therapists
nutrition therapists, 179
dieting, 184
regaining weight after, 46
dietitians, 74
diet pills, use of, 220
diuretics, abuse of, 219-220
dyspepsia, 217-218

E
EAT (Eating Attitudes Test), 75-76
Eating (film), 2
eating disorders. *See also* anorexia
    nervosa; binge eating disorder;
    bulimia nervosa
    as adaptive functions, 53-64
    age at onset, 19
    assessment of, 65-84
    as common, 1-3
    common states of being in, 53-54
    cultural influences and, 45-51
    diagnostic criteria for, 3-4
    distinguishing from disordered eating,
        3
    duration of illness, 19
    emotional limitations in, 53-54
    emotionally fulfilling behaviors, 54-55
    historical background, 1-21
    in males, 23-28
    onset of, 55-56
    prevalence of, 18-20
    prognosis and mortality rate, 20-21
    sexual abuse and, 19, 58-60
Eating Disorders Awareness and
    Prevention, Inc., 247-248
Eating Disorders Awareness Week, 248
eating disorder self, 56-57
    contacting and transforming, 110-112
    dialoguing with, 111-112
EDI (Eating Disorder Inventory), 76-77
EDNOS (Eating Disorders Not Otherwise
    Specified), 17-18
education, 161-162, 249
    in group therapy, 143-144
    on nutrition (*see* nutrition education)
EKG, 214-215
electrolyte disorders, 218
emotions, fear of, 5
empathy, 86-87, 114, 118
esophagus, rupture off, 218
exercise, compulsive. *See* activity disorder
exercise addiction, 29-30, 73
exercise resistance
    meaning to individual, 41-42
    risk factors for developing, 41
    signs of, 40-41
    in women, 39-44
expectations, parental, 163-165

F
Fairburn, Christopher, 15, 17, 21

family. *See also* family therapy;
    significant others
    and activity disorder, 37, 73
    attempts at control, 155, 230
    boundaries in, 169-170
    educating in therapy, 161-162
    emotions experienced after discovery,
        156-157
    environmental contributions, 61, 72-73
    and exercise resistance, 41
    expectations of, 163-165
    father's role, 171-172
    feelings of, 91-92, 155
    genetic contributions, 61-64
    guidelines for, 85-94
    lost child in, 168
    mother's role, 169-171, 172
    patterns of, 72-73, 155
    role of patient in, 167-169
    structure of, adjusting, 169-172
family therapy, 157-176
    addressing abuse issues in, 172-173
    challenging family patterns in, 173-174
    goal of, 176
    goal-setting in, 166-167
    important tasks in, 158-176
    multifamily group, 174-176
    termination of, 175-176
    therapist's tasks in, 158-176
fathers. *See* family
fat phobic persons, 185-186
feminine ideal, 48
feminist perspectives, 51
fenfluramine and phentermine, 198,
    201-202
friends. *See also* significant others
    assessment by, 65-68
    guidelines for, 85-94
    meeting, in therapy groups, 145

G
Garfinkel, Paul, 58
Garner, David, 58, 76
gender conflict, and eating disorders, 51
genetic studies. *See* biological
    predisposition; heredity
goals, personal, 70
    in bulimia, 166
    setting in therapy, 116-117, 166-167
group therapy, 143-153
    benefits of, 143-145
    considerations in forming groups, 148-
        149

ground rules, 150-151
journal entries about, 152-153
multifamily, 174-176
therapist's role, 150
topics for, 151-152
types of, 145-147
Gull, William, 6, 23

H
halfway houses, 226-227, 234-235, 266
help, asking for, 86-87
heredity, 61-64
historical background, 1-21
history, psychiatric, 71-72
homosexuality, male, 25-26
hormone replacement therapy, 209, 215
hospitalization, 224-225, 227-232. *See also* inpatient treatment programs
partial, 224-225
reasons for, 228-229
setting criteria and goals for, 227, 230-232
Hsu, George, 26
Hudson, J. I., 58-59
hunger signals, 184

I
information gathering
guidelines for, 68-75
inpatient treatment programs, 223-245
cost of, 234
curative factors of, 232-234
described, 256-260
options, 223-226
insight, assessing, 75
International Eating Disorders Conference, 13, 15
interventions, 89-90
"I" statements, 87

J
Janet, Pierre, 6, 9
John, Elton, 2
Johnson, Craig, 106

K
Katzman, Melanie, 145
Kaye, Walter, 199-200
Klonopin, 198, 205
Kratina, Karin, 177, 182

L
laboratory tests, 82-84
normal results, 80
laxative abuse, 218-219
Levenkron, Steven, 1, 118, 165
lithium, 197, 205

M
Maine, Margo, 172
males with eating disorders, 23-28
gender identity studies of, 25-26
obesity and, 27
treatment and prognosis, 27-28
meal plans, 184
structured/unstructured, 183
media influences, 45-46
medical assessment, 65, 79-84
medical history, 72, 73-74
medical management, 211-221
of anorexia nervosa, 212-216
of bulimia nervosa, 216-219
medication, 63, 81, 195-209
anorexia nervosa and, 198, 199-200
antidepressant, 72, 197, 200-201, 202
binge eating disorder and, 201-202
bulimia nervosa and, 72, 200-201
nutritional rehabilitation and, 196-197
prescribing, 206-208
in preventing relapse, 198
Mehler, Philip S., 84, 211
men. *See* males with eating disorders
methylphenidate (Ritalin), 198
monitoring behavior, avoiding, 93, 173
Monte Nido residential treatment program, 237-245, 264
mood disorders. *See* affective disorders
mood stabilizers, 204-205
mortality rate, 20-21
Morton, Richard, 4, 23
mothers. *See* family
motivation, assessing, 75

N
nutrition
depression and, 71-72
supplementation of, 189-190
therapist's knowledge of, 124-125
nutritional rehabilitation, 177-191
medication and, 196-197
treatment models, 187-189
treatment phases, 178-179
nutrition education, 178-179, 187-189

nutritionists, 177, 178. *See also* nutrition
  therapists
  finding and choosing, 181-186
  what to expect from, 182-186
nutrition therapists, 179
  finding and choosing, 181-186
  frequency of visits to, 187
  interviewing, 181-186
  topics discussed with clients, 180

O
obesity, 21
  and binge eating disorder, 13, 16,
    186, 220-221
  biological predisposition to, 16
  in males, 27
obsessive-compulsive disorders, and
  eating disorders, 63, 71, 74-75, 196
outpatient treatment, 223
Overeaters Anonymous, 101-107
overtraining syndrome, 34

P
parotid gland enlargement, 216
Paxil (paroxetine), 203
PBIS (Perceived Body Image Scale),
  77-78
perfectionism, 167
personality characteristics
  activity disorder and, 37
  eating disorders and, 49
pharmacotherapy, use of, 196-208
  See also medication
phentermine and fenfluramine, 198,
  201-202
phototherapy, 206
physical exam, 81-84
physicians
  nutritionists and, 185
  training in eating disorders, 80
Pope, H. G., Jr., 58-59
power, need for, 49-50, 54, 122, 168
prevention of eating disorders, 247-253
prognosis, 20-21
  for males, 27-28
Prozac (fluoxetine), 63, 197, 200, 203
psychiatrists
  role in treatment, 193-195
  what to look for, 193-194
psychodynamic therapy, 95, 96-97
psychological assessment, 65
psychosomatic disorders, 79

psychotherapy. *See* therapy
psychotropic medication, use of, 196-209
purging, 9
  as additive, 10
  complications of purging, 216-219

Q
quantitative electroencephalographhy
  (QEEG), 207-209

R
rapport, 160
recovery, possibility of, 114
recovery houses, 226, 234-235, 266
refeeding syndrome, 214
Reiff, Dan, 156
Reiff, Kim, 156
residential treatment programs, 225-226
  curative factors of, 232-234
  described, 263-265
  guide to choosing, 235-237
  Monte Nido, 237-245
Robbins, Tony, 107
Rosenthal, Norman, 206

S
saints, medieval Italian, 49-50
scapegoat role, 167
Schauss, Alex, 191
Schwartz, Mark, 59
seasonal affective disorder, 206
selective serotonin reuptake inhibitors,
  200, 201, 203, 204, 205, 206
self, disordered, 48, 53-54. *See also*
  eating disorder self
self-esteem, 55-56, 119-120, 249-250
self-fulfilling prophecies, 104, 105, 107
self-image, deficits in, 56
self-sacrifice, 49-50
self-soothing
  with food, 13
  lack in ability, 55
self-worth, 119-120
sexual abuse
  addressing in family therapy, 172-173
  eating disorders and, 19, 58-60
  exercise resistance and, 41
Sheppard, Kay, 103
significant others
  accepting limitations, 93
  assessment by, 65-84
  considerations during treatment, 90-93

guidelines for, 85-94
and interventions, 89-90
support system for, 94
talking with person with disorder,
86-89
society
on exercise, 29, 36
obsession with thinness, 2, 41, 45-46,
48, 49, 120, 248249
obsession with weight loss, 2, 26,
43-44
Spitzer, Robert, 15
statistics, on eating disorders, 18-21
Strober, Mike, 62
Stunkard, Albert, 15
substance use, 74
versus eating, 104
substance use disorders, 63
support groups, 94, 147
support systems, 69. *See also* significant
others
group therapy as, 144
in inpatient treatment, 234
for significant others, 94
symptoms, 4-7, 74-75
physical, 81-84
psychodynamic view of, 96-97

T
talking with loved one with disorder,
86-89
teeth, of bulimics, 217
Tegretol, 205
tests, standardized, 75-78
therapists
choosing, 122-123
guidelines for interviewing, 123-124
nutrition knowledge of, 124-125
role in group therapy, 150-151
therapy, 57-58. *See also* family therapy;
group therapy; inpatient treatment
programs; nutrition education;
residential treatment programs;
therapy, individual
for activity disorder, 38-39
for exercise resistance, 43
for significant others, 94
therapy, individual, 109-142
behavioral agreements, 116-117
challenging patients in, 118-119
concurrent uses of types of, 121
critical techniques in, 113-119
empathy with patient in, 114

excerpts of sessions, 125-142
goal of, 111
limiting control battles in, 115-116
long-term nature of, 114-115, 124, 223
nurturant/authoritative, 118-119
therapist-patient relationship, 110
therapist's task, 110-113
topics dealt with, 119-122
thinness
bulimics' drive for, 9
cultural emphasis on, 41, 45-46, 48,
49, 50, 51, 120, 248249
equated with being in control, 6,
49-50
males and, 25, 26
treatment. *See also* therapy
assessment process in, 68-78
assessment strategies and guidelines,
68-75
philosophical approaches to, 95-107
treatment programs, described, 255-266
Trexan (naltrexone), 197-198
tube feeding, 214
Twelve Steps of OA, 101-107
twin studies, 62, 63

U
university-associated programs, 260-263

V
Vandereyken, Walter, 103-104, 105
vitamin and mineral supplements, 190
vomiting, self-induced, 79-80. *See also*
bulimia nervosa
complications of, 216-218

W
Walsh, Timothy, 17
Weintraub, Michael, 201-202
West, Ellen, 4-5
White, Francie, 39, 43
Wooley, Susan, 58-59

X
Xanax (alprazolam), 198, 205

Y
Yates, Alayne, 29, 30

Z
Zerbe, Kathryn, 171-172
zinc deficiency, 190-191
Zoloft (sertraline), 200, 203